WAR BRIDES
*The stories of the women who left everything
behind to follow the men they loved*

This book is dedicated to my War Bride friends Doris (Field) Lloyd and Zoe (Blair) Boone and to my mother Lucy (Hennessy) Jarratt

WAR BRIDES

The stories of the women who left everything behind to follow the men they loved

MELYNDA JARRATT

DUNDURN PRESS

TORONTO

Project Editor: Michael Carroll
Copy Editor: Jason Karp
Printer: Webcom

Library and Archives Canada Cataloguing in Publication

Jarratt, Melynda
    War brides : the stories of the women who left everything behind to follow the men they loved / by Melynda Jarratt.

ISBN 978-1-55488-386-8

    1. War brides--Canada--Biography. 2. War brides--Great Britain--Biography. 3. Women immigrants--Canada--Biography. I. Title.

D810.W7J39 2009   940.53082   C2009-900302-3

1   2   3   4   5   13   12   11   10   09

Conseil des Arts du Canada   Canada Council for the Arts   Canada   ONTARIO ARTS COUNCIL   CONSEIL DES ARTS DE L'ONTARIO

We acknowledge the support of the **Canada Council for the Arts** and the **Ontario Arts Council** for our publishing program. We also acknowledge the financial support of the **Government of Canada** through the **Book Publishing Industry Development Program** and **The Association for the Export of Canadian Books**, and the **Government of Ontario** through the **Ontario Book Publishers Tax Credit program**, and the **Ontario Media Development Corporation**.

Care has been taken to trace the ownership of copyright material used in this book. The author and the publisher welcome any information enabling them to rectify any references or credits in subsequent editions.

J. Kirk Howard, President

Printed and bound in Canada.
www.dundurn.com

Cover Images:
Left: Isobel 'Zoe' (Blair) Boone and son, Gordon, in Rowena, New Brunswick, 1950.
Top: RMS *Mauretania* arriving at Halifax, Nova Scotia on 24 August 1946.
Right: John and Morfydd (Morgan) Gibson of the Black Watch Regiment on their wedding day, 6 September 1944.
Bottom foreground: Rose and pen copyright © iStockphoto.com.
Bottom background: Letter from Private Marshall Boone of the Carleton York Regiment to his fiancée, Zoe Blair, when he was a prisoner of war in Germany.

Dundurn Press
3 Church Street, Suite 500
Toronto, Ontario, Canada
M5E 1M2

Gazelle Book Services Limited
White Cross Mills
High Town, Lancaster, England
LA1 4XS

Dundurn Press
2250 Military Road
Tonawanda, NY
U.S.A. 14150

Contents

List of Illustrations

Maps

Acknowledgements

I have wanted to write a history of Canadian War Brides for twenty years now, since I first started working on my Masters Thesis in History at the University of New Brunswick in 1987.

Over the past two decades I have met thousands of War Brides and I've always known that inside each one of them is a wonderful story just waiting to be told but the opportunity to sit down and actually write the book never came my way. So when I was approached by Tempus Publishing in the fall of 2006 to write a history of Canada's War Brides I naturally jumped at the chance.

There are many people who helped make this book possible. First of all I'd like to thank Sophie Bradshaw and Lisa Mitchell of Tempus for giving me the chance to fulfill my dream. If it hadn't been for their interest in the War Bride story the book would never have been realized.

The first person I went to for help was passenger lists researcher, Debbie Beavis, webmaster of www.warbrides.co.uk, whose War Bride 'listserv' gave me the medium through which to contact many of these women, their children and grandchildren who are connected through the Internet. Debbie's 'listerv' is now in the capable hands of Patricia Tanner, webmaster of WeddingsPastAndPresent.com. Tricia continues to be as helpful as her predecessor was in assisting researchers and writers who are working on War Bride projects.

Linda Granfield, author of *Brass Buttons and Silver Horseshoes*, grabbed the torch and passed the message around to her many contacts across Canada. Thank you Linda, you're always there to give me encouragement.

Dolores Hatch did the same and before I knew it, the phone was ringing, my email inbox was filling up and I'd come home nightly to find my mailbox stuffed with large, medium and small envelopes with handwritten stories, photographs, and documents.

Eswyn (Ellinor) Lyster, War Bride and author, reviewed the introductory chapters and gave her sage advice which only comes from having 'been there' and lived through the experience of being a War Bride herself. I don't know what I'd do without her.

Annette Fulford, the granddaughter of First World War War Bride Grace (Gibson) Clark – and War Bride expert in her own right – also pitched in, providing a wealth of information based on her own research and helping me with last-minute details, especially the bibliography. The entire last chapter is her contribution to this history of Canadian War Brides. Expect to hear more from Annette Fulford on this subject in the future.

There are many other individuals who helped me to gather stories: Irene Maher of the Colchester Historical Society in Truro, Nova Scotia; Don Chapman of the Lost Canadians; and Zoe Boone, Vice President of the New Brunswick War Brides Association.

In addition to these contact persons, there were War Brides, their daughters, sisters, grandchildren, husbands and friends who took it upon themselves to help me shape the stories in this book and/or assisted their War Bride by sending me text and images electronically by email: Gloria Mott niece of the late Dora (Adams) Addison and daughter of the late Doris (Shelton) Butt; Marion Vermeersch daughter of the late Doris (Sayers) Barr; Leesa Swigger, Maureen Dawm, Robbie Bell and Joni Lang children of the late Margaret (Hill) Bell; Jane Veraart friend of Joyce (Hilman) Bezeau; Marina Black daughter of Margaret (Budge) Black; Zoe (Blair) Boone; Marian Boulay daughter of Rose (O'Reilly) Boulay; Rita (Bannister) Buckrell; Angela Michaud daughter of the late Betty (Sheppee) Campbell; Michelle Rusk daughter of the late Olive (Rayson) Cochrane; Dane Carmichael son of Margot (Coombes) Carmichael; John Clark and Anne Clark UE, husband and daughter, respectively, of Irene (Parry) Clark; Mary Dale; the late Johan (Hillis) DeWitt; John Bristow son of Margaret (Perkins) Bristow Eaton; Lynn Fitzgerald daughter of Madeline (Rusbridge) Chunn Fitzgerald; Vernie Foy; Karen Gero daughter-in-law of Mary (Hardie) Gero; Myfanwy and Meredith Burbidge, daughter and granddaughter, respectively, of Morfydd (Morgan) Gibson; Russell Weller grandson of the late Phyllis (Head) Grover; Gwendolen (Cliburn) Hall; Jackie Farquhar daughter of Betty (Lowthian) Hillman; Rob Hoddinott son of the late Marion (Elliot) Hoddinott; Dorothy (Currie) Hyslop; Carole Coplea daughter of the late Alice 'Mac' (McGregor) Hooker; Sandra Pond daughter of the late Ann (Biles) Lawrence Johnston; Maria Landry daughter of Joan (Smedley) Landry; Doris (Field) Lloyd; David Ludwig son of Gladys (Gardiner) Ludwig; Horace MacAuley husband of Peggy (Coppock) MacAuley; Valerie MacDonald daughter of the late Elizabeth (Kelly) MacDonald; Beatrice (Davidson) MacIntosh; Christine Trankalis and Julien Olson, daughter and husband, respectively, of the late Lilian (Gibson) Olson; Cindy Gaffney and Pat Lunn, daughter and sister, respectively, of the late Jean (Keegan) Paul; Jackie Pearase of the *North Valley Echo*, Enderby, British Columbia; Julie (no. 13) Pronovost daughter of Henrietta (Stevens) Pronovost; Pat Pyne; Joan (Fisher) Reichardt; Kay Ruddick; Peggy (Sayer) Sheffield; Carol Coristine, Manager New Media Distribution of CBC.ca and Mary Sheppard daughter of the late Mary (Fletcher) Sheppard; Diane Shuttleworth daughter of Joni (Jones) Shuttleworth; Sheila Simpson daughter of Edna (Burrows) Simpson; Susan Willis daughter of the late Mildred (Young) Sowers; Wilson Stauffer husband of Martha (McLachlan) Stauffer; Bea (Morris) Surgeson; Joe Taylor; Marguerite Turner, President of the Halifax Dartmouth War Brides Association; Mary (Mitchell) Vankonnaught; Sheila Walshe; Kathy Panter daughter of the late Barbara (Cornwell) Warriner; Kathy Eddington daughter of Elizabeth (Adams) Wasnidge; *The Fredericton Daily Gleaner* and Laverne Stewart for the story on Delice (de Wolf) Wilby; Michael Worthylake son of Pauline (Portsmouth) Worthylake; Barbara Steuart and Jim Wright, daughter and husband, respectively, of Betty Wright; and last, but not least, Shelley Harynuk daughter of Gwen (Harms) Keele Zradicka.

My cousins, Patsy Hennessy and Sharon Olscamp, my friends Jan Walker (who happens to be the daughter of War Bride Bridget (Murphy) Sims and Sandy Coutts- Sutherland helped by reviewing the text and providing encouragement at critical junctures. My friend Sharlene Keith and long time editor/writer Meris K. Brookland typed up the many handwritten submissions. K provided some excellent editorial advice, even writing the first drafts of some of the stories you see here. Also Todd Spencer, a promising history student at my *alma mater*, the University of New Brunswick, did some research at the Harriet Irving Library in the microfilm reels and graphic designer Mila Jones provided the maps.

There were also many people who submitted stories which could not be included in this volume due to lack of space. Thank you everyone for your submissions. Perhaps they will appear in another volume on this subject!

And last but not least, I'd like to thank my husband Dan Weston who spent many late nights alone, preparing supper for me so that I'd have something good to eat when I came home. Without his day to day support I wouldn't have been able to get to the end of this book.

Melynda Jarratt, BA, MA, Diploma Digital Media

Foreword

In the fall of 1990, I was preparing to depart for basic training for the United States Armed Forces. My family had gathered for a farewell dinner in Fredericton and to offer their best wishes before seeing me off for the next six months. The women of my family, including my grandmother, Jean (Keegan) Paul, a British War Bride from Couldson, Surrey – whose story is the first in this book – were gathered in the kitchen telling stories in Maliseet about the brave men they knew from the Tobique Reserve who left for military service during the Second World War. Some they spoke of fondly, others posthumously, and in the rare occasion, jokingly.

"Will nee he come home again?" my grandmother asked. Unsure if this was misplaced Maliseet I turned to my mother who was smiling at me nodding her head. She repeated my grandmother's words. Totally confused, they offered me this story of a soldier preparing to leave for basic military training during the Second World War. "Will nee he come home again" was the tale of a man who missed his community so much that he returned only a few weeks after initially departing. After much embarrassment from people within the small community and realizing the importance of his pledge to defend his country and the well-being of his family and loved ones, he again packed his bags and left for what turned out to be a distinguished military career.

I believe the moral of my grandmother's story is about commitment to your country and your loved ones. Without doubt, the courageous women who left their families and homes for the ones they loved, epitomizes the moral of her story and an important part of our Canadian history. Melynda

Jarratt's writings capture the essence of the many stories retold to her about why these women chose to follow love and begin a new chapter in their lives in Canada.

The Honourable T.J. Burke, Q.C.
Attorney General and Minister of Justice
Province of New Brunswick

Preface

The Battle of Love
by Melynda Jarratt

Basically we girls came out to Canada, by and large not knowing what to expect, the vast majority of us dug in, adapted, compromised, made homes for our husbands and families and became good contributing Canadian citizens.[1] (Dorothy (Currie) Hyslop, Scottish War Bride, St Stephen, New Brunswick)

When Canada joined Britain in its declaration of war against Germany on 10 September 1939, the last thing on anybody's mind was marriage.

But less than forty days after the First Canadian Infantry Division landed at Greenock, Scotland, on 17 December 1939, the first marriage between a British woman and a Canadian soldier took place at the Farnborough Church in Aldershot on 28 January 1940.[2] That marriage, and the nearly 48,000[3] which followed over the course of the next six years, formed one of the most unusual immigrant waves to hit Canada's shores: all women, mostly British, and all from the same age group, the story of the Canadian War Brides of the Second World War is one worth telling.

Ninety-four per cent of Canadian War Brides were British, and the reasons are fairly obvious: the Canadians were the first to come to the defence of Britain after the declaration of war and they stayed there for nearly six years. And even though GI Brides received a lot more press, Canadian War Brides outnumbered their American counterparts by more than 10,000 and were the mothers of 7,000 more children by the time the war was over.[4]

Nearly a half-million Canadians served in Britain during the Second World War, the majority of them passing through the Victorian Hampshire town of Aldershot which became known as the Home of the Canadian Army. Canadians lived in the UK for so long they became part of the landscape. Stationed in military barracks and billeted with families throughout the country, it was only natural that they would meet local women, fall in love and marry – and that's exactly what one in every ten Canadians did.

As the number of Canadians in Britain increased, so too did the weddings: in 1940 there were 1,222 marriages; the number more than doubled in 1941 when there were 3,011; in 1942 there were 4,160; and in 1943 they climbed again to 5,897. From January to June 1944 there were 3,927 marriages and another 2,273 from July to December.[5]

By December 1944 marriages were no longer exclusively to British women as the Canadians were marrying French, Belgian and Dutch women they were meeting on the Continent. But the vast majority – 44,886 – of the 47,783 marriages that took place before the last of the Canadians left for home, were to British War Brides.[6]

Back in Canada, the marriage boom certainly didn't go unnoticed; as War Brides began to trickle into the country in 1942, 1943 and 1944, stories about them began to appear in the press and not all of it was kind.

It didn't take long for someone to react. In January 1944 an unidentified British wife wrote a two-page article in *Maclean's*, Canada's national magazine. In it she talks about the reception she's received since arriving in Canada three months earlier and recounts the warning she was given by her husband shortly before she left England:

> 'After the last war,' he said, 'there was a certain amount of gossip about British war brides. Some of the Canadian boys married poor types of girls. Some fine British girls married no-good Canadians. As a result some of the marriages turned out disastrously and caused gossip. People talked about the marriages which failed. They appeared to forget the many British brides who came to Canada and proved splendid wives and mothers.'[7]

The writer, who goes by the pseudonym 'One Of Them', feels she always has to explain why she married a Canadian and defends her sister War Brides from one of the most stinging criticisms that these 'Limeys' are taking the 'cream of Canada's young men out of circulation.'

She also comments on the aloofness of Canadians whom she resents for giving her short shrift when she makes a mistake or says the wrong thing. 'One Of Them' feels Canadians just don't seem to appreciate what life is like for the average British citizen, with the severe rationing, queues, bombing, and tragedy around every corner.

The *Maclean's* article touched a nerve across Canada. An article which appeared in the Toronto *Globe and Mail* in April 1944 faces the issue head on and encourages Canadians to extend a warm welcome to British wives:

> There actually seem to be people who feel that there is something sinister and unnatural in the circumstance that if you expose a normal Canadian youth to several million normal females of his own race for two or three years at a stretch, he is apt to up and marry one of them.
>
> Most British war brides who have traveled to Canada to begin the job of making new homes are received as warmly as they deserve ... [but] in far too many cases the reception ranges from polite hostility to studied rudeness. Particularly if she is setting up housekeeping in a small community the girl from abroad is likely, sooner or later, to meet the girl her husband left behind him, a thwarted mother-in-law, or simply a few third parties who have no legal standing in the discussion at all but feel that their duty to a jilted friend compels them to 'take sides'.
>
> There is hardly a family in Canada that, somewhere in its genealogical history, cannot find a British bride. The type of British bride that the Canadian overseas forces have started to bring back home now will differ from the earlier models only as models in women differ generally from generation to generation.
>
> In the main, they will be pretty much the same kind of women who helped to make our country and the people in it what they are. Most of them will need all the help and kindness their new country can spare them.[8]

In reponse to such concerns, the Department of National Defence wisely issued British wives with a publication called *Welcome to War Brides*. The 40-page booklet included an introduction by Princess Alice, the granddaughter of Queen Victoria and wife of the Governor General of Canada.

Welcome to War Brides also contained some common sense advice, from the obvious: 'If you should unwittingly convey the impression that you regard Canada as in any way a dependency of Britain, you are likely to find that many people will temper their welcome with coolness', to the downright depressing,

'[In small towns] you simply must conform … or live like a hermit and disappoint your husband and his people.'[9]

It also included a glossary of familiar terms with their Canadian equivalents. That booklet would have come in handy for English War Bride Vera Brooks, who made more than one mistake with her use of the vernacular:

> I tried to help some of the girls cope with two or three children, saying 'Keep your pecker up,' which later we discovered was a very rude expression. In England it means chin. We made a lot of these mistakes. Another was to knock someone up, which we'd always used to mean to awaken somebody. We found it was more polite to say 'I am warm' instead of 'I am hot'. The ironmonger's turned into the hardware store. The clerk was a clerk, not a clark. 'Are you one of the clarks?' I asked in a store one day. 'No, I am one of the Browns,' the clerk replied.[10]

Meeting the Canadians

British women met Canadians in all kinds of places and under every circumstance imaginable: from huge dance halls where the sounds of big band music like Glen Miller and Tommy Dorsey urged young people to get up and dance, to standing at a post-box mailing a letter; from having a drink in a pub, to skating; from being introduced on a blind date, to escaping German bombs in air-raid shelters; from meeting a relative's pen pal, to walking down the street: from the planned to the accidental, Canadian men and British women met and when that happened they did what has been going on since the beginning of time: they fell in love and married.

The women Canadians met were just as likely to be working in a munitions factory or driving an ambulance as they were to be a member of the Women's Land Army (WLA) or the NAAFI (Navy, Army and Air Force Institute). By 1944 nearly a half-million British women were in uniform, including the Auxiliary Territorial Services (ATS), the Women's Auxiliary Air Force (WAAF) and the Women's Royal Naval Service (WRNS).[11] Tens of thousands of them became War Brides.

Like many young women her age, nineteen-year-old Johan (Hillis) DeWitt of Glasgow, Scotland wanted to join the WAAF but her father wouldn't hear of it. At the time, there was considerable public criticism of the women's services, due in large part to unfounded rumours which held that innocent young girls were being exposed to all manner of immoral behaviour.[12]

Despite her pleas to the contrary, Johan's father refused to budge. Instead, he would only let her join the Women's Land Army, a British solution to the farm crisis sparked by the war. The Land Army put women on farms and freed up men for more important work in the services and elsewhere. Johan's story of meeting her husband shows just how accidental a meeting could be:

> One day when she was in the barn cleaning up the cow manure, two young Canadian soldiers passed by. One of them was Luke DeWitt, who had been recuperating in the nearby hospital. Her first impressions weren't too positive: here she was, up to her elbows in cow manure, and standing in front of her laughing were two young men. 'I was a heck of a mess ... I don't know in the name of heaven how Luke and I got together but he must have felt sorry for me.'[13]

The fact that nearly all the available young British men had joined up and left their local communities only increased the certainty that eligible Canadian servicemen and British women would meet. Under normal circumstances, fathers, uncles and brothers may have put a stop to the amorous adventures of their female relatives, but most of the men were gone, based elsewhere in the UK or fighting, at first in the Mediterranean and Africa, and later in Italy, and Northwest Europe. There was little they could do to prevent Cupid's arrow from striking their daughters, sisters, aunts – and in some cases, even their wives.

There was talk about Canadians stealing British women, sometimes even married British women – and certainly, that did happen. More than one British woman divorced her husband and married a Canadian instead. There were bigamists too, of both sexes, but in the files of the Canadian Wives Bureau the male bigamists of Canadian origin outnumber the women by eight to one.[14]

As if the divorce and bigamy weren't enough to contend with, there were an estimated 22,000 Canadian babies born to unwed, single British women during the war. The most famous of these so called War Children is blues guitarist Eric Clapton, whose father is Montreal-born serviceman Edward Fryer.

Eric's mother, Patricia Clapton, met Fryer in the days before the D-Day landing and nine months later, young Eric was born. Patricia married another Canadian and came to Canada as a War Bride in 1946, leaving her son behind with his grandparents who raised him as their own.[15]

British Attitudes Towards The Canadians

For the most part, Canadians were welcome in Britain. They were, after all, fellow cousins in the Empire. Nearly fifty per cent of all Canadians could claim British ancestry and many of the young men serving in the UK had relatives living in England, Scotland, Ireland and Wales. Some Canadians were actually born in Britain and had emigrated with their families as children, so they were, for all intents and purposes, going back home.

Although Canada was a Dominion, it was still perceived as a colony by many British, which bothered some Canadians – especially the politicians – but nobody could ignore their shared history; the First World War had proven Canada's commitment to the Mother Country and the Second World War wasn't going to be any different.

Britons recognized that Canadians were performing an important duty, but it didn't mean they always had to like these young 'colonials' as they were sometimes disparagingly called. The first winter of 1939–1940 didn't do much for the Canadians' reputation: It was the coldest winter on record since 1894 and the men didn't like anything about Aldershot: the food was different, the barracks were freezing, and the people were 'strange and reserved.'[16] 1941 wasn't any better.

The Canadians who arrived in the first few years may have had their reasons to dislike Britain but some of them also gave Britons a few reasons to dislike Canadians. Away from home for the first time, undisciplined and untrained, they didn't always behave the way their hosts would have liked, especially when it came to drinking.

British attitudes towards alcohol and the presence of so many pubs represented a huge cultural shift for these young men. In the first few years there was more than one complaint about drunken Canadians tearing up a village. This 1941 letter from a woman in Reigate, Surrey sums up the feelings of many Britons about Canadians that Christmas:

> The damned 3rd Division has now been inflicted on us and they seem just as rough and tough as their predecessors; last night, Xmas eve, they were rolling along in the middle of the road till all hours yelling at the top of their voices, the dead drunk being dragged along by the not so drunk. If anyone wants to know what your wife thinks of Canadians, just say 'they stink'. I heard yesterday that a local girl not quite sixteen was expecting triplets any moment and the Canadian responsible has debunked.[17]

Given that kind of boorish behaviour, it's not surprising that more than one Canadian wasn't embraced by his British girlfriend's parents. This War Bride describes how her husband had to 'sell himself' to her parents:

> They, in common with a lot of other parents over there, looked suspiciously at Canadians. Definitely, they agreed, we should be hospitable to Canadians, for they had volunteered – not been called up – to come and stand shoulder to shoulder with the motherland. They were grand fighters in the last war and probably would be just as good in this one. But to have a Canadian as a son-in-law?
>
> Too many people had heard the story of the 'pub' down in Brighton which Canadians had wrecked, and the story had lost nothing in the retelling. There were those drunken Canadians my father himself had seen in Piccadilly Circus.
>
> With all this, it was to a definitely hostile atmosphere that I brought my husband-to-be home for the first time. Through him, my people met other Canadians and I think I can say that in all England there is not a more loyal pro-Canadian family than the one my husband and I left behind.[18]

Over the course of the war, relations between Canadians and their British hosts became considerably more relaxed and cordial. United by the shared experience of German bombing during the Blitz, incidents like the one at Reigate were rare in the last half of the war. With training and discipline, the Canadians put their best foot forward and, although they weren't perfect, over time they began to understand the British and accept their different ways.[19] As Canadian sacrifice on the battlefield became increasingly evident at Dieppe, then Sicily, Italy and Northwest Europe, Canadians and Britons got to know each other very well and one of the best ways to seal that relationship was through marriage.

I Do

Getting married in wartime wasn't as easy as saying 'I do'. In those days, it was expected that a young man would ask the parents for permission to marry their daughter. Assuming the answer was yes, only then could the fusillade of paperwork begin.

Forms had to be filled out, appointments made, medical exams taken, and although the rules changed over time, a Canadian serviceman had to obtain permission to marry from his commanding officer before a wedding date could be set. If he was under twenty-one, he even had to get permission from his parents back in Canada. If she was under twenty-one she had to do the same with her parents. The bride-to-be also had to get a letter of recommendation from her employer attesting to her character, a meeting with the chaplain was set, and a licence had to be purchased before any vows could be exchanged.

Reverend Father Raymond Hickey was the Roman Catholic Padre of the North Shore (New Brunswick) Regiment. The North Shores were of English, Scottish, Irish and Acadian[20] descent and many of the young French soldiers whom he ministered spoke not a word of English.

One of Father Hickey's tasks was to counsel young couples who were contemplating marriage. In his book *The Scarlet Dawn*, which chronicles his experiences with the North Shores during the Second World War, Father Hickey explains how he learned a lesson about love in a chapter called 'Love knows no language'.

Joe came back from a seven day leave to Edinburgh, came in and 'Father,' said he, 'I come to get married.' 'Fine Joe,' said I, 'marriage is a fine sacrament; a good girl Joe?'

'Oh yes, Father, Irish.' 'Irish,' was the answer that Joe knew would score a bull's eye with me. 'Yes I know Joe, but know her well?' I asked. 'Oh yes, real well, Father,' was the reply. Joe had already told me that he had met her for the first time on that leave. Now it took Joe a day to go and another to return; his Irish Mary was working all day in a factory, so with rapid calculation I figured out just how well Joe knew her. This was a chaplain's duty, so I set out to side-track Joe's marriage. 'Now look Joe,' said I, 'have you thought this all out? Have you told her everything? Does she realize what she's doing? For example, have you told her of the cold winters we have back home, with our ice and snow? And another thing Joe, how is your little Mary O'Brien, with her Irish brogue, going to get along in your village where you speak mostly French? Have you told her all this Joe?' Joe's only answer was a shrug of his shoulders. With a promise to Joe to shove his case through, we said goodnight and I sat down to write Miss Mary O'Brien the things her Joe wouldn't speak. Here was my letter:

'Dear Miss O'Brien:

I'm the Catholic chaplain of the regiment your friend Joe is in. He tells me you intend to marry. Now Joe is a fine good boy, but has he told you of the conditions you will be going to in Canada? For example, we have terrible winters where Joe and I come from; we have nine and ten feet of snow; it's awfully cold, and there's ice from October to June.

And, secondly, Miss O'Brien, have you considered the language question? How are you going to get along with your Irish brogue – which I admit is sweet in your County Down, but out of place in Joe's French-speaking village?' And with a bit of fatherly advice I closed my letter.

Back by return mail, came the answer. It was written post haste in lead pencil on, I think, paper she tore off the wall in her wrath. Here was the answer:

'Dear Father Hickey:

Thank you for your letter. As to your first difficulty – I like snow, and secondly, love knows no language.

Yours truly

Mary O'Brien.'[21]

All this bureaucracy was designed to slow down hasty marriages and it seemed to work: only the most determined couples could be expected to go through that entire process and still come out the other end with stars in their eyes. The 'permission to marry' form would give a date upon which the couple could legally marry and with that piece of paper in hand, they could purchase a marriage licence. The licence was good for a certain period of time and if the marriage didn't take place within the prescribed dates, a new licence had to be bought.

There are so many examples of weddings gone awry that it seems they were the norm, rather than the exception. It was impossible to say when a fiancé would be called away to duty, so marriages that had been planned months in advance could often be called off at the last minute or, vice-versa, hurried preparations had to be made at a moment's notice when it was known a soldier was due for transfer or repatriation back to Canada. How they managed to pull it off is nothing short of miraculous in some cases.

Still other women's hopes of marriage would be dashed when her fiancé was repatriated before the paperwork was complete. This appears to have happened quite frequently if the number of fiancées who came to Canada to get married after the war is any indication.

For the husband, there was little preparation: he wore a uniform. But all the nice things that a young bride dreams of such as a white dress, flowers, cakes and fine food for guests at the reception had to be purchased using ration cards. More often than not, she ended up getting married in a two-piece suit, the cake was made without sugar, and the menu was whatever could be cobbled together from rations, including the serviceman's friend, Spam®.

Transportation of War Brides

Between January 1942 and August 1944, the transportation of servicemen's wives and children was administered by the London Office of the Immigration Branch of the Canadian Department of Mines and Resources. At first the numbers were barely noticeable, and the reasons why so few came during the war years are fairly obvious: the exigencies of the fighting services, the very real danger of travel on the seas and the ban on the westward movement of wives and civilians ensured that only a very small number of dependents could make the dangerous journey to Canada.

But with victory in sight, everything changed when the Department of National Defence took over the transportation and travel arrangements of servicemen's dependents in August 1944. The Army was put in charge of moving wives and children of all three services, Army, Navy and Air Force, and one of the first things it did was to set up the Canadian Wives Bureau on the third floor of a fashionable and expensive store called Galleries Lafayette on Regent Street in London.

Established as a Directorate of the Adjutant General's Branch at Canadian Military Headquarters, the Bureau was responsible for arranging dependent's passage to Canada, collecting and caring for them en route to their ships and providing information and welfare services. The Bureau also encouraged the formation of wives' clubs in the UK, where brides held social gatherings and listened to talks on life in Canada.

Although smaller numbers of War Brides and their children had made their way to Canada between 1942 and 1945, the overwhelming majority, (45,320 of 64,451), were brought to Canada in 1946 in a massive year-long effort that began with the sailing of the *Mauretania* on 5 February.

English War Bride Eswyn Lyster and her young son, Terry, came to Canada on the *Mauretania* which departed from Liverpool in the early morning hours. The *Mauretania* was 'the vanguard'[22] of more than 45,000 Canadian servicemen's dependents scheduled to sail for Canada over the course of the next twelve months. A famous photograph of the ship's departure paints a vivid picture of the huge vessel in the soft morning light, smoke billowing from its stacks as two tugs help it along its way. In this brief excerpt from her memoirs, Eswyn describes the five-day ocean voyage:

Terry and I sailed from Liverpool on the *Mauretania* in a group of about 1,000 Canadian War Brides, in the early hours of February 5th. This was the first dedicated War Bride sailing, although small groups had made the crossing while the war was still on. From the dock the *Mauretania* had looked like a floating warehouse, and most of us assumed that no amount of water could unsteady it. We were wrong.... The Atlantic in February gives a watery impersonation of the Canadian Rockies. The good ship *Mauretania* tilted much too far one way, slid into a valley; tilted as many degrees the other way, and rode a sloping wall of water until nothing could be seen from the porthole but sky. Not that anybody was looking. The process was repeated endlessly for five days with predictable results.[23]

That sailing marked the beginning of what the Canadian press affectionately dubbed 'Operation Daddy'[24] in reference to the thousands of women and infants on board the huge ocean-going ships. But for members of the Canadian Wives Bureau, the Immigration Branch, the Red Cross and for the women themselves, it was a huge logistical undertaking that took on the dimensions of a D-Day assault. By the time it was all over, 43,454 War Brides and their 20,997 children were transported to Canada.

The Darker Side

Interestingly, more than 4,500 of the 48,000 War Brides who married Canadian servicemen refused to take the government up on its offer of free passage to Canada. While it is true that about half of the War Brides who decided to stay in Britain and Europe did so because their husbands found employment, there is evidence of a seamier side to the War Bride story.

Riddled throughout the files of the Canadian Wives Bureau and Immigration Branch are the most personal and intimate details of these people's lives, including lists of hundreds of War Brides who are either refusing to come to Canada because they are getting a divorce from their Canadian husbands, or who are being refused transport under the War Bride transportation scheme because their settlement arrangements have been deemed 'unsatisfactory' by the Immigration Branch. In the files are these couple's full names, addresses and sometimes quite shocking revelations about the reasons why the women aren't coming to Canada.

In a day when everyone seems to be so concerned about privacy, it's surprising that the files are actually public record and open for anyone to see. Reasons given include everything from 'husband in jail' to the unsavoury 'VDS' (which stands for Venereal Disease Symptoms); from 'wife insane' to 'divorce pending'; from 'husband cannot be located' to 'husband doesn't want wife'.

Although the reading may be titillating, the fact is that these five per cent of cases were rare in comparison to the ninety-five per cent of War Brides who did come to Canada to happily join their husbands. What happened when they got there is another story.

Boarding the Ships

Each wife had documents to provide, forms to fill out, medical appointments to keep, and more forms to fill out before packing her luggage and finally boarding a ship in Southampton or Liverpool. Each night before the ship would sail, wives and children would descend upon one of the brides' hostels in London, such as the Mostyn Hostel, where they were organized by the Red Cross for departure to Canada the next day.

Unfortunately for those brides travelling between 1942 and 1945 the accommodations and services provided to dependents was by no means as impressive: sailing in wartime, on reconverted troopships with no special considerations for the needs of babies in nappies, and without the dedicated assistance afforded to wives in 1946 through the Red Cross Escort Officers and VADs (Voluntary Aid Detachments), the wives who came during the war years had a vastly different experience than those who came at the height of the War Bride transportation in 1946.

Doris Lloyd, an English bride who arrived in New Brunswick in November 1944, remembers how she and her daughter, along with twenty other War Brides and their children, ended up spending four days in a dismal Scottish hostel while waiting for a winter storm to break. Once on board their ship, the *Ile de France*, twelve women and their one or two children each were crowded into cabins with twelve bunks, one bed for each mother and her children. As seasickness set in, they approached the Red Cross for help and were told to take care of themselves. Doris was not impressed.[25] By 1946, however, the kinks were worked out of the system and few brides would share that experience.

Travelling in style on refitted luxury liners such as the *Queen Mary* and the *Aquitania*, the War Brides who came to Canada in 1946 had a luxurious trip by comparison. For these brides, the transatlantic trip was equivalent to a modern-day cruise, with fine food, lodgings and services.

In this newspaper article dated 11 June 1946 the author makes it quite clear that the Wives Bureau had taken 'every precaution' to ensure the comfort of its special cargo:

> Every possible precaution was taken to protect infants from accident or illness during the voyages ... No children were allowed to travel in ships considered unsuitable, such as the *Ile de France* and the *Lady Rodney* which have steep companion ways and narrow alleys. Ships especially equipped for children are the *Letitia*, the *Queen Mary*, the *Aquitania* and the *Lady Nelson*. All have babies' cots adjacent to the lower berths reserved for mothers, up-to-date hospitals, maternity wards and full staffs of doctors, nurses and Red Cross workers.[26]

But no matter if you were on the *Ile de France* in 1944 or the *Queen Mary* in 1946, seasickness was a serious problem for many on board and there was little that could be done except to lie in bed and suffer until the ship docked at Pier 21 in Halifax. English War Bride Pat Pyne recalls coming down with seasickness on day three of her voyage on the *Letitia* and in her diary she wrote:

> Peg (another War Bride) and I were the only two at our table today for dinner and there were only a few at breakfast. Our steward told us not to take any sugar in our tea or coffee if we didn't want to get seasick. We haven't been feeling too good ourselves today but are both most determined to not be sick.[27]

Making matters worse for the seasick was their proximity in closed cabins to other sick wives along with their nauseated, crying children in nappies, not to mention the threat presented by stormy weather during the sometimes turbulent ocean crossings. In the diary she kept of her work as a Canadian Red Cross Escort Officer on board the War Bride ships, Kay Ruddick wrote of a harrowing storm that hit the *Queen Mary* on 27 August 1946:

> Terrific sea; around midnight, wave hit the ship and was so huge, splashed into the portholes on top deck and hit the bridge, down the gangway into the Captain's cabin ... Electrical equipment put out of commission and ship stopped for two hours, bobbing like a cork ... brides, babies (1000 brides and 1,000 babies on board) ship's crew sick all over the place! Men, civilians

and other passengers, turned to, to help us look after the babies. By morning the seas had calmed down and the 'cleanup' started ... wet mattresses galore, not to mention gallons of javex used to clean the cabins and decks.[28]

After spending up to two weeks at sea, the vast majority of War Brides and their children arrived at Pier 21 in Halifax, the principal gateway to Canada for returning servicemen and their dependents during and after the war.

From the ship, they were escorted into a waiting area in Pier 21 where Red Cross personnel would care for the children while the wives were processed through Immigration. From Halifax, the next step of their journey began with trains called War Bride Specials, equipped and staffed by military personnel and Red Cross Escort Officers. At every whistle stop across Canada, these War Bride trains brought dependents to their husbands and new families from Cape Breton to British Columbia. Thus marked the end of the fairytale and the beginning of real life in Canada.

Settling In

After the initial shock of arrival wore off, the War Brides settled into the regular ebb and flow of life in Canada. At the beginning, War Brides' groups formed in towns and cities with the help of the local YMCA or the Red Cross and women tried to help each other with a friendly network of support. But the fact was, with new babies arriving one after the other, there was little time to go to War Bride meetings and most of these groups soon disbanded.[29]

In retrospect, had some War Brides known what was in store for them in Canada, they probably would have turned around and gone straight back home to their parents. But it wasn't so easy in 1946 to just get up and leave and even if it had been, many still would have decided to stay. 'You made your bed, now you have to lie in it' was a saying that reflected the social expectations of women for whom marriage was supposed to be forever: divorce was simply not an option.

In response to concerns raised in the media about the fate of British War Brides, in May 1947 Canada's Department of Veterans Affairs released the results of a cross-country survey of War Brides that intended to show how they were faring in their marriages to Canadian servicemen. Using New Brunswick as the example, the study found that the majority of these marriages were 'as successful as even the most optimistic could expect',[30] and it offered up statistics showing that the War Brides' marriages were no less likely to fail than any other Canadian union.

The reason the DVA released the report had as much to do with public perception that some War Brides had been lured to Canada with false promises as it did with the reality that others were in fact returning to their homelands after their marriages had failed.[31]

We will never know how many women went back home to Britain and Europe after coming to Canada as War Brides. Once the war emergency was over, Immigration no longer counted these women as a distinct group so they blended into the statistics for outward migration. We can only imagine how many War Brides would have liked to go back but they did not have the financial resources to do so and there was no help from the Canadian government.

Correspondence in the Canadian Wives Bureau files shows the difficulties some War Brides had in adapting to life in Canada and the kind of help they could expect from Canadian authorities. Some clearly wanted an escape, but not all War Brides were planning to leave their husbands behind. As this January 1947 letter to the Canadian Wives Bureau shows, there were also economic reasons for going back home:

> My husband, baby and myself wish to return to England. My husband has been offered a good position out there but we haven't the money to pay both our fares. I am a War Bride and I haven't lived in Canada over a year. Two people told me I can apply for my fare through the government because of this. Is this true and if so would you be so kind as to give me the necessary information ... [32]

There were as many reasons why a bride would want to leave as there were reasons to stay and whether she acted upon it depended on a whole set of circumstances unique to her situation. We do know, however, that the majority stayed in Canada. As any married couple will attest, it isn't easy starting out, and so it was for the War Brides in the postwar years.

With so many returning veterans, jobs were scarce and it was difficult, if not impossible, to find adequate housing. Cultural differences, language, ethnicity and religion caused problems for many women as they tried to fit in. English War Bride Henrietta Pronovost couldn't speak French when she arrived in St Gabriel de Brandon, Quebec but she says she knew enough 'to tell when they were talking about me'.[33]

And although outhouses were a normal part of Canadian life, they certainly weren't for city slickers used to plumbing and electricity in big cities like London. How many women found themselves facing down an angry barnyard rooster on the way to the 'biffy' is impossible to tell, but at least they can laugh about it now. British War Bride Betty Campbell came from Plymouth, England to Arthurette, New Brunswick. She had a run in with a rooster named Jimmy Duke who took a disliking to her.

> We lived six miles out in the woods in Birch Ridge. The outside toilet was 400 feet from the house and my sister-in-law had a very ugly rooster named Jimmy Duke. One day I had to go out there. When I opened the door to come out, there stood Jimmy Duke. My sister-in-law was wondering what had happened to me so she came out to see if I was okay. There she stood, laughing at Jimmy Duke and me inside, crying. Any time I came home from somewhere or stepped outside, he came running as soon as he saw me or heard my voice, so I had to learn to keep my mouth shut. And guess what? I always had to have an escort to go outside.[34]

Added to the mix was the fact that many of the husbands had been repatriated ahead of their wives and had spent the last six months or more back in their home towns, hanging around with their war buddies at the Legion, drinking and reliving the good times – and the bad – overseas. Others suffered what we would call post-traumatic stress disorder which was exacerbated when their wives and young children arrived in Canada.

'He wasn't the same man I married,' is a saying that was heard often among the War Brides. Hopes and dreams of a happy life in Canada were sometimes buried under infidelity, poverty, unemployment, alcoholism and debt. For these War Brides, returning back home to Britain was not only an admission of failure, but it was financially impossible, especially if there were children involved.

Undoubtedly, rural life was a shock for women raised in cities with modern transportation and communications systems: dirt roads that turned into mud in the spring, no electricity or telephones and lack of access to education and healthcare were all important concerns. But if your husband treated you well and you were in love, nothing else really mattered.

The War Brides Today

It would be impossible to tell the story of every Canadian War Bride in this short volume: every woman's experience was unique, ranging from the 'idyllic to the tragic'.[35] They shared much in common: meeting and falling in love with a Canadian soldier in Britain, marrying and coming to Canada, settling into a new culture and adapting to a new way of life. But far from the stereotypical War Bride with her tea-cosy and loveable accent, the War Brides are as different from one another as they are to any other immigrant group.

Without question, there are couples who probably should never have married. But behind the sordid tales of unhappy War Brides is anecdotal evidence which shows these women have had mainly successful marriages, filled with happiness and plenty of love to pass down to their own children and on to the next generation.

And no matter what happened in their personal lives, if you ask the War Brides today if they would do it all over again, most will give a resounding 'Yes!' For many, their lives were enriched both materially and emotionally by coming to Canada and the list of their accomplishments is lengthy: a loving husband; a good home; fine well-educated children and grandchildren; as well as a standard of living far better than what they might have had in their homeland.

Many played important roles in their communities, first as volunteers with their children's schools and later, as the children grew up, taking leadership roles in organizations, service groups, arts, culture, religion and even politics.

Many wives worked outside the home, providing a second income to make ends meet while gaining a wider circle of friends and deeper ties to their community. Others became famous in their own right; English War Bride Joan Walker won the Stephen Leacock Award for Humour in 1954 for her book *Pardon My Parka*, a hilarious look at her experiences coming to Canada as the wife of a Canadian serviceman. Betty Oliphant became the head and inspiration of the National Ballet School of Canada, and was considered one of the country's leading professionals until her death in 2004. And in 2006, Jean Spear was honoured by Queen Elizabeth II when she received the Member of the Order of the British Empire (MBE) in Buckingham Palace.

In the 1970s when the last of the children flew the nest, and later, as husbands started to pass away, many returned to their immigrant roots and revived long defunct War Brides organisations in villages, towns and cities across the country. The revival began in Saskatchewan, then spread like wildfire across Canada until nearly every province had an official War Brides Association. Today, the War Brides may be in their eighties, but the groups provide a tangible connection to a sisterhood, which despite their differences, share so many similarities.

The groups also symbolize Canada's continued fascination with the War Bride story more than sixty years after the end of the Second World War. Every year, there are War Bride reunions from Regina, Saskatchewan to Halifax, Nova Scotia; from Peterborough, Ontario to Fredericton, New Brunswick, and even though they always say 'this will be the last one' there always seems to be another.

In 2006, the sixtieth anniversary of the War Brides' arrival in Canada was celebrated across the country. Six of ten provinces declared 2006 Year of the War Bride and in November, the largest gathering of War Brides since 1946 made a pilgrimage to Pier 21 in Halifax on board VIA Rail's special War Bride train. Age and time have not slowed them down. They are still the bright young lasses who caught the sparkle in a Canadian's eye and fell in love with him in the midst of the Second World War.

The War Brides came to Canada at a time when there was a renewed sense of optimism that things could be better after six long years of war. Anything was possible, so long as one was willing to work for it. Together with their husbands and families, they helped shape the Canada we know today, reinforcing British cultural traditions and fostering emotional ties with the Mother Country that have been passed on with pride to the next generations. Whether they were English, Scottish, Irish or Welsh, their legacy is alive in the one in thirty Canadians who can count a War Bride in their family tree.

1

Maritimes and Newfoundland

When we think of the War Bride experience one of the first things that comes to mind is the long train journey across the vastness of the Canadian landscape, but War Brides who came to the Maritime provinces had geography on their side.

For women headed to Halifax, the long transatlantic journey ended the moment her ship landed at Pier 21. When War Bride Marguerite Turner of Leeds, England arrived in March 1946 she was thrilled to see her husband Jim waving at her from atop the building facing the *Aquitania*. 'I remember it clearly. He was standing on the roof, wearing a brown pinstripe suit and he had a brown fedora and I was standing on the side at the rail of the ship and he was dead opposite me with two other chaps'.[1]

That kind of a reunion was unusual; most British wives had a long distance ahead of them and the vast majority did not meet their husbands in Halifax. For those men waiting patiently in Quebec, Ontario and especially out west, another five more days would pass as their wives made their way across Canada by train.

In 1946 Canada consisted of 11.5 million people living in nine provinces and two territories, stretching nearly 4,000 miles from Nova Scotia on the east coast to British Columbia on the west.

The Maritime region, where Halifax is located, consisted of three eastern provinces, Nova Scotia, New Brunswick and Prince Edward Island. Together they had a combined population of just over one million people[2] and of these, most lived in a rural setting, either on a farm or out in the country, far away from the closest city or town.[3]

Compared to Ontario and Quebec, the Maritimes were a mainly rural population. In 1946 there were only three or four big cities in the whole of the region, the main ones being Halifax, followed by Saint John and Moncton, New Brunswick, the hub of the Maritimes where trains travelling east and west would pass through. The whole of Prince Edward Island had only 95,000 people and the majority lived on farms.[4] Most people in the Maritimes worked in the resource-based economies of farming, forestry, fisheries and mining as had their forefathers for generations.

The three provinces share a unique cultural heritage that is tied to 400 years of European settlement as well as a pattern of immigration that brought newcomers mainly from France (known as Acadians), England, Scotland and Ireland. There is also an Aboriginal presence stretching back more than 10,000 years with Mi'kmaq and Maliseet settlements throughout the region, and even Black Loyalists – former slaves – who were promised their freedom for supporting the British during the American Revolution. The French-speaking Acadians shaped the character of the region and there were immigrants from other countries such as Lebanon, Italy and Eastern Europe, but for the most part Maritime Canada in the postwar years was English speaking and place names like New Glasgow, Newcastle and Hampshire reflected its British heritage.

Newfoundland is often mistakenly included as one of the Maritime provinces but it isn't today and it certainly wasn't in 1946. As Newfoundland had not yet joined the Confederation – and wouldn't until 1949 – War Brides who went to Newfoundland were, in fact, going to another country and when they arrived in Halifax they still had a long way to go by ferry before they were home.[5]

But War Brides who were headed to Halifax or Dartmouth could have taken a taxi to their new homes or driven to surrounding communities like

Map of Maritimes, Canada including Newfoundland and Labrador. The Maritimes included Nova Scotia, Prince Edward Island and New Brunswick. Newfoundland did not become part of Canada until 1949 so War Brides who travelled there were headed to another country.

Truro in a couple of hours. Depending on the weather, those destined to the far-flung reaches of Cape Breton or New Brunswick would be in their husband's arms in less than a half-day by train. And although Prince Edward Island was accessible only by ferry, War Brides who were headed to PEI were at home, bags unpacked and sipping a cup of tea a long time before their shipmates who were going to Quebec and Ontario.

London-born War Bride Beatrice MacIntosh came to Halifax on the *Mauretania* in March 1946 destined for South Harbour, Cape Breton. She had no idea of the hardship she caused her husband who had the wrong date of his wife's 'imminent arrival' in Halifax. His long journey by snow-shoe, dog sleigh, foot, ferry, bus and horse sleigh in the middle of a cold Cape Breton winter amounted to a journey of epic proportions.

He assumed that the War Brides for Cape Breton would be sent by train from Halifax to Sydney. It was February, mid-winter, and the roads were not open. He started out by snow shoes to Big Intervale. He was joined by a local friend who also wanted to travel to Sydney. From Big Intervale they got a ride by horse and sleigh to the foot of North Mountain. Carrying the snowshoes (one pair between them) they followed a snow track made by the mailman … They finally reached Pleasant Bay and went to a hotel … The next morning they gave their backpacks to the mailman (he had a dog team), left their snowshoes at the hotel and walked behind the mailman all the way to Cheticamp, crossing both MacKenzie and French Mountain. Quite a walk!

In Cheticamp they stayed a night at Aucoin's Hotel, owned by a man nicknamed 'Johnny on the Spot'. The following morning they took a large six passenger bus to the Strait (Hawkesbury), where they changed to an Acadian Lines bus. They had only gone a few miles when the bus had problems so the driver pulled into a hotel where they stayed that night. There was a dance in a hall close by, so the passengers all went. The bus driver got very intoxicated and couldn't drive the bus the next morning. He was fired and another driver came to drive the bus. At last, they arrived in Sydney, only to find out that I had sent a cable to South Harbour telling Kendrick that the boat I was supposed to travel on, the *Ile de France*, had been wrecked in a storm and I had to wait for further notice about another boat.[6]

Beatrice MacIntosh's experience aside, for most War Brides who went to the Maritimes the journey by train was not so important. Their biggest challenges lay in adapting to the cold Canadian climate and adjusting to a rural lifestyle far from towns and city centres where the things they had taken for granted in Britain, like shopping, transportation, and culture, were now but a distant memory.

The Only Place She Wanted to Be
Jean (Keegan) Paul

Jean Keegan was born in Coulsdon, Surrey, England in 1926. She married Charles Paul of the Tobique Indian Reserve in New Brunswick.

Jean Keegan was just a teenager from Coulsdon, Surrey when she fell in love with a young Aboriginal soldier, Charles Paul, of the Tobique Indian Reserve in northwestern New Brunswick.

One of four daughters of Charles and Mary Keegan, Jean came from a comfortable, middle-class background and lived in a large English city with all the modern amenities. No one in the family would have imagined that Jean would end up on an Indian Reserve in Canada but once she met Charlie Paul, that's the only place she wanted to be.

Jean's older sister Pat was stationed with the WAAF at the Kenley Aerodrome and she only came home to Coulsdon on leaves, but she remembers when Jean and Charlie Paul started going out together.

'They met at a dance near the old Cane Hill Hospital in Coulsdon,' says Pat, who is now eighty-three and lives in Warlingham. 'There were a lot of Canadians around the area and my mother really liked "Buck", as we called him, so she didn't mind Jean going out with him. They all used to go to a pub called the Midday Sun where the Canadians and their girlfriends gathered.'

Jean's father was only thirty-nine when the war started so he rejoined the King's Own Regiment and was stationed in Formby, Lancashire. The three younger girls lived at home with their mother and when Coulsdon was under attack from German bombing the two youngest, Kathy and Mary, were evacuated to northern England. That left Jean and her mother at home so the two of them would go to the dances, her mother as the chaperone. Mrs Keegan was attractive in her own right and was often mistaken as a sister to Pat and Jean, to her great delight.

Pat says other people may have thought that Charlie was different but nobody in their family gave much thought to the fact that he was a Canadian Indian. 'I remember after they married a girl came over to look at Jean's baby Christine and said, "Oh she's white!" I was amazed. I never even thought of Charlie or his brother Jim as not being like us.'

But in the weeks before Jean and Charlie married, her mother's friendly disposition towards Buck had changed.

'I was on my first leave home and Mum greeted me with tears,' Pat recalls. 'She said that Jean was pregnant, and what was she going to say to dad? What was she to do?'

The first thing they did was make wedding arrangements. Jean and Charlie were thrilled: they were in love and wanted to get married – everything was unfolding as planned as far as they were concerned – but Pat remembers her parents weren't very happy about it and neither was the Catholic priest, Father Tindal at St Aidan's Church.

All food and clothing was rationed so a friend of Mrs Keegan helped out by lending Jean a fur stole for the wedding ceremony and she even hosted the reception. Soon after, Charlie was sent to Italy with his regiment, the Carleton York, and after Christine was born, Jean went to Liverpool to stay with an aunt. Charlie contracted malaria and was diagnosed with arthritis that bothered him his whole life, but once he recuperated from his illness he was sent back to serve in northwestern Europe and at the end of the war he was repatriated to Canada.

Soon it became time for Jean to make her own travel arrangements through the Canadian Wives Bureau. Pat recalls that the padre of Charlie's regiment tried to dissuade Jean from going to the reserve and so did the British Red Cross, but Jean wouldn't listen to any of it. She was going to be with her husband and nothing would change her mind.

'It's what she wanted,' Pat says. 'Jean was very headstrong and always got what she wanted.'

In May 1946 twenty-year-old Jean and her daughter Christine crossed the Atlantic with hundreds of War Brides on board the *Aquitania*, arriving at Pier 21 on 21 May. From Halifax they made their way by train to McAdam, New Brunswick where they were met by the Roman Catholic priest, Charlie and Mrs Valreia Hunter, a volunteer with the Canadian Red Cross Train Meeting Committee who faithfully recorded Jean's arrival in the diary she kept of War Bride arrivals at McAdam.

The priest, Jean, Charlie and Christine were taken by canoe to the Maliseet Indian Reserve above Perth, New Brunswick. Reserve life was a very trying experience for a woman from a fine home in urban England. The community was located at the juncture of the Saint John and Tobique Rivers where the people eked out a meagre existence from the land, relying on the seasons and nature to bring what they needed to survive. Jean adapted to this rough life: she learned the ways of the people and became fluent in the language and ways of the Maliseet tribe. It was another twenty years before she was able to return to England for a visit.

There was little or no employment on the reserve so Charlie found work as a river guide during the fishing season and a hunting guide during the hunting season. In the fall, they would pick potatoes and in the summer they'd follow the blueberry trail as had generations of Native Indians before them.

Their daughter Cindy remembers growing up with her three brothers and sisters in grinding poverty in a shack on the edge of the reserve where rats would scamper across the floor. They didn't have a fridge or electricity and the bathroom was an outhouse in the back. When the Indian Agent would show up on the reserve to do his annual assessments he'd leave behind a barrel of flour and leftover army rations for every family. The convent school was run by nuns and they'd give the children a treat of hard tack and cod liver oil to battle malnutrition and rickets.

When Cindy was still a youngster her father built a small house for the family near the church. It was a step up and Jean was pleased with the new surroundings. When Jean's grandfather died she was asked what she wanted from the inheritance; a bathtub and running water was her request, and that's what she got.

Jean never complained about her life on the Tobique Reserve and her English family had no idea of the living conditions until her mother came to visit when the last child was born. It was quite a shock to see the way people lived on the reserve but Jean wasn't asking for sympathy from anyone: her husband was good to her and even if they weren't rich, they loved each other.

'I didn't know till years after what a brave and courageous woman my sister was,' says Pat. 'She was always the bossy and daring one, but lovely with it. There is no way I could have done what she did, even for love, but I'm proud to have been her eldest sister.'

Over the years, their situation improved considerably. Jean's younger sister Kathy married an American and moved nearby to Maine, USA, so for the first time Jean had her own family within reach. At one point, Jean's mother even came to stay with Kathy in Maine but she ended up going back to England. Charlie was elected Chief of the Tobique Reserve and in the late 1960s he became involved with the Union of New Brunswick Indians. With the children all grown up, Jean and Charlie left the reserve and moved to Fredericton in 1971 where he worked for the Union as a member of the Executive.

Cindy remembers going for a visit to see the relatives in England and everyone thought Jean had really 'made it' now. Jean lived in a nice home in the city and she even went to the hairdresser!

Jean and Charlie Paul had six children. Most grew up to have university educations and all have been successful in their own right. Charlie was recognized for his work with the Aboriginal community with an honorary PhD by St Thomas University in Fredericton, and could now carry the title Dr Charlie Paul. He and Jean were further honoured when they were invited to sit next to the table of Prince Philip and Princess Anne during a Royal Visit in 1986. While in England, they never got that close to the Royals. Had anyone bothered to ask, they would have heard the story of Sachem Gabe Acquin, Charlie's grandfather and the founder of what is now St Mary's First Nation in Fredericton.

Gabe Acquin was a leader in the Wolastoqiyik (Maliseet) community and was frequently coming and going from the Lt Governor's residence along the Saint John River in the 1800s. During the Royal Visit of 1860 Gabe took the Prince of Wales for an unscheduled canoe ride along the river. The Prince was supposed to be at church and couldn't be found. He showed up late for the service and shortly after that Gabe was invited to England by the Royal Family to visit and demonstrate Wolastoqiyik culture to the people of London.

In 1991, Jean was diagnosed with cancer and the four Keegan sisters came together for the very last time for Christmas in New Brunswick. It was an emotional gathering for the sisters and they were grateful to spend the last moments of Jean's life at her side. When Jean finally slipped away soon after the New Year, her family, friends, and Natives from all over Maliseet and Mi'kmaq territory came to the funeral mass which was conducted in both the English and Maliseet languages in her honour.

Jean died sixteen years ago but her memory lives on. In December 2005 her grandson TJ Burke, the first Aboriginal member of the New Brunswick Legislative Assembly (now Attorney General and Minister of Justice in the provincial Liberal government), introduced a motion to have 2006 declared Year of the War Bride in honour of his grandmother.

The idea soon caught on, and before the year was out, nearly every province in Canada followed suit: in villages, towns and cities across the country, Canadians celebrated the Year of the War Bride in 2006, honouring this very special group of citizens who helped build the Canada we know today.

Postscript: Charlie Paul died in 1997 knowing that he and Jean did the best they could for their children. Their oldest daughter, Christine, is a hairdresser and moved back to Tobique First Nation Reserve after living in Fredericton. Stewart has been the Chief of Tobique since 1987. Nick has a Masters Degree in Social Work and works in Tobique. Cindy has a Bachelor of Arts and Bachelor of Education and was a teacher for many years. She lives in Fredericton. Lindsay was a journalist and served on the Tobique Band Council. Pam, the baby, has a Bachelor of Social Work and works in Fredericton. Today, there are sixteen grandchildren and sixteen great grandchildren of Jean and Charlie Paul.

Rather Than Lose Him, I Married Him
Betty (Lowthian) Hillman

Betty (Lowthian) Hillman came to an isolated farm in Hawkin's Junction, New Brunswick.

Betty Lowthian was an Academy Girl dancer in the Isle of Wight dance troupe called Concert Party when she met her Canadian husband, Doug Hillman of Millville, New Brunswick.

Concert Party was a wartime entertainment company that grew out of Nesta Meech's dance school in the Isle of Wight. Betty remembers it consisted of 'a comedian, a contortionist, a baritone, a soprano, a pianist, a male tap dancer named Mr Ward, and the six-member Academy Girls dance troupe', of which Betty was one.

The war was on and the Isle of Wight was transformed into a training centre for the British Army, with Canadian and Americans also being trained there for the Dieppe raid. The performers would travel by private bus to different army camps to entertain the troops.

Betty was a member of Concert Party for four years, from the age of fourteen to eighteen. 'I finished school at age fourteen and the next year I tried to join the forces,' she explains. 'But when I saw the recruiter I was told to come back in three years. By being in the Concert Party I felt I was helping the effort in my own small way.'

She recalls that they had beautiful costumes made by their dressmaker, Mrs Sloper, and sometimes they would back up Nesta Meech when she sang. They did all kinds of routines, including tap and soft shoe dancing, and after their performances there was always a big meal in the Sergeant's Mess.

On two occasions, they did a show at Camp Hill Prison. The convicts were in charge of the curtains and when the show was over they gave the beautiful young dancers flowers called rose buttonholes that were grown in the prison gardens. A guided tour of the cells and a buffet lunch followed. Not surprisingly, the prisoners were very happy when the Academy Dancers performed!

Betty Lowthian was born in 1927 at Newport, Isle of Wight. Her mother's father, Charles Price, was a sea captain who owned two merchant ships, the *Wessex* and the *Moultonian*. Charles was captain of the *Wessex* and Betty's father, Albert Lowthian, later became first mate. Betty's paternal grandfather, William Lowthian, came from Carlisle, Cumberland County and he worked for the railway. Her mother Florence met Albert when he was stationed on the island with the Argyle and Southern Highlanders.

Betty had an idyllic life growing up on the Isle of Wight. Her favourite memories are of Christmas when the neighbourhood would be full of the sounds of caroling and her mother and aunts would make Christmas pudding. She remembers one Christmas when the milkman stopped at every

house with his horse and cart. He ladled out the cream and milk for his customers and by the time he got to the end of their road he was rather tipsy
since everyone wanted to give him a Christmas drink.

Betty was only twelve years old when the war broke out and her life was
soon transformed. The island was a target for the Germans because it had a
shipyard and housed two aircraft factories. Everyone was supplied with gas
masks and trained how to put them on in case of a gas attack. Betty's family
had their own air-raid shelter and she recalls that some nights the warning
siren would go off three or four times so they didn't get much sleep. A search-
light at the bottom of their field would pinpoint oncoming night bombers as
the target for ack-ack gunners.

Betty attended Parkhurst School until age fourteen and then joined the
dance troupe. When she wasn't performing with Concert Party she worked
in her aunt's café, Ma Freemon's, in the evenings and weekends. She also
worked as a shop assistant for the Maypole Dairy.

One evening in 1944 Betty was working at Ma Freemon's when Doug
Hillman came in and asked her for a date. He was in the Provost Corps
(Military Police) and he looked smart, but she was a bit dubious at first.

'I thought he was good looking so eventually I agreed to go see *Gone
with the Wind* with him. I was sixteen and he was twenty-one.'

Over the next two years Betty and Doug saw as much of each other as
they could. Doug had already asked her to marry him when she was sixteen
but at the time she thought he was crazy. By age eighteen she had to make
up her mind.

'He was coming back to Canada and I had to make a decision,' she says.
'Rather than lose him, I married him.'

Doug and Betty were married on 6 September 1945 and she came to Canada
ten months later in July 1946. Leaving her family was very difficult and the trip
across the Atlantic memorable, but nothing could have prepared Betty for the
new life she would live on a mixed farm in Hawkin's Corner, New Brunswick.
From the beautiful surroundings of Newport to an isolated, rural farmhouse
and a household of three men – her husband, his brother Les, and their uncle,
an eighty-seven-year-old bachelor – Betty was in for a culture shock.

Doug met Betty at the Woodstock, NB train station and the next day they
proceeded by car to his uncle's farm. Ladies from the Women's Institute met
with Betty and went out of their way to make her feel welcome, knowing
full well there was no other woman in the house and that it was not going
to be easy for a young English girl in these new surroundings. They gave

her a big shower the following day where she was presented with three handmade quilts and over ninety gifts.

No amount of presents could overcome the cultural gap Betty found herself in. The language and the life were utterly different from what she was used to. She came from a house with electricity and modern plumbing, but in Hawkin's Corner she couldn't decide what was worse: the outhouses, the wildlife or three very stubborn, argumentative men.

On one of her first walks along the railway tracks she thought she encountered a bear but it turned out to be a groundhog, which was the source of great amusement to the men. With her husband gone in the woods all day Betty was expected to help with the chores such as milking the cows. But the cows knew she was afraid of them and one day they chased her out of the barn and into a stream. One of the neighbours, Mrs Marr, rescued her from that predicament and also did the milking that day, but Mrs Marr's husband had a pet crow which would perch on a tree in the yard waiting for a treat. When the crow was outside Betty was afraid to leave the house!

Then there was the water: all the water for cooking came from the aforementioned stream. When Betty dipped her pail into the stream she saw tiny fish swimming around and it turned her off. She quickly changed to drinking milk instead, but then she had that little problem with the cows. Her husband thought the best way for Betty to bond with the cows was to give her one as a pet so he presented her with a calf aptly named Newport!

About a year after her arrival in Hawkin's Corner, Betty became pregnant. When she was four months along, Doug sold eight pigs to pay her fare back to England. A few months later, he made the trip himself, arriving before their first daughter was born. It was a good thing Betty did go back to England because she was very ill with toxemia and eclampsia after giving birth and she was in the hospital for a month.

Doug found a good job as a foreman with an engineering firm and they decided to give it a try in England. It was eleven years before they returned to Canada to stay.

Although she has been back several times and many of her relatives have come to visit, Betty says firmly, 'Canada is now my home but England will always be close to my heart.'

Postscript: Betty and Doug Hillman had five children. Doug passed away in 1987 and Betty moved to Upper Kintore, New Brunswick where she lives next door to her daughter Jackie.

There Was A Colour Bar
Mary (Hardie) Gero

Coming from a regimental family in Scotland, it was no surprise when Mary
Hardie married a soldier. What no one could have anticipated was that her
husband would be an African-Canadian with Black Loyalist ancestors.

Mary Hardie met Albert (Al) Gero of Truro, Nova Scotia in 1943 when he
was on leave in Edinburgh, Scotland. He was billeted in the same building where Mary's sister-in-law lived and they struck up a conversation
on the stairs. Al was an African Canadian serving with the Cape Breton
Highlanders. In the course of their stairway conversation he suggested that
Mary write to his sister in Nova Scotia. Soon after, Al asked Mary to write
to him.

Al was soon shipped off to Italy and he and Mary started writing to each
other. The relationship blossomed into romance and over the course of the
next two years they saw each other whenever they could. They decided to
get married and even had a date arranged but it had to be cancelled because
Al couldn't get leave.

There were a lot of servicemen from other countries in Scotland during
the Second World War and the people were good to them knowing the sac-
rifices they were making in defence of Britain. And so was the case with Al
Gero. Mary's widowed mother had no problem with Al being of a different
colour and if she did, all she had to do was deny them permission to marry
since Mary was under twenty-one years of age. What Mary's mother was
concerned about was that her youngest child was moving so far away.

Meantime, Mary wanted to do her part for the war effort so she joined
the WRNS in July 1944. All of her brothers were in the military and one
had even been reported killed piping in the troops at Dunkirk. His wife
began to receive a widow's pension but in fact he was a prisoner of war at
Stalag 13 in Germany. No one notified the family that he was alive; he just
returned and shocked everyone after the war.

Mary first served in Liverpool and later at the Fleet Air Arm in Abbotsinch,
which was close to Glasgow. One of the greatest moments in her life was
meeting General Bernard Montgomery, 'Monty'. She was going up the
steps to Saint Giles Cathedral in Edinburgh as he was descending with his
guards. He came over to shake her hand and they spoke for a few minutes.
She will always remember that moment.

Mary and Al were married on 12 October 1945. The best man was Phillip Fontaine, a friend of Al's from the service who was a Native Indian from Manitoba. The minister who married them was the Revd Cecil Thornton, which seemed appropriate; Mary had been the first baby he baptized and the last War Bride he married.

Unusual for the times, a large reception with a sit down meal for 200 guests was held at Tollbooth Hall, which is part of the Royal Mile. They spent one night together at her mother's house and then both reported for duty the next day.

Two months later Al returned to Canada and Mary followed in July 1946 on the SS *Georgic*. Al and his brother Michael met her in Halifax and they drove the sixty miles to Truro in Michael's new truck. Knowing what the rationing was like in Britain, Al had asked Mary if she wanted something special to eat when she arrived in Canada. Waiting for her on the front seat of the truck were what she asked for – bananas – the first she had tasted in years.

Al told Mary that he lived with his family on a farm in Truro but when she got there she found out it wasn't a farm like in Scotland. The 'farm' was a house, a field and one goat. The outdoor toilet was another surprise; coming from Edinburgh she had never seen an outhouse before. There was no running water either, but she learned how to clean her laundry on a scrub board and to maintain chamber pots in the winter.

The biggest adjustment for Mary was realizing that there was a colour bar in Truro. In Scotland, the people treated everyone the same, whether they were white or black or Indian. This was especially so for servicemen who were risking their lives for Britain. Al had been wounded twice in Italy and Mary thought that meant something. But in Canada in 1946, race was an issue.

Although nothing was said to them outright, it was obvious the locals could not accept the fact that a white woman was married to a black man.

One day she and Al were walking up Young Street where they lived and a man was coming up the hill behind them. Al said, 'Look at him, he's staring at us, he just can't stand it that we're together.'

There were two large posts on the street and Al said to Mary, 'You watch; that man is staring at us so hard he's not watching where he's going and he's going to walk right into one of those poles.'

Sure enough, that's exactly what happened. 'He got a few bumps on his head after that,' Mary said.

Mary's mother came to Truro when their first child was born in 1947 but they didn't stay there much longer. The next year Al went to Montreal to get a better job and Mary soon followed with their baby son. At first Al worked at Hollander's Furs dying the skins for the coats but later he became a pipe fitter which was a better living for their growing family. From 1949 until 1954 Mary and Al had four more children. Her mother came to visit the family in 1950 and stayed for two years, 'My mother was a big help to me,' Mary says.

In Montreal, Mary had a lot of the conveniences she didn't have in Nova Scotia, such as indoor plumbing and a washing machine. She and Al also didn't have the problems they faced in Truro; no one gave them a second glance. Getting an apartment was not a problem for them and their children didn't experience any racism in the diverse cultural environment of Montreal.

Mary and Al lived in Montreal for seventeen wonderful years; then in 1963, despite being quite content in Quebec, they moved back to Nova Scotia. Al was getting lonely for his family, particularly his mother who was getting elderly. Three weeks after they arrived, Al had a heart attack and died.

When Mary and Al lived in Montreal she didn't have to work, but now she was a thirty-six-year-old widow with five children to support. She found a job at the Colchester Hospital as a cook, and later a cook supervisor. Mary worked at the hospital for twenty years and when she retired she took her first trip back to Scotland. After that she went every two years, the last time in 2000.

Mary never remarried or even dated another man after Al died. She had a good life, a good marriage and good children. She never regretted her decision to come to Canada, but once in a while she entertains the notion that she should have moved back to Quebec after Al died so the children would have had more opportunities. Now that she's in her eighties she's content to be in Truro with three of her children and their families living close by.

Postscript: Mary Gero has fourteen grandchildren, nineteen great-grandchildren and one great-great-grandchild.

No Harmony in Harmony Junction
Elizabeth (Kelly) MacDonald

Elizabeth (Kelly) MacDonald was born in Edinburgh, Scotland in 1920. She married Addison MacDonald of Souris, Prince Edward Island and ended up in Harmony Junction.

My mother and father met on a blind date while he was on a furlough in Edinburgh. She actually had two dates that night but after being introduced to Addison MacDonald she never bothered with the second.

My father was a farmer from Souris, Prince Edward Island (PEI), a small island province made famous by author Lucy Maude Montgomery in the children's book *Anne of Green Gables*. PEI is in the Northumberland Strait off the coast of New Brunswick and Nova Scotia and the only way to get there until the government built the Confederation Bridge in 1997 was by ferry from the mainland.

My mother came from a family of nine children and so did my dad. His father died in a tractor accident when he was four years old so my grandmother in PEI was widowed with a large family to raise. She never remarried.

My parents went on three dates and married on their fourth. Before the wedding, my grandmother in PEI wrote to my mother and, invoking the uncertainty of the times, implored her to delay marriage until the war was over. But my parents adamantly refused – my mother found out later that his family had a hometown girl in mind for him and that was the real reason for the letter.

They remained in Edinburgh for most of the war. In between my father's war assignments my mother lived with her parents except for a short period in London when dad was stationed there.

My mother's home in Edinburgh was often filled with my father's brothers and friends who would drop in to visit. For some it became a home away from home. Five of my father's brothers served overseas and two of his sisters also joined up – one brother died and is buried in Holland. My mother's sister and three brothers served as well, one brother spending time in a prisoner of war camp. His wife told me that the only person her husband could ever talk to about his experiences was my father.

As was common among veterans, my father never talked about the war. He would talk about people he met, the food he ate, and the beauty of the countries he was in but not what happened to him while serving his country. I learned a number of years later that when he was quartermaster in Italy, he lost his stripes for shooting another soldier who was raping an Italian girl.

My sister Elizabeth Anne was born in December 1942. She was adored and pampered by all her grandparents, aunts and uncles. She and my mother came to Canada via Pier 21 in 1946 following my father's repatriation. Mum never remembered much about the voyage on the *Queen Mary* because she spent much of it seasick – another War Bride took care of Elizabeth.

My mother and sister were met in Halifax by my father, his brother and two of their friends. They continued on by ferry to PEI where they lived for six months in Harmony Junction, outside of Souris with my grandmother (Nanny), my uncle and his wife.

Mum in her hat, heels and fur stole was not prepared for what awaited her in Harmony Junction: it was a very unhappy time for my mother because she missed her large rambunctious family and she was scorned by those she lived with.

Mum was a city girl who loved clothes and was used to city ways. I believe PEI was insular and not terribly forgiving of those who 'came from away'. When she dressed up for church, Islanders took it to mean she thought she was better than them. When she tried to cook, her in-laws (except for Nanny) laughed at her and set her up to fail. She was used to certain standards and Islanders thought of her as strange and uppity. If Mum washed the floor my aunt would rewash it. If she did a washing my aunt would complain about the quality of her work.

My grandmother taught Mum to cook and bake. One day Mum baked ginger snap cookies and was so proud of them. Another uncle came for a visit and after trying one he took the cookies outside and buried them before the other aunt came home and made a fuss.

Nanny would wake Mum up when the others were in bed and teach her how to cook. She had to do it when my aunt and uncle were not around because my aunt would criticise and lie about ingredients. Finally after months of this covert operation Nanny announced that Mum would be cooking dinner. The relatives were gleeful, looking forward to her failure and an opportunity to yet again make her the target of their vitriol. Much to their chagrin, and my mother's surprise, dinner was a success.

My mother did make friends and she loved Nanny but living with my aunt and uncle was excruciating for her. She would often trudge down to the next farm, even in deep winter, and visit with her friends despite the two-mile walk.

My father opened a butcher shop in Souris and they moved to a house just down from the Catholic church. Here she was under less scrutiny and made new friends. She and Dad loved to dance – he was a great mimic and loved to laugh. My mother's new friends discovered she was a gifted singer and soon she was called upon to sing at ordinations and country fairs.

My brother Richard was born in 1947 and I followed in 1949. My grandmother Kelly came for her first visit to Canada when I was born and it was a wonderful thing for Mum to have the support of her mother.

The only other problem was the amount of drinking of my father and his friends. My mother did not drink at all, which was unusual given her parents owned a spirits store in Edinburgh. Dad came home one night to find her sitting up at the kitchen table with boxes packed. She said she couldn't stand it anymore and was going home to Edinburgh.

That was when they decided to leave PEI and Dad went to Ontario to find work. In no time he had a job with Ontario Hydro but it took one and a half years to save enough money to send for my mother and the children.

During this time my mother was alone on the island; she lived for Dad's letters and watched while his business was sold. She also had to put up with a few men trying to seduce her and some nights had to barricade the doors of the house.

My father asked her to come to Ontario to look for a house and she was gone for a month. My parents asked the relatives to look after us but aside from eleven-year-old Elizabeth – who went to an aunt so she could babysit the kids – they refused to look after Richard and me so we were sent to the orphanage in Charlottetown to be cared for by the nuns.

One oft-told family story was that I had long strawberry blonde hair that Mum would put in braids. When she returned from Ontario and collected us from the orphanage she burst into tears when she saw me because the nuns had cut off my hair. The nuns could not understand why she was upset as they saved my braids for her: it was the first thing they did. Mum kept the braids for years.

After we left PEI for good my father's family sold what was left of our belongings and we never received a cent. My mother was happy to be gone from the island and began to make a new life for her family in Ontario. The only person Dad and Mum wrote to was Nanny. Dad used to say that when he retired they should go for a visit and not tell anyone they were there. It never happened.

Through Dad's job we traveled the province of Ontario: Chippewa (now part of Niagara Falls) where their youngest Mary Estelle was born in 1954; Whitedog Falls (on the Ontario Manitoba border); Red Rock Falls; Little Long Rapids (north of Kapuskasing) and finally Pickering.

When we were in Pickering we had a surprise visit from one of my PEI uncles and his wife. Thereafter he and my Dad kept in touch and in time we all met the relatives, even those made infamous in family stories. It was interesting to us how they spoke only in glowing terms of our mother.

My father died at a young age in 1969 and it broke my mother's heart. She lived to see eighty-one.

When I think of my parents I think of theirs as a love story; a story of forging a new life in a world away from home and family. When I close my eyes I see my young, elegantly dressed mother standing on Pier 21 not knowing what life was about to throw her way; not knowing that she would face it with great courage and dignity; not knowing she was going to make a difference to this new country of hers and that she was going to teach her beloved children that courage and dignity in adversity made them very proud children indeed.

Contributed by Valerie MacDonald, daughter of Elizabeth and Addison MacDonald.

Time Is Short
Mildred (Young) Sowers

Mildred (Young) Sowers was born in Buffalo, New York in 1924. Her parents returned to England in the Depression and lived in Thornton Heath. She married Harold Sowers from Fredericton, New Brunswick.

One summer evening in 1941, seventeen-year-old Mildred Young and her friend Joan were in Croydon when they met two Canadian soldiers looking at photographs in a shop window.

One of the soldiers, Harold Sowers, was a member of the Carleton York Regiment and he and his friend Eddie were stationed nearby at Caterham. The four young people struck up a conversation and agreed to meet again later.

Mildred and Harold liked each other from the start and within a few weeks she took him home to meet her parents in Thornton Heath. Mildred's younger brother, Lawrie, was away in the Navy and her older brother Billy had been killed in an air raid in August 1940. As the only child left at home, her parents were naturally concerned about this Canadian soldier, but they welcomed Harold and he soon became a fixture at the Young household.

Everything was going smoothly for Mildred and Harold until they missed the bus back home one evening. There wasn't another from Croydon back to Thornton Heath for over an hour so they walked several miles home. Coming up Norbury Avenue, they saw Mr Young waiting by the front gate, obviously upset.

Mildred was sent inside and Harold got a stern warning: 'If anything has happened to my Mildred, there is nothing I wouldn't do to you!'

Mildred and Harold became engaged in 1943. Harold would not consider marriage until after the war ended because so many women who married servicemen were widowed and he didn't want Mildred to be one of them. Soon after VE Day Harold returned to England and they set a date of 24 July 1945. His regiment was being repatriated to Canada so in order for him to remain overseas until the wedding he had to join the 3rd Battalion of the North Shore Regiment, where he served with the Occupational Forces in Germany.

When the time came for Harold to travel to England for the wedding, he only got as far as Calais, France. The British Railway was on strike and only British soldiers were crossing the English Channel to Dover. Harold was desperate to get across; he couldn't miss his own wedding! He tried every way he could think of to get through. He even tore all the Canadian badges off his tunic and tried to sound British, but that didn't fool the guards; they knew he was Canadian.

Meanwhile, back in Thornton Heath, everyone was busy making arrangements for the wedding. The circumstances which transpired over the next days and weeks were so unusual that a light-hearted account of the ceremony appeared in the *New Brunswick Telegraph Journal* back in Canada.

Wedding Bells Ring Loudly Three Times Before Final Take
Sgt. Major Harold Sowers and Bride-Elect Had Tough Time Getting Married
Reception Before the Marriage
The Minister's First Marriage in the Parish
All Ended Happily

Already postponed once, the marriage of Company Sergeant Major Harold D.E. Sowers of Sheffield, New Brunswick, now overseas, and Miss Mildred Young of Norbury Avenue, Thornton Heath, was scheduled to take place on a Monday not long ago.

The guests assembled at the church where the ceremony was to take place and at five minutes to the hour when the bride and groom were to stand before the minister and become man and wife, a messenger arrived with a message which postponed the ceremony until 3 o'clock, as the Sergeant Major, the groom, was delayed by circumstances beyond his control. Three o'clock arrived. The minister, waiting patiently to begin the ceremony, and the bride-to-be glanced anxiously at the church door, waiting for the groom to arrive, but the groom did not show up. The bride had gone to a lot of trouble for the occasion, so the reception was held anyway – before the marriage. Even the wedding cake was cut and eaten.

Next day, the Sergeant Major arrived from Germany. He had been held up along with 10,000 other servicemen at Calais because of a rail strike. So arrangements were made to have the marriage take place the following Saturday.

Saturday came and over twenty of the original guests who wanted to witness the marriage they had been invited to the previous Monday were on hand, as well as the groom, who arrived bright and early for his wedding. This time the groom and the guests waiting patiently, the groom gazing at the church door waiting and hoping to see the bride appear, but this time there was a groom and no bride. Ten, fifteen, twenty, twenty-five minutes passed slowly, and still no bride. Then there appeared another messenger, this time with a message from the bride, saying that the automobile in which she was riding to the church had broken down.

One of the guests ran out into the road and thumbed a passing motorist to beg for help. Away they sped to the bride's home to pick up the trail from there. The bride was not home and they could not locate the broken down automobile, but after searching for some time, they came across the vehicle on a side road. There was the bride, nearly in tears. Practically snatching her up bodily, they hustled her into the other automobile and sped away to the church.

To the tune of the Bridal Chorus, the happy couple, finally united, met in front of the minister, who gave a sigh of relief as he commenced the wedding ceremony. The Revd J. Freeman was the new vicar at St Oswald's Church, and this was his first marriage in his new parish. What a time he had to get it started!

Wearing a heavily brocaded satin gown with a long train and embroidered silk net veil surmounted by a headdress of feathers, the bride was given away by her father ... The groom wore, along with other necessities for a marriage, a beam on his face as he gazed at his bride and deep in his heart apparently had a thought – the third time always takes.

A second, smaller reception was held at the bride's home, this time with the groom, after which the happy couple left for their honeymoon in Seaford.

The newlyweds had one month together before he was repatriated to Canada at Christmas 1945 and it was six months before they were reunited.

Mildred sailed on the *Lady Nelson* from Southampton, arriving at Pier 21 in Halifax on 21 June 1946. A War Bride train took her on the short trip to Moncton, New Brunswick where Harold and another couple were waiting. The next day they drove to Harold's family home in Sheffield, a small farming community outside of Fredericton, and along the way she was treated to fresh strawberries from a roadside stand, her first taste of New Brunswick.

An English War Bride was quite an attraction in Sheffield with her accent and funny expressions. The first time Mildred saw a moose, she called it a 'gentleman moose', a phrase that sent everyone into fits of laughter.

Mildred was a city girl and living in the country was difficult to get used to but she learned how to stretch pennies, earning extra money trapping muskrats and selling pelts. Harold's sister Dean and her husband Tommy lived on a farm nearby and they shared their livestock and vegetables. Deer and moose meat were plentiful in season. With times rough for everyone, people looked out for each other and Mildred managed to cope.

Next door lived Celia, who also happened to be a War Bride, and Mildred was fortunate to find a second family away from home with her friend Jean's parents, who were from England. Being near people from her homeland helped ease the initial culture shock she experienced and made her adjustment to Canadian life easier. She spent her first Christmas in Canada at their home, but was homesick for her family and Jean's mum provided a shoulder for Mildred to cry on that Christmas Day.

Their first child, Malcolm, was born in March 1947 and Linda in July 1948. Harold was working in construction and like many other women whose husbands worked away from home, Mildred was left to raise the children mostly on her own. It probably wasn't what she expected out of marriage but she made the best of the situation by being the best mother she could be.

She had an uncle, George Young, who lived in Toronto and he visited New Brunswick occasionally. During the summer of 1958 Mildred's parents came over from England and they all had a reunion in Sheffield but Mr and Mrs Young were alarmed to see the very harsh living conditions their daughter had to cope with in rural Canada.

Moving to Fredericton in 1960 dramatically changed life for everyone; the new house had modern luxuries like indoor plumbing and television, though Mildred still cooked on a wood stove. Malcolm and Linda attended a large school in the city and it wasn't long before they made new friends and had lives of their own. Harold was still employed with the same company but was working in an office now and had time to socialise as well.

Mildred wanted another child but had several miscarriages; finally in 1961 she became pregnant again. Susan was born in September and she was thrilled, focusing her attention on the new baby. She often wrote to her family about her little daughter, hopeful they might come to Canada again to see her.

Mildred's father died in 1962 but she could not afford to attend his funeral, which was a great disappointment. Uncle George died a few years later, leaving her a small inheritance so she returned for her first visit home in May 1966. Mildred spent two nostalgic weeks with family and old friends in familiar places. It was a wonderful visit but she was glad to return to her family in Canada. She said that she could not live in England again. Canada had become her home.

Shortly after Mildred's return her daughter Linda got married. It was difficult for Mildred to accept, soon followed by the news that she and Harold would be grandparents.

As the year drew to a close, personal circumstances had clearly begun to affect Mildred. On 16 December 1966 she wrote a letter to her brother Lawrie, in which she told him, 'Time is short, so a brief letter will have to do. I'm not looking forward to Xmas too much. If you were here, you would understand.'

It was obvious from the melancholy tone of her words that Mildred was not her usual cheerful self. She ended her letter by saying she was going to town later that afternoon. Mildred had no way of knowing how short time really was, or the tragedy that awaited her before the day was over.

Later that evening, Mildred and Harold were returning from a Christmas party when Harold lost control of their car on an icy bridge and crashed. Mildred was in a coma for several hours and passed away the following day, 17 December.

Contributed by Susan Willis, Mildred's youngest daughter. Susan moved to England in 1998. Today she lives in Essex and works as Domestic Violence Services Manager for the national charity Refuge.

A Union Jack on Her Grave
Mary (Fletcher) Sheppard

Mary (Fletcher) Sheppard was born in Liverpool in 1921. She married George Sheppard of Corner Brook, Newfoundland in 1940. George served in the Royal Navy as an Able Seaman on a number of ships including the HMS *Nelson* and the *King George V*.

Crossing the ocean in 1947 as the wife of a Newfoundland sailor was the single defining decision of my mother's life.

Until she met my father when she was eighteen, she was a giggly factory worker in Liverpool who loved to dance, see the latest films and ride her bike down to the docks to see the ships moored in the Mersey.

Seven years later, she was the mother of two girls, very pregnant with a third and on a ship going to Newfoundland. She thought she had extracted a promise from my father that he would stay in England. And he did try. They stayed two years after the war and were making a go of it, just barely, when a telegram came from home to say his father was ill and he wanted to see his eldest son one last time.

Granddad met them at the train station, healthy as a horse and they both knew they'd been had. But they agreed they would wait until the baby was born to see what was to be done.

She stayed. The facts were simple. England was absorbing hundreds of thousands of men home from the war and jobs for foreigners were scarce. Meanwhile, Bowater had promised any man who volunteered to fight that his job at the paper mill was guaranteed when he came back home.

But her heart never settled. It was always understood in our household that 'home' was not the house we lived in. It was that mythical place across the sea where roses bloomed in May, houses were built of brick and rainwater made the softest hair on earth.

This business of 'home' not being where her children were raised and not being the house that she and father had bought and finished, furnished and refurbished over the years was a constant threat to us bonding as a family. How could we be a family like in *Father Knows Best* when our mother's home was somewhere else?

Like the other War Brides, she had to start again. She had no mother to confide in, no sisters to console her or to help with babysitting, no lifetime neighbour who knew her as the cute kid from Fortescue Street or teacher who knew of her academic successes. She was her dad's little princess when she stepped on that ship, and while she didn't know it then, she would never see him again.

We lived in a newly built postwar veteran enclave. The house had four walls and not much else when they moved in. There was no running water, the road was barely passable and the veterans' houses were built on top of a hill that was swept with deep snow and high winds most of the long winter.

She had never seen snow and with three small children, twins on the way, no family support, no road and water that had to be hauled up the hill by the buckets, snow was hell. She never did get to like it. In winter, it kept her prisoner; in spring, it kept her garden from blooming well into June.

The common ground for War Brides was the Legion. It was there, at Branch No. 13 that my mother felt comfortable talking with the other War

Brides and raising money. She must have helped cater hundreds of dinners and weddings and auctioned off dozens of novelty cakes made in our
kitchen.

I think it was the volunteer work at the Legion that brought her out of
her domestic cocoon. And once that happened, she became a force to be
reckoned with. Sure, there were now nine children underfoot, but there was
greater work to be done.

I was in grade three the year my mother went on a campaign to get water
and sewers to the neighbourhood. She did radio phone-in shows, wrote
letters to the editor, talked to politicians until she was blue in the face. And
finally, the diggers moved in and after more than ten years of community
water tap at the bottom of the hill, we could turn on hot and cold water and
flush a toilet.

She went on a mission to get my father's war pension sorted out. That
took her twenty years, but in the end, she got what she felt my father
deserved for his many wounds. Over the years, she learned when to call the
Premier's office and how to get action.

I think that eventually, say after forty years of marriage, my mother finally
accepted that marrying her Newfoundland sailor was indeed a good thing.
By that time, she'd gone 'home' a few times and compared the cost of raising
nine children in England versus Newfoundland. The Rock won out, hands
down. She was shocked when in the 1990s, her sister was robbed of her TV
while she was asleep in her bed in a little village near Liverpool. That wasn't
her England. But she never stopped referring to England as home.

She's dead now. I sometimes think we did her an injustice by burying her
on an isolated hill overlooking the Bay of Islands. I keep meaning to buy a
British Union Jack to put on her grave so there's a reminder that here lies a
woman who is forever far from home.

*This article is used with the permission of CBC.ca and the author, Mary Sheppard.
Mary is the executive producer of CBC News Online.*

The Town That War Brides Built
Marion (Elliot) Hoddinott

Marion (Elliot) Hoddinott was born in Glasgow, Scotland in 1923. She married Walter Hoddinott and came to Newfoundland where she helped build a
new town consisting almost entirely of War Brides.

Marion Elliot was seventeen years old and working in a munitions factory when she met Walter Hoddinott of Corner Brook, Newfoundland.
Walter joined the Royal Navy at the outbreak of war in 1939. At the time,
Newfoundland was British and when the call went out for commonwealth
volunteers Walter joined up.

Marion and Walter were married in Glasgow on Valentine's Day 1942.
Soon after, Walter shipped off and Marion settled in to a small apartment in
Clydebank. Walter Jr was born nine months later.

Walter was demobilized in July 1945 and it was nearly eight months
before they were reunited in Corner Brook. Against doctor's orders, she left
England on 17 March 1946, eight months pregnant with her second child,
but she was young and healthy and weathered the crossing like a trooper.
Soon after, a second son, Robert, was born.

In 1945 the Government of Newfoundland announced the Post War
Resettlement Program and the farming community of Cormack was born.
Cormack was about fifty miles from Corner Brook on the west coast of
Newfoundland. The area was cleared of timber, the soil was conducive to
farming and there was a railway and road connection at Deer Lake, twelve
miles away. Construction began in 1946 and Walter and Marion were
approved for the program becoming one of more than fifty War Bride families in the new town of Cormack.

Each family was supposed to receive training in farming methods, fifty
acres of land (ten acres cleared) a six-room house, a barn for livestock, a cow,
a horse, pigs and cash for machinery and seed. This was a generous scheme
but, like so many other government initiatives, it was ruined by politics,
greed, mismanagement and even fraud. Conditions faced by the families
participating in this experiment led to extreme hardship, heartbreak and in
many cases, divorce.

Walter and Marion went off to St John's with the two boys in the spring
of 1947 to take training in farming techniques. In September they travelled
by train to Deer Lake and were met by a government agent who put them
on a 'Cat train' headed for Cormack. A Cat train is made up of a bulldozer
pulling a series of large sleds linked together like rail cars and designed to be
pulled over mud, dirt or snow-covered logging roads. The road to Cormack
was a muddy, rocky track through the woods, passable only by the Cat trains
and Bombardier-tracked snow machines. An all-weather road, which was
part of the Trans Canada Highway across Newfoundland, would not be
built to Cormack for another ten years.

After a six-hour trip, the family reached their new home just before dark. They entered the house to find it was only a shell with a large wood burning stove in the kitchen and no furniture. The government agent in Deer Lake had given them a few supplies to get them settled including a kerosene lantern, kerosene, a few days food supplies, a metal pot and kettle.

Walter took the pot down to a brook nearby and brought in water for tea. He then gathered enough wood scraps to feed the fire and set about making a meal for the family. While Walter seemed happy and excited with this new adventure, Marion was feeling lost and miserable. After they ate, the two boys were put to sleep. Since there were no beds, heavy quilts and blankets were arranged on the floor and would serve the family for many weeks until beds arrived from the agent in Deer Lake.

The final insult came when Marion had to go to the bathroom. Walter took her by the hand, led her to the woods and told her to squat behind a nearby tree and do her business. Then he handed her some thin bark from a birch tree to use as toilet paper.

Marion had grown up in Glasgow where there were electric lights, hot and cold water, indoor bathroom facilities, gas for cooking and heat and public transportation right outside the door. Nothing in her wildest dreams prepared her for going into the dark woods and squatting on the ground like a wild animal. Marion spent the first night in her new home crying herself to sleep.

The days and weeks to come were unbearable. The temperature dropped and the first snow came. Daily chores of hauling water from the brook for cooking, washing clothes on a wash board and chopping wood to feed the big stove's insatiable appetite were back breaking. Neither she nor her boys had proper clothing for the weather outside.

Walter had gone into Deer Lake several times in the first two weeks to see the agent and get more supplies. It took him a whole day to walk the twelve miles to town and hitch a ride back. Left alone with the boys, Marion was afraid of the wood stove and was terrified that savage beasts were waiting to pounce on her outside.

On the third week at the farm Walter made a trip to town and didn't return until the early hours of the next morning. At 2 a.m. she heard someone on the steps outside and opened the door to find two strangers holding up a very drunk Walter.

Now her fear and loneliness turned to rage. She didn't speak to him for a week. It didn't occur to Marion until much later that he was feeling the same frustration and handled it in the only way he knew how.

As the fall progressed Walter dug a well near the house, and cut and split enough fire wood for the winter. He finished two rooms in the house with material on hand and built a table, two four-foot benches and a kitchen cabinet. Marion now had a furnished kitchen and one bedroom.

The winter brought mountains of snow and freezing temperatures, Marion had never experienced anything like it in her life. During the frequent storms, snow would actually blow in through cracks in the outside walls.

Wildlife was plentiful so Walter put out a trap line and brought home beaver, otter, muskrat, fox, martin and occasionally a lynx. He taught Marion how to prepare a fur pelt and dry it in the kitchen on drying boards which would stand behind the wood stove. He also shot moose, snared rabbits and bagged partridge to eat. This food was new to Marion and it took her quite a bit of time to adjust but it was a break from their supplies of salt beef, pork, fish, canned meats and bologna which made up most of their diet.

As their first Christmas in Cormack approached, Walter had accumulated quite a collection of furs from his trap line. His plan was to take the furs to Deer Lake and sell them to an agent for the Hudson's Bay Company. While Marion had dreams of curtains, gifts for the boys and maybe some treats, Walter had other ideas: he sold the furs and returned with a Belgian mare named Queenie. Marion was furious, wondering what they were going to do with a horse.

Then Walter dropped a bomb on the family. He was taking Queenie to a logging camp to haul wood and he'd be back in mid-March.

In early January Walter set out with Queenie for the camp. Marion struggled alone with the two boys. The deep snow, constant cold, hard back-breaking work, and long lonely nights without her husband all conspired to make her long for Scotland.

In September, shortly after arriving, Marion had made friends with a neighbour who was also a Scottish War Bride. Helen Reid had arrived in Cormack in 1946 and endured all the same hardships as Marion. Every day they would visit each other and reminisce about home, crying on each other's shoulders. Later Marion would say that Helen was the only thing that kept her from going insane.

Walter returned from the logging camp in March with enough money to buy seed and pay off his bills with the merchants in town. Walter's brother Gordon had taken up the farm next door and together they planted potatoes, turnips, carrots and cabbages. The crops seemed to do well but a frost in August killed almost everything and the potatoes that survived were too small to sell.

The whole summer had been a waste so in September Walter went back to work in the lumber camp. That winter was a repeat of the previous and Marion was growing more despondent.

The spring of 1949 arrived with renewed hope. Vegetables were once again planted and were doing well. Then disaster struck; in September Newfoundland was ravaged by a hurricane. This coupled with news that some of the logging camps were closing caused many of Cormack's original residents to throw their hands up in defeat.

Some went back to their home towns, others took their families to larger centres to find work. Many went back to the fishing industry. Unfortunately many War Brides returned home with their children and Marion was one of them. Walter joined her the next year in Scotland, but jobs were scarce and rationing was still in effect. Realizing it wasn't much better in Scotland, they returned to Cormack in 1951 with the boys and a new baby, a daughter named Marion.

Things had improved immensely between 1949 and 1951. Newfoundland had joined Canada and signs of prosperity were everywhere. The roads were vastly improved, mail was delivered weekly and Walter joined with most others in Cormack to form a co-op. They built a general store and started a full-time school from kindergarten to grade eleven. It was easier to get to town and regular visits to doctors and dentists were now possible. Marion and other women in the community worked tirelessly at fundraising to build Saint George's Anglican Church, the first church in Cormack.

Farming, however, was still precarious. The weather was unpredictable and promised government marketing initiatives failed to get off the ground. Walter found seasonal work and never went back to farming. Two more children came along and Walter fixed up the house, replacing the wood stove with an oil furnace thus ridding Marion of the dreaded chore of cutting and splitting wood. She didn't get electricity until 1964 and it was another ten years before she had inside plumbing but Marion was a lot happier.

Marion was killed in a car accident on 23 December 1982, just two weeks shy of her sixtieth birthday. Shortly before she died, Marion had ended a feud with her sister-in-law, also a War Bride, who lived next door. Although their husbands were great friends and the children of both families grew up together, something caused Marion and Margaret Hoddinott to steadfastly refuse to speak to one another for twenty-five years.

Marion was a devout Christian, and she offered the proverbial olive branch to Margaret. Although she and Margaret would never be close friends, she did enjoy the company and felt good about her Christian act. On the morning of 23 December, Marion went along with Margaret to Deer Lake to do some shopping. The car was hit broad side and both Marion and Margaret were killed instantly.

War Brides Marion and Margaret Hoddinott were buried on 26 December 1982, on a cold, stormy, old-fashioned Newfoundland winter day.

Postscript: Walter died in Toronto in November 1985. Marion and Walter are resting peacefully together in a cemetery at Pasadena, Newfoundland. Their story was submitted by Rob Hoddinott, their second son.

Everything Will Be Fine
Rose (O'Reilly) Boulay

Rose (O'Reilly) Boulay was born in Co. Cavan, Ireland in 1920. She followed the advice of her husband's regimental padre and married Horace Boulay of Belledune, New Brunswick, a small village near the border with Quebec.

Rose O'Reilly was only seventeen years old when she left Co. Cavan, Ireland and emigrated to London, England with the dream of becoming a nurse.

At the time, Rose was working in the 'greener pastures' of Dublin, about fifty miles away from the rural farm where she grew up in Ireland. Rose had two brothers and two sisters living in London and when her older sister came home on vacation she persuaded Rose to go back with her to London. The plan was to work for a year and then begin her nursing course. But when the war broke out, Rose's plans were put on hold and she worked for the war effort instead.

Rose filled shells for aircraft at the Royal Ordnance Factory in Swynnerton, Staffordshire. The factory was in a rural area in a camouflaged setting and the shift workers were bussed in; at night the bus windows were blackened and its headlights were covered so just a little slit of light would show as it made its way to and from the factory, dropping off and picking up workers.

Rose met Sgt Horace Boulay of the North Shore Regiment during a visit to her sister's in London at Christmas 1942. Horace was from Belledune,

New Brunswick a small village along the shores of the Bay of Chaleur near the province of Quebec. Although Horace's ancestors were from Quebec, his Catholic grandfather had married into an Irish family in Belledune and the next generation, including Horace, were brought up speaking English.

Rose and Horace wrote to each other during the next two years and whenever he was on leave he would go to London and they would visit with Rose's sister. When Horace asked Rose for her hand in marriage, she hesitated and told him that she would have to think about it.

Southern Ireland was neutral during the war and there were travel restrictions for military personnel. That meant Horace would not be able to meet her family in person and this was cause of some concern because her parents didn't know what kind of a man she was marrying.

To assuage her family's concerns, Father Raymond Hickey, the Roman Catholic Chaplin of New Brunswick's North Shore Regiment, wrote to Rose saying that he knew Horace's family well and that they were a good Catholic family.

Rose kept his letter, which included some good old-fashioned advice for anyone contemplating marriage:

Dear Miss O'Reilly:
I am the chaplain of the North Shore Regiment and one of my boys, Horace Boulay, spoke to me about your intention to marry. Now, Horace is a fine boy, from a fine Catholic family. I know them well, and Horace is a good Catholic himself. I hope Horace has told you of conditions in Canada, how we live, etc., then you will not be disappointed. So long as you love one another and are sincere about everything, then everything will be fine. I hope you can be very happy and you can be, by deciding to be right now.
Sincerely, Father Hickey

At the same time, Horace wrote to Rose's mother and asked for her hand in marriage. With the ringing endorsement of Father Hickey, Mrs O'Reilly gave her blessing, along with an invitation to visit Ireland when the war was over.

Rose and Horace were married on 29 April 1944 at St Agnes Catholic Church in Cricklewood, London. One week later Horace was sent to Southampton awaiting the invasion of Normandy and on 8 June he landed on the Normandy coast as a dispatch rider bringing messages to and from the front lines. From there on he served in France, Germany, Holland and

Belgium, earning the Military Medal for bravery in the field. Having survived the war, Horace returned to New Brunswick with the North Shore Regiment in August 1945.

Nine months later, Rose followed her husband to Canada, but before she left, she went to Ireland for a three-week visit to say goodbye to her family. 'It was a big decision to leave my home and family,' she said, 'but it was part of growing up.'

On 4 April 1946 Rose boarded the *Aquitania* at Southampton, and arrived in Halifax less than a week later on 10 April. It was a pleasant crossing and on board the train bound for Bathurst she will always remember the landscape of trees and snow. A snow storm prevented her from getting off the train in Bathurst so she had to continue her journey to Belledune. There Rose was met by Horace and her in-laws who welcomed her with open arms. She finished her long trip by horse and sleigh to the family farm.

The literal translation for Belledune is 'pretty sand dunes' which in the heat of the summer are a sight to behold along the Bay of Chaleur; but in the winter all Rose would have seen from the sleigh was ice and snow along the shoreline and she would have felt the penetrating chill of the Bay's northerly winds.

Despite her snowy introduction to New Brunswick, Rose says that she didn't really experience any culture shock because the living conditions were very similar to Ireland in the 1930s and '40s. There were a rich mix of French, Irish and Scottish families who had settled in the Belledune area since the early 1800s and other than adapting to married life, she was very lucky because she didn't have any difficulties settling in. 'Horace's family became my new family and life on the farm became my way of life,' she says. 'I have no regrets.'

Father Hickey's advice so long ago to a young Irish girl lasted fifty-five years: 'So long as you love one another and are sincere about everything, then everything will be fine.' Rose and Horace visited Ireland many times before he passed away in 1999. They had three children, four grandchildren, one great-grandchild and another two are on the way.

Postscript: Rose Boulay still lives in Belledune. Since Horace died she has visited Ireland with her daughters and granddaughters.

2

Quebec

I'll certainly be glad when this is all over

(A.L. Jolliffe, Director of Immigration Branch, as quoted in a 1945 letter he wrote about English War Brides going to Quebec)

British women who married servicemen from Quebec during the Second World War faced a unique set of circumstances that set them apart from other War Brides who married into English families in Canada.

It was difficult enough adjusting to married life with a husband you barely knew, coping with the loneliness of rural life miles from the nearest city, and learning an entirely different way of running a household with wood stoves, no electricity or running water. But to be faced with the additional burden of learning a new language – and in many cases, a new religion – would have been a test of any woman's resolve, not to mention her coping skills.

One War Bride came to an isolated island of less than a thousand people where she was the only person who wasn't French. 'If I wanted to speak English, I had to talk to myself,' she says of those first few years in Quebec.

Another complained that 'Even the dog spoke French'[1] – which may seem funny when we think about it now but it probably wasn't then –

Map showing location of Quebec.

especially for a young woman from a relatively sophisticated background who was faced with some extraordinary challenges in Quebec.

It's hard to say whether War Brides who married into French-speaking families in Quebec knew what they were getting into. If a couple made their way through the bureaucratic process of filling out forms, getting permission to marry, meeting the padre and passing the necessary medical examinations, one would assume that the issue of language must have come up at least once. On the other hand, young lovers aren't likely to listen to anyone's opinion – especially when the opinion is that they shouldn't marry because of language.

There is no doubt that Roman Catholic chaplains actively discouraged marriages between their Catholic soldiers and non-Catholic women; even commanding officers in the French regiments did the same. In January 1943 there had yet to be a marriage of a member of Le Régiment de la Chaudière in Britain – and the regiment had been there for two years.[2]

War Brides who came to a traditional, French Catholic family in Quebec did their best to fit in but what they soon found was that being accepted wasn't simply a matter of learning the language or taking Holy Communion every Sunday. The famous Canadian novelist Hugh MacLennan described the tensions between prewar French and English Canada in his landmark of

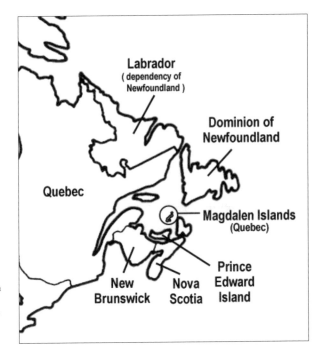

The Magdalen Islands are a tiny cluster of islands located in the Gulf of St Lawrence off the coasts of Quebec, Nova Scotia, Prince Edward Island and New Brunswick. Although the Islands are part of the province of Quebec, many of its inhabitants are of Acadian descent.

nationalist fiction *The Two Solitudes*. While many War Brides probably never even heard of Hugh MacLennan or his prize-winning novel before coming to Canada, if they had read his book it may have prepared them for what to expect when an English woman and a French Canadian man fall in love.

The more MacLennan's two characters love each other, the more the prejudice against them increases. This leads them to the discovery that 'love consists in this, that two solitudes protect, and touch and greet each other.'[3]

The Canadian government was not unaware of the problems which these marriages presented for British War Brides. Language, culture and identity are still a hotly contested issue in Canada and always have been. So when the inevitable began to happen and French-speaking Canadians started marrying British women, the alarm bells went off. It was especially worrisome for those headed to rural Quebec. How are these English women going to manage?

It was the responsibility of the Immigration Branch to investigate the settlement arrangements of all War Brides coming to Canada. As the correspondence shows, in 1944 and 1945 some concerns were being expressed at the highest levels about how to deal with the sensitive issues raised by a number of British wives – three in particular – who were preceding their husbands to Quebec. The problem seems to be that nobody spoke English in the homes where the wives were supposed to settle. The Directorate of Repatriation (Repat) wanted direction, knowing full well there would be a lot more cases just like this to follow.

It was out of individual cases that policy was developed and from what we can see of the response that Repat got from A.L. Jolliffe, then Director of the Immigration Branch, language was certainly not going to become a political issue when it came to the War Brides.

In a perfect example of bureaucratese, Repat was going to have to figure out a way to tell English War Brides what they were headed to in Quebec without actually saying that language might be a problem:

> [Y]ou raise the question as to whether English is spoken in the household … We think that it would be inadvisable to the language question with relatives at this end … [and] it would be unwise to refuse to permit women to sail on the basis of difference of language. We will make sure they are informed in general terms of the location of the husband's home and the fact that the same is a French-speaking community. Such intimation, together with the information obtained from the husbands, should be sufficient to enable the women to decide whether or not they wish to proceed in advance of the head of the family to Canada.[4]

Interestingly, on the back page of this same letter is one single sentence, typed in the middle of the page, which doesn't appear to be intended for general consumption but must have summed up the Director's feelings about the whole War Bride transportation and the headaches it was starting to cause for him: 'I'll certainly be glad when this is all over.'[5]

Of course, some Quebeckers spoke English and a few English War Brides were bilingual; and there were English enclaves in Quebec – especially Montreal – so some British wives actually married English-speaking Quebeckers and came to live in an English environment. Their difficulties with the French language began when they realized that they were a tiny dot in a sea of French. According to the 1941 census, of the more than three million people living in Quebec eighty-five per cent of the population spoke French; sixty per cent spoke French only; twelve per cent spoke English only and twenty-seven per cent were bilingual.[6] It was a rare British War Bride in Quebec for whom language didn't become an issue, either in learning it, or learning how to cope with it!

Joan Walker was a British War Bride who ended up in Val Dor, Quebec, a northern mining community. Trained in Parisian French in an elite Swiss finishing school, Walker was a self-professed city slicker who had worked as a journalist on Fleet Street in London before marrying a Canadian. Inspired by her experiences settling in to life in Quebec, she wrote a hilarious novel for Harlequin called *Pardon my Parka* which won Canada's highest award for humour, the Leacock Award, in 1953.

In a chapter called 'Icit on parle Quebecois' (translation 'We Speak French Here') she describes her rather embarrassing introduction to a Mr Boisevert, a local man they hired to build their house:

During our long introductory session with Mr. Boisevert, I also gave tongue in what I had always been led to believe was French. I spoke about the exact shade of blue I wished for the room and how the front door must match it to a nicety. I mentioned the fact that a coloured bath, john and basin in the bathroom would not come amiss and would be preferable to the usual white. Dusty pink. I was about to expand on the desirability of a tiled floor when Mr. Boisevert looked at me numbly and turned eyes like those of an agonized fawn upon Jim saying, 'Mumble-mumble-mumble-ICIT!'

I swallowed.

Was it for this that I spent so much time in finishing school in Switzerland, learning French and apparently a lot of useless accomplishments?

'What,' I demanded of my spouse, 'is the word that sounds like ee-sit? And why can't the dumbcluck understand me?'

'Ici-here,' he said. 'They tack a "t" on the end of some words ending with a vowel ... Boisevert was explaining that you don't speak the same French as they do here ... Try speaking slowly and drop that Parisienne accent. And for the love of god, don't be idiomatic. Translate more or less literally as you go along'

I tried and it worked. Mr. Boisevert brightened visibly. The only snag was that it didn't work in reverse. All it did was release a torrent of Quebec French on my unsuspecting head.[7]

Like Joan Walker, a good sense of humour and a loving spouse would have made the transition to life in Quebec a little bit easier and that is something that holds true for War Brides who married into any Canadian family – no matter what their mother tongue, race, ethnicity or religion. In the stories that follow we meet four British women whose lives turned out very differently in Quebec. How they dealt with the challenges they encountered have as much to do with their own willingness to adapt to life in Quebec as it does to the support of their husband, his family and the friends they made in the communities where they lived.

She Did the Right Thing
Joan (Smedley) Landry

Joan (Smedley) Landry was an eleven-and-a-half-year-old schoolgirl living in London, England when the Second World War was declared. She was evacuated to a village near Wisbeach, Lincolnshire and returned to London in September 1940 in preparation for her evacuation to Canada as a Guest Child of the Canadian government.

A day or two before I was supposed to sail to Canada, our home was bombed and we lost everything including my travelling papers. I could not board the ship to Canada without documentation so I was not allowed to join the other Guest Children on the ship. Luck was on my side: on Friday 17 September the *City of Benares* was torpedoed by the German U-Boat U48 and sunk with the loss of almost 100 children.

Still being underage for the workforce, I had to be evacuated once again, this time I was sent to a different location, Chatteris, Cambridgeshire, where I joined a London Jewish school. I did not know anyone there but I loved school and the teachers were excellent. I got on very well and by the time I was fourteen had a tenth grade commercial course. However, I was unhappy as I was continually being taken from one home to another. The people just did not want to have the responsibility of evacuees in their homes and did whatever they could to get rid of us.

Although I was heartbroken at leaving school and my teachers did their best to persuade me to stay, it reached the point where I could no longer stand living this way and I asked my mother's permission to return to London. By then I was of school leaving age and I had no trouble finding secretarial work as all the older workers were in the services.

One Sunday afternoon in 1942 my two older sisters and I were resting on the grass in St James Park near Buckingham Palace. A group of young servicemen speaking another language were sitting not far from us. One of the young men got into a conversation with my eldest sister Minnie. He spoke some English and told us that he was a French Canadian from the Magdalen Islands, Quebec.

The soldiers were just passing the time away before taking the train to return to camp. We went to the station to see them off and before leaving the young soldier took Minnie's address. A few months later he turned up on our doorstep with a friend named Conrad Landry. From then on, Conrad would come to see us whenever he was on leave in London.

Then came D-Day, 6 June 1944. Conrad was a driver mechanic and drove a machine gun carrier. He was with La Régiment de la Chaudière and was among the first Allied soldiers to land in Normandy. It was two months before the regiment was given twenty-four hours behind the lines to rest and wash up and Conrad was able to write me a few lines to let me know that he had come through hell and was still alive.

The next time we saw each other was New Year's 1945. It was then we realized that our friendship had turned into something deeper and Conrad asked my mother if she would allow me to marry him. I was seventeen.

By this time we had known Conrad for three years and although it was not easy for my mother she gave her consent. Upon his return to the regiment Conrad began gathering all the information and necessary forms which were needed in order to obtain permission to marry.

This was not easy to obtain as the Canadian Army was advised to dissuade soldiers from marrying girls from a foreign land. However, after several months of having had forms completed, being interviewed by the padre of the regiment and receiving my medical certificates, we were informed that we had been granted permission to marry on or after 9 May 1945. Meanwhile, I had decided to become a Catholic and was receiving instruction from a priest once a week. I was finally conditionally baptized in the Catholic Church on 5 May 1945 and confirmed by the Bishop the following day.

We were married two weeks later on a beautiful sunny day. I wore my eldest sister's wedding dress as it was difficult to find such clothing in London. The church ceremony was lovely and I somehow managed to catch my heel in my chair and sent it flying down the altar steps. Conrad went to pick it up while thinking that we were off to a good start with me throwing chairs around. My mother had been saving canned goods from our weekly rations for several months and was able to give us a small reception with about thirty guests.

Before Conrad returned to his regiment in Germany, we went to the Canadian Wives Bureau to apply for my repatriation to Canada. My name was put onto a list and we were told that it would probably be a while before I would be able to travel to Canada as the list was very long. Should I become pregnant, I would not be allowed to travel after my sixth month and once the child was born, it should be at least three months before we could travel.

Conrad was demobilized and sent back to Canada in August and soon after I found out I was pregnant. I tried to arrange it so I could go right away but it was eleven months before I saw Conrad again, this time with a little baby. Meanwhile, my sister Jeanne had also married a young man from the Magdalen Islands, a friend of Conrad's, Aurelius Bourque, so she was also waiting impatiently to rejoin her husband.

We finally both received notices in early July 1946 that we should be prepared to travel at twenty-four hours notice from 12 July onward. We were later advised to go to a London hostel on 18 July where the War Brides would be gathering in readiness for the trip.

We stayed overnight in the crowded hostel. We were not allowed to leave the premises but our families were allowed to visit with us until 10 p.m. when they were asked to leave. I saw one young woman leave with her parents. My mother stayed with us until the very last minute. It was heart wrenching tearing ourselves away from her: our mother would be alone for the first time.

The next morning as we left to board the bus to the railroad station, she was waiting for us outside the door. I don't know if she had even gone home the previous night. When the bus started off, she was running alongside with tears streaming down her face not looking where she was going. We were afraid that she would get hurt in an accident. Jeanne and I were both in a terrible state, torn between the love for our mother and of our husbands who were waiting for us in Canada.

We arrived in Southampton where we boarded the ship the *Queen Mary*. All the luxurious furnishings had been removed from the cabins and had been replaced by bunks around the walls, hammock-like cots were attached to the lower bunks for the babies. We were given disposable nappies (the first we had ever seen) and also the rules and regulations about what was expected of us while we were on board as well as meal times and the services that were available to us.

There was a full nursing staff to take care of anyone needing their services and a nursery where we were allowed to leave our babies for no longer than one hour at a time. This permitted us to do other things, such as having our meals in peace or doing the hand washing which was hanging up all over the cabin and the bathroom. There were twelve women with their babies and young children which made for a lot of washing. It was a tight squeeze and a rush to get to the bathroom.

When we felt the ship leaving port, most of us were on deck. It was very difficult seeing the shores of England gradually disappear from sight and not knowing when we would see our loved ones again or what to expect in our new homeland.

We all gasped when we went into the dining room for the first time and saw all the food on the tables with the beautiful white bread and fresh rolls that were light as a feather. Our steward said that he had never seen anyone eat as much bread as us War Brides. No wonder. We hadn't seen white bread in almost six years!

The captain spoke to us over the PA system on our first day out. He told us that there were some returning servicemen on board, that we were not allowed to roam all over the ship and should remain in our own quarters. He also warned that anyone found in the company of a serviceman or a member of the crew would not be allowed to set foot on Canadian soil. We later heard that about ten War Brides were not allowed to land.

The *Queen Mary* made a record crossing and we arrived in Halifax harbour on 23 July 1946. It was very foggy and we were unable to see a thing until the fog suddenly lifted like a curtain and we saw the crowds on the wharf. We were told to return to our cabins and it was announced over the PA system that those travelling to the Maritimes would be the first to disembark.

I had to ask our steward whether the Magdalen Islands were in the Maritimes. As he did not know, he took me along to the chart room where the officer there pointed out the Islands on a huge wall map. They were located in the Gulf of St Lawrence off Quebec, Prince Edward Island, Nova Scotia and New Brunswick. He was quite surprised when he learned that I was from London and going to such an isolated place. He told me that he felt very sorry for me but wished me luck, which was not very encouraging.

Jeanne and I were the first passengers to disembark; a sailor carried our hand luggage while another carried the baby down the gangway. People came out of the crowd to greet us while a band played in the background. There were also huge banners that said 'Welcome to our War Brides'.

Suddenly through the crowds I saw my brother-in-law Aurelius making his way towards us. I asked if Conrad was with him and he laughingly pointed to someone at my side. It was Conrad. I had not recognized him in his civilian clothing.

We stayed overnight in Halifax and the next day we took a bus to Souris, Prince Edward Island where we boarded the SS *Lovat* to the Magdalen Islands, arriving early the following morning.

The Islands looked like a picture postcard with the sun shining on a very calm sea and everything looked so clean which was in such contrast to the London we had left behind in ruins. I have often said that it was a good thing I saw the Islands in summer before the winter.

It wasn't every day that two British War Brides arrived at Cap aux Meules so there were a lot of people on the wharf. There I met Ethel Maclean, an English woman who had written to me and answered any questions I had about the Islands. We continued to Conrad's parents' home while Jeanne went to her in-laws. My mother-in-law greeted us warmly and the baby just fell into her arms, this was her first grandchild. Later on I met my father-in-law and the other members of the family. That evening a party was held in our honour. Jeanne and Aurelius were also present and since only a few people spoke any English it was not easy to converse with them, yet I could still feel the warmth of their welcome.

Even during the war in London we had gas, electricity and indoor plumbing. On the Islands in 1946 there were none of these conveniences, which I soon found out when I asked for the washroom and was taken to the outside toilet. Automatically before leaving I looked around to pull the chain but there was none. I later learned from Jeanne that she had done the same thing.

I had to get used to pumping and heating any water that was needed. I never could light the gasoline lamp or the gasoline iron; I was sure that it would blow up in my face so unless there was someone there to light them for me I used the paraffin lamp and the iron which I heated on the stove.

My mother-in-law did her best to help me and I did my best also, but since neither of us could speak the other's language it was very difficult for us to communicate and led to some misunderstandings. We were alone all day while the men were out fishing, so I used a sort of sign language. I would point to something and she quickly understood that I wanted to know the name of it. She would then tell me and I would repeat it. She was very patient with me. When Conrad arrived home, I would very proudly say any new words that I had learned during the day. Quite often they were mispronounced and Conrad would have to correct me so it would be the source of great laughter.

My mother-in-law was a very good cook but the methods of cooking and the foods here were something that I had to get used to, such as the salt meat boiled dinners and the salted fish. Today I still am not fond of these foods but I was never a fussy eater having been brought up to eat whatever was on my plate.

I gradually learned enough French to hold a conversation on a one to one basis if the person spoke slowly; but if there were several people talking and joking together, then I would be lost and I was always asking Conrad, 'What did they say?'

I realize today how difficult it must have been for him trying to translate conversations for me, but at that time I felt rather left out of things because I could not understand.

I had been used to having public transport whenever I wanted to go anywhere. When I arrived on the Islands in 1946 there was none. There were a few privately owned vehicles and maybe a couple of taxis but the only other method of travelling was on Sundays when people would go to church or visit the sick in the hospital. They would go by trucks which had been fitted with seats and a ladder to climb up into the back. During the winter months, when the roads were blocked, the only way to get around was by horse-drawn sleighs.

That first winter was very difficult. I had never seen so much snow in all my life and thought that the winter would never end. In London, the snow would melt almost as soon as it touched the ground. During the winter months the mail was often late because there was only one plane a week, and that was when conditions allowed the plane to land. Since there was no airport, the plane landed on the beach in the winter when the surface was hard enough.

I was used to going to the public library and taking out as many books as I wanted. I was a real bookworm, often taking out five or six books a week. Here there was very little reading material in French and none at all in English. I was so happy when friends in England took out a subscription for me for *The Overseas Daily Mirror*, a popular newspaper. Even though the news would be a month late I would read every word, even the advertisements. Later I received a *Woman's Own* subscription, a magazine I used to buy before leaving England. Besides some short stories it had recipes, knitting and sewing patterns which I would save as there was nothing like that here.

When I realized that I would have to do all my own baking, including my bread, I had no idea how I was going to manage. I watched my mother-in-law carefully when she was making her bread and tried to figure out the recipe as she did not have one and did not measure anything. When I tried to handle the dough it stuck to my fingers, yet it didn't with her. Then there was the problem of learning how to use the big old wood stove. You had to know exactly how much wood to put in otherwise it was too hot or not hot enough.

I had brought with me from England my knitting needles, some patterns and a bit of wool, also my embroidery hoops, floss and transfer patterns. I did all my children's knitted clothing but soon realized that it was not acceptable for me to knit on Sundays. I embroidered pillowcases using empty flour or sugar bags which had been bleached.

On Sundays I would write letters. From the day I left England until she passed away in June 1968 I never missed a Sunday without writing to my mother. Occasionally, when I was feeling too lonely and down I would take the truck to Grindstone and visit the sick in the hospital, even though I did not know anyone. When I returned home again I felt better having seen someone who was worse off than me. I was thankful for my family's good health and thought about what we had instead of what we did not have.

About six months after our arrival, my mother immigrated to Canada, going to Ontario where she was able to rejoin her mother whom she had not seen in thirty-three years. Not long after her arrival my sister Jeanne and her husband Aurelius decided to move to Ontario with their baby. When they left it was another difficult moment for me; I felt even more alone.

I cried a lot during the first two years. It was not easy to adapt, everything was so different. I tried to keep myself busy to ward off feeling homesick and lonely but it didn't always work.

I had a nice baby carriage which I had brought with me from England but the roads were too rough to go very far. In any case, where would I go? The English-speaking community on the Islands was too far away. If I wanted to speak English, I had to talk to myself.

We'd been living with my in-laws for almost two years when Conrad asked whether I wanted to remain on the Islands or move to the mainland. I gave it some thought and could not see the sense in moving away as we didn't know a lot of people elsewhere and at least here we had Conrad's family and I was already attached to the people of the Islands. So it was my decision that we should stay here. I honestly believe I made the right decision and have never regretted it.

Conrad bought a piece of land and began building our home. We moved in a week before Christmas 1948, just three weeks before our third child was born. I learned to cook on my new wood and coal kitchen range. I don't know how, but I made beautiful bread and other baked goods. I also taught myself to sew on a second-hand Singer sewing machine. I recycled a lot and used worn-out articles of clothing which I carefully unpicked and pressed, and these served as patterns as there were no patterns to be found here.

When our first child started school, I tried helping her with her home-work. Everything went well until we came to French. It was she, and later the other children, who taught me how to pronounce and gradually I was able to read using my little French–English pocket dictionary whenever there was a word that I did not understand. A lot of words were not even in my small dictionary. From then on I would read whatever I could get my hands on.

I found writing French was even more difficult. I have improved a lot but I still make grammatical mistakes. When people ask me if it has been difficult for me to learn French I usually reply that I have taken my first grade nine times; they look at me in a funny way until I explain that I had nine children.

By the time I reached my thirty-second birthday I had my ninth and last child. When she started school I began thinking about myself for a change. I applied and obtained a part-time job with the local post office where I worked for twenty-one years. I was glad to get out of the house, to talk with adults and do something other than housekeeping and cooking.

It wasn't long before I was invited to join different committees and become a member of a board of directors and so over the past forty-odd years, through my volunteer work, I met many interesting people and learned a lot about the problems of others in society. All this helped in my personal evolution as a woman. I hope that in return, in some small way, I was able to do my part for the Islands and its population who welcomed me so warmly all those years ago.

Postscript: Joan and Conrad Landry have nine children, twenty grandchildren and two great-grandchildren. They celebrated their sixty-first wedding anniversary in May 2006 and still live in the Magdalen Islands today. In 2006, Joan was honoured to receive the Caring Canadian Award from Canada's Governor General, Michaëlle Jean.

She Finished What She Started
Henrietta (Stevens) Pronovost

Henrietta (Stevens) Pronovost was born in Paddington, London, England in 1922. Within one week of joining the NAAFI she met her husband, Jacques Pronovost of St Gabriel de Brandon, Quebec.

My father was wounded in the First World War and his left arm was so crooked and scarred that it looked like a laced-up old boot. He was a painter by trade so his injury made it very difficult for him to work. My mother helped out with the finances by cleaning houses and as the oldest of seven children I had chores to do at home while she was at work.

I went to school at Portobello Road Senior Girls School in London. Like other girls my age, I left school in 1936 when I was fourteen and got a job at Whiteley's Department Store, Bayswater where I worked as a learner cashier. At Christmas that year I was chosen to be one of Santa's helpers. Queen Mary opened the Santa Claus event and I was asked to present her with flowers but I had to practise my curtsey first. I didn't think much of it but my parents and grandparents were very proud that I had met the Queen.

When the war started I was employed as a stock records clerk at Woolfe & Company in Southall, Middlesex, where they made tires for planes and army trucks. Three years later I decided to join the Navy, Army and Air Force Institutes (NAAFI) where I worked in the army cafeteria. I met my husband Jacques Pronovost the very first week.

Jacques was from St Gabriel de Brandon, Quebec, a small town about an hour north of Montreal. He was a member of the famous Royal 22nd Regiment and had been in England since 1940. Jacques's mother was a First World War Scottish War Bride so he spoke English as did the rest of his family in Canada.

Nobody said anything negative about marrying Jacques except my father: he had served with French Canadians during the First World War and he didn't like or trust them. Dad said they were too bossy with their women and yelled at them a lot. My mother had little choice but to give her blessing, but warned it would be a bad marriage. I found out later that they were both right.

We were married on 13 May 1944 and Jacques was repatriated to Canada in August 1945. Eleven months later I left England on the *Queen Mary* arriving in Halifax, Nova Scotia as a War Bride with my little girl Barbara who was then just fifteen months old.

I didn't get seasick but when Barbara and I were walking down the passageway the ship lifted sideways and she hit her head. Barbara remained under observation in the hospital on board until we docked in Halifax. From there we took an overnight train to Montreal where my husband, his five brothers and six sisters welcomed us at the station.

We lived for a while with his parents in St Gabriel de Brandon. At first, my mother-in-law was very understanding and we got along well. I had been raised an Anglican and even though she had converted, I felt no pressure to become a Catholic. As for language it was never an issue because my husband and his family were all fluently bilingual. And although I never learned enough French to hold a conversation, I knew enough to tell when someone was talking about me.

It wasn't long before I realized that my husband was not the same man I knew in England. He made me feel like I shouldn't have come to Canada and although he wasn't physically abusive, he was argumentative and bossy. I wasn't allowed to have any opinions and he just did whatever he wanted. I very quickly realized that my father was absolutely right about my husband. If I was going to survive in this country I'd just have to accept the situation and carry on.

We left his parents' home and moved to Montreal when Jacques found work there. Housing was tight and we shared an apartment with friends from England, Teresa Lalonde and her husband, another French Canadian from the Royal 22nd Regiment.

Teresa was an English War Bride and she had come to Canada in 1945. The living arrangements could have worked but my husband complained a lot and argued with our friends. It was very unpleasant so we moved back to St Gabriel de Brandon. I never saw Teresa after that.

By this time I was pregnant again so my husband applied for a house with the Central Housing and Mortgage Corporation. We didn't stay there very long before we moved again; that seemed to be the story of my married life, always moving and babies arriving every year.

I ended up with fourteen live births and one stillborn – eight babies were delivered at home and even when I gave birth in the hospital I had very little help from anyone in my husband's family. They would take one child each and then return them to me the day I came home from the hospital with a new baby. I remember giving birth to my eleventh child on a Saturday night at home and Jacques left for work in Labrador the next day. On Monday morning I had to get the older kids off to school.

At this time my husband went to work for the Iron Ore Company in Labrador for about a year so I was left alone to care for my eleven children. I didn't seem to be very popular with my husband's family so my husband told me not to bother them. While my husband was in Labrador, my children came down with measles and the nine-month-old baby also contracted the disease. It turned into meningitis and she died.

It was a very difficult time for us all so when I found out I was pregnant again my husband offered my youngest sister in England airfare to come and help me while he was away. I would have preferred he stay at home but he wouldn't hear of it. My sister stayed one year and was a big help. My husband worked in Labrador for another four years, returning home only every few months.

We moved back to the city after he'd finished his stint in northern Quebec and we lived in Laval, which is now part of Montreal. I liked it there. I had friendly neighbours and could take the bus when I needed to go where I wanted. My older sons found jobs and in 1971 they gave me airfare for two of the children and me to go on a visit to my family in England.

After twenty-five years I was so very happy to see them all. I was supposed to be in England for two weeks but I stayed for six and was reluctant to go back. One day I went for a long walk with my mother and told her I didn't want to return to Canada. She knew everything about the way my husband treated me because my sister had told her what happened during her stay. My mother said I had to return and finish what I started – raising the children. Once they were old enough she said I could return if I wanted so I went back to Quebec with that thought in mind. I never saw my mother again. She died very suddenly a few months after I returned to Canada.

My children grew up, got married or had partners and families and I enjoyed being 'nannie' to them all. I'd found myself a job and was saving money to leave my husband when he became sick and was diagnosed with lung cancer. I couldn't leave him. He eventually passed away in January 1991.

In all the years we were married, going back to England in 1971 was the only vacation I ever had. My oldest daughter Barbara is a long-distance truck driver and in 1995 she invited me to accompany her on a trip to Western Canada and the United States. For the first time since I was in this country I had the opportunity to see some beautiful scenery and meet friendly people. I went with her on the road until I was seventy-nine years old and loved it!

Now I sit at home and reminisce and watch my family grow. They've all turned out to be good, kind human beings and those with children are good parents. I'm very proud of them all. Today I have eleven living children, eighteen grandchildren and nineteen great-grandchildren. I think I made a big contribution to Canada and am proud that I did, but would I do it again?

Now that's the $64,000 question!

Postscript: Henrietta Pronovost lives with her oldest son, Bob, in Hawkesbury, Ontario. Her daughter Julie (number thirteen) helped her to write this story.

She Made Her Own Bed
Joyce (Hilman) Bezeau

Joyce (Hilman) Bezeau was born in Leicester, England in 1925. She married
Bob Bezeau, a French Canadian from Baie Comeau, Quebec.

The day Joyce Bezeau left for Canada, her father refused to come down to
the train station to see her off.

Instead, he called her into the front room of their house, hugged her and
said, 'It's your own bed you have made and you will have to lie in it. Don't
think it will be easy and don't come crying home in six months.' Then he
cried.

There were a lot of tears in Joyce Bezeau's life over the next couple of
years but true to her father's words, she never came crying back home.

Joyce was born into a privileged, but strict Roman Catholic home in
Leicester, England. She had six siblings and their home was a bustling
center of activity for the entire extended family. They survived the Leicester
Blitz of 18 November 1940 but the house was so badly damaged that they
couldn't live in it for another two years.

Joyce remembers that terrible day. Her sister Kitty came running in and
cried out to them all, 'Why are you not in the cellar? Don't you know that
the bombs are dropping and the town is on fire?'

They just made it into the cold, damp cellar when they heard the whistle
and the explosions of the bombs. 'The whole house sounded like it would
collapse on top of us ... the back of the house was badly damaged ... the
yard was full of rubble and bricks and all the windows were broken ...
electric wires and street car cables were in the front garden.'

By 1942 Joyce had been working for three years at Jennings & Leeson,
a wholesalers located on Frog Island in Leicester. She wanted to join the
WAAF but her father wouldn't give his permission saying Joyce was 'easily
swayed' and the forces were 'no place for gullible girls' so she had to stay
with the company.

One weekend, Joyce and a friend from work, Betty Thornton, secretly
decided to go to London for a weekend. Knowing they would never get
permission from their parents, Joyce told her mother she was staying at
Betty's and Betty told her mother she was staying at Joyce's. They thought
someone should know where they were going so they told Joyce's brother,
Ray, who insisted that if they go ahead with their plan they must promise

not to take the last train home as it would be full of GIs and could mean trouble with drunks, fights and stabbings.

Joyce and Betty thought that would just add to the adventure but vowed to take the early train back and off they went. They stayed overnight at a dreadful B&B and in the morning went to see Buckingham Palace. The next stop was St James Park nearby, the park that changed Joyce's life.

Betty and Joyce sat on a park bench. Two Canadian soldiers walked by and one turned back to ask for a match. They gave him a box of matches. The match borrower (named Gareau) was speaking to the other soldier (named Bezeau) in French. Gareau's English was very good when he spoke but Bezeau spoke only French.

It never occurred to Joyce that Canadian soldiers could not speak or understand the English language. After all Canada was part of the British Empire, wasn't it? So Joyce just kept talking away in English. Every so often 'Buzzo' as Joyce now knew him, would say 'No' when he should have said 'Yes' and Joyce would say 'Don't say "No" say "Yes".' He would laugh and say 'Yes'.

Betty could speak a little high school French so the four young people spent the afternoon together and at the end of the day the soldiers saw the girls off at the station. As they settled into their seats, elated with the stunning success of their escape weekend, Betty turned to Joyce and said she was awfully sorry, it must have been boring for her since Bezeau couldn't speak a word of English.

Joyce said, 'Don't be silly, we've been talking all day.'

'I know you have,' said Betty. 'But tell me one thing that he said.'

Joyce tried to remember, but all she could think of was, 'Don't say "Yes" say "No".'

So began the romance between Joyce Hillman and Bob Bezeau.

Bob was in the Royal Canadian Engineers (RCE) and his main job was blowing up or building bridges. In 1944, as the fighting moved up into Holland he was shifted over to the infantry and found himself in the midst of heavy fighting. In his letters to Joyce he started talking about marriage.

Joyce's sister Olive was in the NAAFI and she asked a few Canadians about the Quebec North Shore, where Bob was from. It wasn't good news. They told her it was total isolation and snowed six to ten months of the year. There was no road in or out but in good weather it was accessible by ferries and planes. And as if that wasn't bad enough, nobody spoke English.

Joyce's family were against the marriage but the more they argued against

Bob, the more desirable she found him. The only good thing about Bob as far as her parents were concerned was that he was Catholic.

Joyce got her way. They were married on a Monday morning, 5 February 1945. Joyce's sister Veronica was in the WAAF (in contrast, she had been allowed to join because her father said she 'needed the discipline') and had never met Bob before. At the wedding, Veronica's way of showing approval of Bob was to yell loudly, 'If I had seen him first, Joyce wouldn't have him!'

By this time, Bob was starting to understand English a little better so he decided to inject his own brand of humour and pronounced, also very loudly, 'Ah, le divorce!'

At the word 'divorce' everyone in the room froze. 'Imagine my horror!' says Joyce.

> The shock waves on the faces of my family and friends was something to see. It was a heart stopper, especially since it had only been ten minutes since we had been pronounced 'man' and 'wife'. But, divorce is not a thing we mess around with in my family. I blessed my father for his intervention and have always a fond memory of him telling Bob, 'You've got the best of the bunch, my lad.'

It immediately became apparent that things weren't going to be easy for Joyce. During their honeymoon in London, it rained non-stop. As they were leaving a restaurant, Bob became very annoyed. Joyce asked him what was wrong and he became extremely angry. It took some time but she finally discovered it was because of the rain.

She thought, 'So what? It rains every day in England!' She said she will never forget thinking, 'Good Lord, what have I done? Here I am married to a wildman for life.'

She put it down to battle fatigue. He had never been angry in the two years she had known him so it must be the war. 'Just wait until I got him into a home of our own,' she said to herself. 'I'll make him happy. He will never be angry again.'

But as she soon found out, the Bob Bezeau she married wasn't the same man she had fallen in love with. The things he had seen in the war changed him.

In the autumn of 1945 Joyce received two notices from the Canadian Army saying she was to sail to Canada. She refused to go because Bob was still stationed at Basingstoke. She enrolled in French classes at night school but due to a lack of pupils, classes were cancelled. The Army notified her a third time and said if she didn't go this time she would be obliged to wait until all the troops had been repatriated and then pay her own way. Fortunately, Bob was now in Baie Comeau living with his sister Marianne, so she packed and got ready to go.

Then came her father's parting words, 'It's your own bed you have made and you will have to lie in it.'

That night before she left for Canada, she sat on her bed in the War Brides hostel and wondered if her dad was right. She started to think she had made a mistake in marrying a French Canadian. She led a privileged life in England; what if it was true that the French hated the English and Bob had changed his mind about wanting an English wife?

The only way to be certain was to go to Baie Comeau. She sailed to Canada on the *Aquitania*, arriving in Halifax, Nova Scotia on 3 March 1946. Once on the train the porter gave her a telegram saying she would not be met by Bob in Rimouski, Quebec but by a M. Bellavance. When she arrived in Rimouski it was discovered that M. Bellavance was in Montreal so the military decided that was where she should go.

Joyce refused, so they woke up the only person in Rimouski who spoke English – the local doctor – who came to the train depot and signed the paperwork to prove she had arrived. She was taken to a small hotel and the doctor phoned Bob to say she would be on a plane the next morning to meet him. Her first plane ride and she was the only passenger! When she landed she saw a stranger in civilian clothes – it was Bob. She felt as if her heart was singing. They got in a taxi and drove for six miles to Marianne's place and her new life in Canada.

When they arrived, Joyce found out Marianne couldn't speak English. Her children were crying loudly and Bob was growing impatient of translating everything for Joyce. They got out of there and went to the Hudson's Bay Company to get her some boots because the shoes she had were unsuitable for winter weather. When they came back, Bob started packing. When she asked where he was going he said he had to go back to work. That's when Joyce found out that Bob worked in the bush for two weeks at a time and he came home every second weekend on Friday for two days. She didn't know how she would exist for the next two weeks without him and live with his sister who did not speak English. The tears started flowing.

To say life in Canada was different is putting it mildly, what with the snow and the language barrier. She began to learn some French from Marianne's children but she was so lonely. Even when he was home from Friday to Sunday, Bob didn't spend much time with her.

She was feeling sorry for herself until Bob pulled her out of her self-pity; 'If you don't like it here why don't you go home to England?'

That made Joyce realize she could expect no help from him.

She met a couple of British War Brides and they became friends, but most of the time Bob was gone and she was on her own. She adapted to this new life. It wasn't what she expected when she married a Canadian serviceman but she stayed and they raised four children. Learning how to speak French helped; she could understand and be understood in this very different language.

Joyce eventually discovered that as long as she didn't drag Bob into her plans he was happy. She passed her driver's licence and even travelled overseas to England and Australia. Three times her parents generously paid her way home and she was ever grateful for it, because there was no way Joyce could afford the trips herself. Then, in the late 1970s, she and Bob moved to Dutton, Ontario, to be closer to their children who had settled nearby. Bob was in his element: he was happy there with all the grandchildren around.

In 1988 Bob had a stroke and then another, more serious stroke. He was hospitalized for quite some time. Joyce said it was sad to see this once energetic man confined to a chair, watching life go by. In 1994 he became ill again and after only a week in hospital he died, thus ending that part of Joyce's life; that of a Canadian War Bride.

Postscript: Joyce still lives in Dutton, Ontario. She has eight grandchildren and three great-grandchildren. She loves her life now.

Postman Do Your Best
Morfydd (Morgan) Gibson

Morfydd (Morgan) Gibson was born in Risca, Wales, in 1920. She married an English-speaking Quebecker from Montreal.

Although my family came from Wales, during the war we were living in Guildford, Surrey. I had gone up to London to get some experience in the working world and lived in digs in the north end with a girlfriend.

One night my friend and I had played a hockey match and our custom after games was to meet up with a friend, who was a Major in the British Army, and have a drink.

As we waited for the Major, two very drunk Canadians decided to sit down with us. One of them was named John Gibson and he told us he was from the Black Watch Regiment out of Montreal. We explained that we were meeting someone, but as they were quite drunk they brushed that fact off and insisted on keeping us company until he arrived.

The Major arrived and our drunken acquaintances called out to him. He took one look at us sitting with two drunken, low-ranking Canadians, turned around and left the pub. It was the strangest thing as we had been quite good friends and after that we never heard from him again.

Our new friends felt bad that they might have been the cause of our friend deserting us so the four of us left to get a meal. When it came time to pay, the man who became my darling husband was nowhere to be found as he had gone glad handing around the place, leaving the other man, who had no money, to pay.

So my friend and I ended up paying. Needless to say they didn't make a spectacular first impression,

After we finally rounded up John, they insisted on accompanying us back to our digs, which were miles away from their camp. Trying to dissuade two drunken servicemen proved to be impossible. Back in our part of London we didn't know what we were going to do with them, as it certainly wouldn't have been possible to allow two men to stay with us! So we left them in an air-raid shelter.

The next day we went looking for them but they had gone. Sometime during the previous evening we had acquired their address, albeit the writing wasn't as clear as it could have been as there had been drink taken. So we made out the address as best we could and added the post script to the front of the letter, 'Postman do your best.' And he did. John wrote back.

We started going for walks and figured we had gotten to know each other well enough and decided to get married.

Our wedding was originally planned for October but had to be moved up to September 1944 as John's unit was being shipped out to the fighting.

Basically the entire thing was planned in one day. There was not time to tell anyone, never mind invite anyone. I made multiple trips from London to Guildford and back that day as I had to arrange for a special licence.

The dress had just been found – they weren't easy to come by – my mother found it somewhere. My sister Connie spent the entire day before the wedding making dresses for our sister Gwyneira and my niece Anne who were going to be my attendants.

The day of the wedding we ended up with quite the guest list; two of my sisters, my parents, my niece Anne, my nephew, David, the cleaning lady and a dog.

The fiancée of the best man spent the wedding at the train station waiting to be picked up by the best man but we did manage to get her in time for the celebration at the pub.

Young David insisted on holding John's hand during the entire ceremony. I think the highlight was trying to get the minister to pronounce my name. John was shipped out four days later and I had no idea when I would see him again.

John was injured and sent back within months and then shipped off to Canada as soon as he was well enough. Then the government started arranging for the brides to go over. John was from Montreal so that's where I was headed. I didn't know much about Canada other than it was cold. My husband had assured me that it was a 'dry' cold so you didn't notice it! Trust me, in Montreal you notice the cold.

We had a special train from London to the ship in April 1944. I remember there was a young serviceman whose detail it was to escort us during the sailing to Canada. This poor man was in charge of eight women, all of whom were pregnant to varying degrees, myself included. Actually there had been some discussion as to whether I was even going to be able to travel as the baby was due in June.

As the war was still on there were several drills during the crossing and the poor man was in charge of us getting all of us up on deck. I can't imagine what he told his family about this assignment. I wasn't, and still am not, a great traveller. I threw up the entire way to Canada and was miserable. Not knowing much about biology I was a bit worried that I would throw up the baby!

I was so happy to get on solid ground only to get onto a train for another 800-mile journey to Montreal, certainly the longest train journey I had ever been on. There were huge distances of vast – well – nothingness really, between the stops. At the time Canada seemed like a huge uninhabited wilderness.

When the train did stop, sometimes only one lone girl would disembark to the platform to be greeted by waiting strangers. I always felt sorry for them and in later years wondered what became of them. Often before a stop there was a great flurry of getting ready as nervous brides readied themselves to be presented to their new family and reunited with their soldier.

As happy as I had been to get off the ship, I didn't prove to be a better train passenger than I was a sailor. I was still quite ill and couldn't manage any food. When the train finally arrived in Montreal I had to be propped up by two Red Cross workers.

I had asked John that he come alone to meet me because I had barely seen him since the wedding but his sister Mary wasn't going be put off. She insisted on coming to the train station with John so that was my arrival in Montreal; bedraggled from days of travel and illness, weak and propped up by nurses. Not the entrance I had hoped for.

To top it off, a newspaper photographer was hovering around wanting a shot of a war hero (John was still on crutches from his injury) greeting his War Bride. John nearly decked him.

We went to live with John's family. There were three siblings plus his parents in a small walkup in Park Extension in Montreal. I thought it was the strangest thing that the house had a staircase on the outside. Turns out this was typical of Montreal houses of the time. I was alone with them most of the time as John had to go back to camp and finish his army tour.

His parents had immigrated to Canada from Scotland when John was just two months old and they had strong Glaswegian accents. I couldn't understand half of what they said and for some reason Poppa kept the windows closed. I wasn't used to that at all; at home we always had the windows open to let in fresh air. I felt like I was suffocating.

When my daughter Myfanwy was finally born John's mother took me to the hospital and I was terrified. I had no idea what was going to happen. When her brothers, Neil and Huw, were born I was much better prepared.

Since I was one of the first War Brides in Montreal I was quite active in the Acorn War Brides Club. We early arrivals helped the newer ones adjust and explained to them how things worked. Many of them ended up in French neighbourhoods of Montreal where it turned out only their husbands could speak English. They found themselves isolated and felt very unwelcome. The club was quite a refuge for some of these women; it was a place where they could go to get things off their chest and feel safe among friends.

My husband spoke French because he learned it at the factory where he worked, but I never mastered the language. I always lived in English neighbourhoods in Montreal and was able to get along just fine. Unlike some other War Brides who belonged to our club, French wasn't something I needed to survive. Even our three children never learned how to speak

French when they were growing up; it just wasn't necessary in the part of Montreal we lived in those days. English people could live an English life in their own neighbourhoods; but it's very different now. You can't live in Montreal today without speaking French.

Later, my husband owned his own manufacturing business and was active in the Cadet Corps with the Black Watch in Montreal. When our three children grew up I took a job at Concordia University (an English university) as a secretary and worked there until I retired. By that time, the children had all left the province of Quebec so about fifteen years ago we moved to Burlington, Ontario, to be closer to our daughter and her family. Today, John and I live in a special care home in Burlington and we are still together after sixty-two years.

Postscript: Morfydd and John Gibson have three children and eight grandchildren. Morfydd's granddaughter, Meredith Burbidge, helped her write this story.

3

Ontario

War Brides who came to Ontario arrived in a province that was more like Britain than any other part of Canada. Geographically, historically and culturally, Ontario had a connection to Britain that would have made it an ideal place for British War Brides to settle.

For more than two centuries English-speaking people had been coming to Ontario, first from the United States after the American Revolution but then mainly from Britain. British immigration was reflected in the familiar place names of cities like London, Kitchener, Waterloo, Kingston, Scarborough, and Peterborough.

Prior to European settlement a native population made up of the Algonkian and Iroquoian linguistic groups lived in the north and south.

Their descendents – Huron, Ojibwa, Iroquois, Cree and Mohawk – were still very much evident on reserves in the 1940s when the War Brides arrived. And although waves of immigration following mining discoveries in the north changed the cultural makeup of the north, in the south, where the largest cities are located, the face of Ontario was white, Anglo-Saxon, Protestant and the most British in character.

Ninety per cent of its nearly four million people[1] could speak English and the majority were of British origin; in fact, forty-six per cent of all Anglicans in the entire country lived in Ontario, as well as forty per cent of all Baptists![2] As Canada's second largest province, Ontario had more people and the greatest share of the country's natural resources. That wealth showed in its good roads, schools, universities and transportation systems that were well developed compared to the other provinces.

In Ottawa was found the seat of Canada's federal government and its provincial capital was Toronto, a large, bustling urban centre along the shores of Lake Ontario where museums, theatres, and art galleries were part of city life. Like the rest of the country, there was a serious postwar housing crunch, but most city dwellers would have had modern amenities like plumbing and electricity. In comparison to their counterparts who were settling into rural Maritimes, Newfoundland, Quebec and points out west, War Brides who came to Ontario's cities would have found the transition to Canadian life relatively easy.

Mary (Mitchell) Vankonnaught was the first War Bride to arrive in Parry Sound, a lumber town near Georgian Bay, about 140 miles from Toronto. In this excerpt from her diary, she describes her journey with her small daughter June from Halifax to Toronto and then on to Parry Sound:

> A train was waiting for the next leg of the journey; the biggest I had ever seen and quite luxurious. We were assigned a sleeping car and then ate in the dining car, traveling day and night until we reached Toronto the next morning. We were taken to a large reception area where reporters were busy taking photographs of and interviewing the war brides. There were several women that were waiting to meet their new in-laws from that area. At last the crowd thinned out, my name was called, and the Red Cross people took us to the train that would take us to Parry Sound.
>
> Three airmen and one soldier were going with us to Parry Sound. We were all introduced to each other and to the Conductor. I was surprised to learn that they all knew Van's aunt and uncle with whom I was going to stay. We were all given box lunches to take on the journey. I was surprised to find that we were the only

passengers – in England the trains were always packed – but the train had not many cars attached.

We had fun. The Conductor and the men told me all about Parry Sound but they added some tall tales such as that the Indians wore headdresses and went on the warpath on occasion and that the bears came into your garden and you had to shoo them away. They amused June and we had a pleasant lunch together. The Conductor said he would let me know when we were close to Parry Sound so that I could freshen up.

When we got to the station, there was a surprise for us. The whole town had turned out to give their heroes a welcome home. It was one of the most exciting times of my life for me too. I found that they were also there to welcome me because I was the first war bride to arrive in town. Van's uncle and aunt were there to meet me. The Red Cross personnel welcomed us and there was a reporter from the local newspaper to record the occasion.[3]

The suburban face of downtown Ottawa or Toronto certainly wasn't reflected everywhere in Ontario; during the Second World War, one-and-a-half-million people lived on farms or in rural areas. So although it may have had the biggest cities, and a huge industrial base, Ontario also had a large rural population that was spread throughout its 354,348 sq. miles (917,741 sq. km) in a diverse geography ranging from the low-lying hills and flat agricultural base of the south to the forests, rivers and lakes of the frozen north.

Cold weather wasn't isolated to the northern reaches of the province; even women who went to cosmopolitan cities like Ottawa had to struggle with Ontario's climate. Vernie Foy recalls that first winter in Canada:

It took some time for me to get used to the weather – especially those very cold days in winter when the front door of the family home would not close properly because of the ice. The laundry being brought in and stood up in the kitchen before it thawed was another shocking experience.[4]

Just because they lived in cities and towns was no guarantee of happiness: whether they went to the populated south or to remote settlements in the north, east or west of the province, War Brides still had to stand on their own two feet. In the following stories we will meet a diverse group of women who settled in Ontario. Having come to one of the most British provinces in the country, one could say they represent the quintessential Canadian War Bride experience.

Map showing location of Ontario.

Margaret's War
Margaret (Perkins) Bristow Eaton

Margaret (Perkins) Bristow Eaton married a Canadian in 1940 and moved to various locations in southern England to be at his side. In 1944 he was taken prisoner of war in Germany.

Margaret Bristow was nineteen years old and working at a shoe box factory in Rushden, Northamptonshire when she met Bill Bristow, a Canadian serviceman from London, Ontario.

Although the so-called Phony War was still on, Margaret had already experienced her own share of tragedy: she was still mourning the recent death of her friend, Bobby Steele, whose ship, *The Royal Oak*, had been torpedoed by German U-Boats in the Orkney Islands in October 1939.

Bill Bristow was also nineteen and he was in England with the Royal Canadian Regiment (RCR). He had signed up in London, Ontario as soon as war was declared and he arrived in Greenock, Scotland, as part of the First Canadian Division on 17 December 1939. In May 1940 he was transferred to Rushden where the Canadians were billeted in private homes.

One Sunday afternoon in May at a band concert in the town park, Margaret and a friend met Bill and another soldier. Bill was very handsome in uniform and if there is such a thing as love at first sight this was probably it. They sat and talked and agreed to meet again. From then on they saw each other as often as they could.

Margaret's father died when she was sixteen so she had to leave school and take a job at the shoe box factory. She had dreams of becoming a nurse, but for a family without means, it was impossible. Margaret's mother lived with relatives so Margaret boarded in Rushden. She took Bill to meet her grandfather and mother and although his stay in Rushden was brief – two weeks – Bill had definitely left his mark.

Things were warming up on the war front, the Phony War was over and the British Expeditionary Force along with the French Army was being pushed out of France through Dunkirk. One morning that May all the Canadians were gone, along with L/Corporal Bristow. They were off to the Continent to form a spearhead to assist the British Expeditionary Force and the French Army to escape from the German *blitzkrieg*.

The First Canadian Division's stay in France was brief and they returned to England unscathed. Bill was moved to Horley, south of London, and did not return to Rushden. Margaret found out later that during this time Bill was sent to Norway. She never did find out what the Canadians did there but two months later, in early July, Bill, now a Corporal, received a forty-eight-hour pass and much to Margaret's surprise he asked for her hand in marriage. She remembers that it was pouring rain and they had stopped in a doorway to avoid getting wet. Of course she said 'Yes!' She was elated.

Since neither of them were of age they both required permission to marry, Margaret from her mother and Bill from his commanding officer. They wanted to have the ceremony in September so Margaret purchased a marriage licence which expired at the end of October. The Battle of Britain was beginning and air raids were stepped up all over England. Life was very hectic, leaves were cancelled, letters not delivered. With the war raging around them they had almost no way to communicate or see each other. Airplanes were flying overhead day and night, anti-aircraft (ack-ack) guns were firing continuously and barrage balloons were everywhere.

By 31 October Margaret hadn't heard from Bill for some time and the marriage licence was about to expire. She figured Bill had changed his mind so she did not renew it. Then on Friday evening 1 November, Bill and his friend, Merle Shantz, showed up at her door. They had walked across

London amidst air raids, bomb damage and bus disruptions and were covered with oil and dirt but she was still overjoyed to see them.

Bill brought Merle to be his best man and asked if they could get married the next day, Saturday. Margaret explained that the licence had expired and they would have to wait till Monday, which they did but legally they still had to wait another twenty-four hours before the marriage could occur. They were finally married on 5 November 1940, Guy Fawke's Day, at the Methodist Church in Rushden.

During this time Bill was stationed at Reigate, Surrey just south of London. The Canadian Army had taken over empty houses in the area and was headquartered there. Bill wanted Margaret to come down to Reigate to be with him and rent a room in the area to live – as many other married soldiers did – and he would obtain a sleeping out pass. Off to Reigate Margaret went and so began the first of many moves she would make over the next five years as she followed Bill from place to place in southern England.

Life went on; there were air raids most nights, some bombs fell very close. Bill was away on duty or training most of the time but they did manage to spend their first Christmas together. Everything was rationed except rabbits so Margaret bought one. Bill had never eaten rabbit nor had she ever cooked one. Margaret remembers thinking that Christmas in England before the war was never like this.

There were other soldiers' wives and girlfriends living in the area and Margaret made many friends. They were in Reigate about six months and were forced to move numerous times. One night in Croydon (about five miles away) the bus depot was bombed. There were well over 100 buses inside the depot and Margaret remembers the way the sky lit up that night.

Bill was transferred again, this time to Chipstead, near London. The first place they lived in Chipstead was a small bedroom in a house on a large hill. Bill didn't want to sleep in the air-raid shelter and one night a bomb fell on the street, blew in their windows and collapsed the roof of the house. They were not injured but decided that it was probably wise to move into the air-raid shelter at night.

They moved again into the home of a lady named Brenda Martin and her two children. Brenda's husband was away in the Navy. By this time Margaret discovered she was pregnant with her first child. Hospitals were reserved mainly for wounded soldiers so babies were delivered at home or in private nursing homes. In January 1942 their daughter Anne was born in a private home for pregnant woman in Purley, about two miles away from Brenda's.

On 19 August the Second Canadian Division was involved in the raid at Dieppe, France. The Essex Scottish was almost completely annihilated and Bill was transferred to the Essex as Company Sergeant Major (CSM) where he became an instructor for new troops arriving from Canada. They were sent to Arundel Castle which was the home of the Duke and Duchess of Norfolk. Once again, Margaret and the baby moved to be close to Bill in Bognor Regis about five miles from the castle.

They lived one street away from the English Channel; the beaches were barricaded with barbed wire and at the end of the long pier on the beach was an ack-ack gun which was in action all the time. One day Margaret took Anne for a walk along the promenade for a couple of miles to visit a woman she had met who was also married to a Canadian soldier. They had tea and Margaret was walking home when a German bomber dropped his load on Main Street in Bognor Regis. The noise was terrible but she continued walking home.

Margaret hadn't expected to see Bill that night but when he heard of the bombing he rushed into Bognor where he was told that Margaret had taken Anne for a walk. He assisted in pulling bodies from the wreckage of the bombing and when he came home, Anne and Margaret were already there. He came into their room and was so filled with joy at seeing his wife and daughter that he cried.

Once again Bill was moved to a new location, this time to Middleton about two miles east of Bognor. Headquarters was in a house in which lived two old ladies who owned a parrot. This parrot would sit in an open window and the passing soldiers took great delight in teaching the parrot a 'new language' much to the chagrin of the old ladies, who were furious. They complained but it was too late. The parrot was now swearing like a trooper and they couldn't remove the words from the parrot's head.

Margaret followed Bill to Middleton and rented a home there. One day in November just before dusk she was walking with Anne in the pram when she heard the air-raid sirens and saw a plane flying quite low towards them. It was a German plane and she could see the pilot. As she looked up, he waved at her. She pulled Anne from the pram onto the ground, put herself on top of the baby and held her breath. The plane continued on to Ford Airfield about three miles inland where it bombed the airstrip, killing some airmen and destroying a few planes.

In the spring of 1943 Bill decided that Margaret should move back to Bognor. By this time she was pregnant with her second child and had to attend a clinic where all the arrangements were made for her to have the baby at home with a midwife in attendance. A boy, John, was born in October and within a few months Margaret moved again, but this time it was to get away from German bombs.

Early in 1944 the Germans began a new series of heavy raids using bigger, more destructive bombs. As time went on they came more and more frequently so Margaret and Bill decided it was time to move the children out of harm's way. In May Margaret returned to her home town of Rushden, about 50 miles north of London, where she rented rooms in a house across the street from her mother.

Then came D-Day and Bill was sent to France with the Essex Scottish Regiment. In mid-July the Canadians were involved in heavy fighting to capture the city of Caen, in northern France. Bill was wounded and captured by the Germans. Margaret received a telegram saying that Bill had been 'believed killed'.

It was a mistake, but one can imagine her feelings at that moment. Bill's mother and father also received the same telegram in Canada.

In late September Margaret finally received a form letter from Bill saying that he had been wounded but he was alive and well and a prisoner of war at Stalag IVB. Needless to say the summer of 1944 was the worst of Margaret's young life. She was only twenty-four years old and thought she was already a widow.

It had been a different story for Bill's parents in Canada. One of Bill's friends had been in touch with his own mother after the battle and told her he had seen his friend Bill lying in a shell hole covered with blood. He thought Bill was dead and wrote to his mother telling her so. This was the story as they knew it in Canada and the local government placed a plaque on the city hall in Chatham, Ontario with the names of all the men killed up to that point in the war. Bill's name was on the plaque.

Correspondence from Bill was all from letters which said very little. She never knew how many of hers got through to him or what had been censored. She sent many parcels to him, including a set of heavy underwear for the winter and over a year later the parcel was returned to her mother unopened. He had never received it.

By 1945 the Allies were pushing the Germans back on all fronts and were advancing steadily through France, Belgium and Holland. As they progressed the Germans also moved their POWs back and Bill was one of many who took part in a forced march to Stalag XIIA, close to the Russian border.

Before Bill went to France he and Margaret talked about what she would do if anything happened to him. She promised that she would take the children to Canada to be with his parents and they agreed if she didn't like it there, she would return to England. Given the circumstances, Margaret decided to go to Canada. She wrote to Bill and told him of her plans but he never received the letter. Her mother and grandfather, who was by then eighty-four years old, did not want Margaret to go but both agreed that it was the correct decision. In early March 1945 she was told to prepare for imminent departure. At this time the children were both under three years old.

Margaret received train tickets to go from Rushden to Liverpool and had to say her goodbyes with the feeling that she would never see her grandfather again: in fact he died shortly after Margaret and the children landed in Canada. They arrived in Liverpool and spent the first night at the YMCA. The next day they boarded the SS *Franconia*, a troopship that had just returned from the historic Yalta Conference where it served as the floating headquarters for Winston Churchill and his staff. The *Franconia* was full of War Brides, their children and soldiers returning to Canada, and since it was to be part of a convoy they had to wait on board for thirty hours while the other ships were loaded.

Although the war was winding down there was still a constant fear of convoys being torpedoed by German submarines. The convoy therefore zigzagged across the Atlantic doubling the usual crossing time. This was before the organized transport of War Brides to Canada with the Red Cross so there was no help with the children on board the ship. All the women pitched in and helped each other. The food was wonderful, they had things to eat which they hadn't seen in years and haven't seen since. Because of Bill's rank (CSM) Margaret didn't have to go into the large dormitory area bunks. She and the children shared a small cabin with another War Bride and her two children. There were four bunk beds so she put Anne and John at each end of the bottom bunk and she slept on the top one.

The *Franconia* arrived in Halifax in the evening of 11 April 1945 and two days later they were met in Chatham, Ontario by Bill's parents, his sister and her husband. She and the children were made to feel most welcome in Canada. At last Margaret's war was finally over.

Back in Europe, Bill's war was still raging. The Germans were bringing their POWs into Germany via forced marches day and night. During one night march Bill and another POW escaped by hiding in a ditch along the side of the road. They spent the next few weeks wandering the countryside trying to survive and avoid being recaptured by the Germans. He told of eating raw turnips and potatoes stolen from fields. As they wandered about, they felt that they had been going in circles and soon discovered that they were, in fact, on an island going round and round. Bill was finally liberated on 9 May 1945 by the advancing American army.

He was taken immediately to hospital in England. As soon as he was well enough he got a pass and went to Rushden to see Margaret and the children. Only then did he discover that they were already in Canada. Bill returned to Canada in August 1945 on the SS *Ile de France*. After six years Bill's war was finally over too.

Postscript: Bill spent many months in the veteran's hospital in London, Ontario. He had severe malnutrition and a piece of shrapnel was still in his shoulder. Through Bill's employment the family transferred from Chatham to Gananoque, Ontario in 1953 where Margaret still lives today. Bill passed away in 1965 as a result of his war injuries; he was only forty-five years old. Margaret's mother came to Canada in 1948 and lived nearby until she died in 1975. Margaret married Frank Eaton in 1968 and was widowed for the second time in 1978. Her children Anne and John are in their sixties and have given Margaret five grandchildren and six great-grandchildren.

If It's OK with My Mother, Will You Marry Me?
Martha (McLachlan) Stauffer

Martha (McLachlan) Stauffer was from Stirling, Scotland. A fortune teller predicted she would marry a handsome young man, have three children and move far away – all of which came true.

I was born in 1926 in Port Glasgow, Renfrewshire, Scotland. I was the eldest of five girls and it was a family joke that having so many girls was a big disappointment to my father. As one of Scotland's leading pipe drummers and a member of the famous Millhall Prize Pipe Band, Dad always teased us by saying he needed a boy for a successor!

My mother worked at the Gourock Rope Works in Port Glasgow before she married my father. At first they lived in Dumbarton but my father got a better job in Stirling before the war so we moved there. Soon after we arrived in Stirling war was declared and Dad joined the

Expeditionary Forces. He was involved in the evacuation of Dunkirk in May and June 1940 and he stayed in the military until the war was over in 1945. That meant my mother and we five girls had to fend for ourselves. My mother worked at a munitions factory making casings for bullets and I got a job in a cotton factory in Deanston on the spinning machines.

Our home on Ochil Crescent in Stirling was situated near the River Forth between Wallace's monument and Stirling Castle. The German planes came over at night and we could see them silhouetted in the search lights. It was scary because we had mines dropped just east of us and my grandmother was in Port Glasgow when the Germans bombed the shipyards. Her friend was killed when the shelter she was in suffered a direct hit.

I remember our shelter at home in Stirling: two double beds put into one room. Mom and five girls slept there. One day my mother said, 'If the Germans land here I will take you all down to the river and drown you.' Luckily, that didn't happen!

After the cotton factory I worked for many months in an aircraft factory but then I applied for a job on Alexander's Buses as a conductress, or a 'clippie' as they called us. I wore a uniform and gave passengers their tickets for their journey, charging them accordingly.

I ran the route between Stirling and Dunfermline which was about twenty-three miles and although I had plenty of rough customers, I never had any trouble. The bus stopped right outside the dog racetrack and owners of greyhounds always wanted to bring their dogs on the bus. I was allowed to have three dogs on board at a time, provided the animal curled up under the seat. One day, a man sat his huge hound on the seat, which was against the rules. We had quite an argument, as these dog fanciers treat their dogs like human beings. He said the dog was too big to go under the seat.

Finally I said, 'Look mister, if you don't get that dog off the seat I'll have to charge you two fares!' Without another word he whistled the dog under the seat.

I continued to work for Alexander's Buses during the war and in December 1945 I was on the run from Stirling to Crief when I met my future husband, Wilson Stauffer, a Canadian serviceman from Oshawa, Ontario.

I had never met a Canadian before. I remember going to a fair with an American soldier one time and except for the fortune teller it was a forgettable evening. We walked around the grounds and came to a fortune teller's tent. My date gave me a shilling to cross her palm and she said: 'You are going to meet a handsome young man, get married and go overseas. You will have three children. You will have no worries, he will look after you.'

Then she said that I would win the football pool or some other lottery so I didn't put much faith in her predictions but as it turns out, she was absolutely right!

When I met Wilson he was in the queue waiting to get on the bus with another Canadian when he called, 'Hey sweetie! Do you have a seat for me?'

I replied as I would to any customer: 'If there is one available. If not, you will have to stand.'

On the last leg of the trip I was in the front seat getting my money ready to hand in at the depot. Wilson came down from the back of the bus to ask if he could walk me home. His friend Victor and he walked with me until we got to the corner. Then Wilson said, 'See you later Vic', and Vic disappeared. When we reached our house we chatted for a while and he asked if he could see me again. I said yes and so began our whirlwind courtship.

At the time Wilson was away from the Queen's Own Rifles and was with No.4 Repat Depot at Whitley, Surrey, England attached to the Salvation Army as a military helper. I too was a volunteer with the Salvation Army and in fact, if it hadn't been for meeting Wilson I would have enrolled in the college and become an officer. But those plans were soon cancelled after we met.

Wilson worked as head projectionist showing movies afternoon and night as well as four shows at the Sergeants and Officers Mess. Since he worked such long hours until 10 or 11 p.m. almost every night he was able to get ninety-six-hour passes every second weekend. He would take a fifteen-hour train from Surrey to Stirling, arrive at 6.30 a.m. Saturday morning and leave at 9 p.m. Sunday night.

On one occasion in March 1946 Wilson had a nine-day pass so we spent as much time together as we could. On the Wednesday, which was my day off, we were alone at my home because my mother was uptown and my sisters were at school. Seizing the moment, Wilson asked me to marry him in a way I will never forget. He said, 'If it's OK with my mom, will you marry me?'

You see, since Wilson was only nineteen years old he had to get permission to marry from his parents and there was some doubt whether his mother would consent!

No sooner had I said 'Yes' to his proposal when my youngest sister Ann walked in the door. We shooed her out of the house by sending her on an errand to get some candy. Meantime, my mother was on her way back home and she ran into my sister on the street. Sensing there was something funny going on my mother walked in the house and demanded to know what we were up to. Needless to say, there were two red faces!

Wilson wrote to his mother to ask permission to marry but I was less worried about what might happen. He said that if his mother refused, he'd ask his father, who would certainly say yes. We both had to go through normal channels: Wilson had to see the padre, camp colonel and get permission to marry from his commanding officer. I had to have a medical and get a character reference from my minister at St Mark's Presbyterian as well as a letter of approval from my parents. We were married on 7 June 1946 at St Mark's in Stirling.

When I received the letter from the Canadian Wives Bureau with a form about my departure, I waited before sending it back until I knew for sure when Wilson was leaving. I didn't want to arrive in Canada before him, something which I had heard happened to a few other girls. As it turned out, Wilson was repatriated in the middle of October 1946 and I left two weeks later on the 26th.

During that time everything was pandemonium to say the least. We packed a good-sized trunk with all the wedding presents and everything I'd need for Canada. And of course Mum and I went shopping for incidentals.

A lot of the neighbours came by to say 'Cheerio' instead of 'Goodbye'. In their own way I suppose they were leaving an opening in case I wanted to come back. There had been stories of War Brides who returned to Scotland and since there was no way of knowing what fate awaited me I could very well have been one of those unlucky women.

After all the packing and unpacking, and checking and rechecking to see if I had brought everything I needed, we arrived at the train station that Wednesday only to find out that I had left my ration book at home. Coincidentally, at the same time this was happening, a reporter for the *Journal*, a local newspaper, had just arrived at my parents' home with the intention of interviewing my mother about my leaving for Canada.

Here is how the reporter described it in an article titled, 'Forgot her Ration Book! 'Journal' Reporter Helps Canuck Bride to Join Husband in Canada' which appeared in the newspaper the next day 27 October 1946:

Waiting at the Stirling Station yesterday (Wednesday) to board the 3:32 Glasgow train which was to carry her on the first stage of her long journey to Canada to join her ex-soldier husband was Mrs. Wilson Stauffer, daughter of

Mr. and Mrs. John McLachlan, 3 Ochil Crescent, Stirling, when in the midst
of her farewells she remembered she had overlooked bringing her ration
book without which she would not have been allowed to leave the country.

Her father immediately made a dash by taxi to collect the all-important document, and his arrival at the house coincided with that of a 'Journal' reporter
who had called to interview Mrs. Stauffer. Hurried explanations were made,
and ration book – and reporter – reached the station with minutes to spare.

We arrived in Liverpool and stayed overnight in a building set up with
single beds all in a row for the War Brides. On the train from Stirling I met
a girl from Dundee, Marian O'Conner. She settled in Calgary, Alberta and
we became very good friends, corresponding until she passed away a few
years ago. We were both very impressed with all the help we got from the
Canadian Army. They took care of our luggage and trunks and put everything on the train.

Marian and I were so excited when we boarded the ship and were able
to get bunks beside each other. I think that made it easier to be going so far
away from home. Although a lot of the girls were seasick Marian and I managed the trip without any mishaps. We were thrilled with the menu: white
bread after all these years of rationing and even roast turkey. We thought
heaven couldn't be any better.

After seven days on the *Letitia*, we arrived at Pier 21 in Halifax, Nova
Scotia on 2 November. As we left the ship our names were checked and
then we were brought over to the train station not far from Pier 21. Marian
and I stayed together for another twenty-four hours until it was time for me
to disembark in Oshawa, Ontario. We had a tearful departure, both knowing
we may never see each other again.

I was the only person getting off the train and I was on the very last
carriage. As I stepped onto the siding, I could see Wilson running down to
greet me. We climbed into a 1934 Pontiac and drove to his parents' home
where we lived for nearly one year.

I was amazed that he drove on the wrong side of the road and that there were
trees growing out of the pavement. Later I realized that they plant trees along
the sidewalks to beautify the city, but at the time it certainly looked strange.

When we arrived at his house there was a big banner that said 'Welcome
to Canada Martha.' Up until then I had been so nervous about meeting his
family but I didn't need to worry: they welcomed me with open arms.

Postscript: Martha and Wilson Stauffer celebrated their sixtieth wedding anniversary in June 2006. They still live in Oshawa, Ontario and true to the fortune teller's prediction, they had three children, one daughter and two sons who have given them two grandsons, three granddaughters, five great-grandsons and four great-granddaughters.

It's a Good Job I Didn't Smoke, Drink or Wear Much Makeup
Rita (Bannister) Buckrell

Rita (Bannister) Buckrell came from Patcham, England. She married a Canadian and settled in the rural farming village of Burgessville, Ontario where her husband's family were strict Baptists.

I was born in Brighton and grew up in the same house as my grandparents at 10 Tidy Street. When my grandmother was alive, everyone got along and our house was a happy one but things soon changed after my grandmother died.

My step-grandfather was a spiritualist and he claimed my grandmother's spirit had instructed him to build two houses on Winfield Avenue in Patcham, one for us and one for himself. In honour of my late grandmother, whose name was Louise Augusta, one of the houses was to be named Louise and the other Augusta.

While the houses were being built in Patcham we continued to live on Tidy Street. I was only five years old but I remember the day my father and my grandfather got into a row over music. That did it. My grandfather made it clear we were no longer welcome on Tidy Street or in the new houses in Patcham. I don't know what the spirits told him but he would not let my mother get any pictures of grandma or any keepsakes. So my dad climbed in the window and picked up what mother wanted – pictures of her ancestors, the Passingham family from Cornwall.

We eventually built a house in the new housing estate at Patcham and I went to school in the village. The estate was growing by leaps and bounds so the school moved to Patcham Place – a large historic building in the old village. There was a big park around the house and the London to Brighton railway track ran through a tunnel under the woods close by. Across the main London Road was the Black Lion Pub which was later owned by boxer Joe Louis. I passed my examinations and in 1938 I began my high school education at Varndean Secondary School.

I was thirteen years old and in my second year of high school when the Second World War broke out. We had previously been issued with gas masks and when the sirens sounded for the first time we figured there was an air raid coming so we all rushed to put on these masks. They were in a round yellow canister and from that day on until almost the end of the war I never left the house without mine. If we arrived at school minus our gas mask we were sent home to get it. I had a three-mile walk so I made sure I never had to do that.

Now that we knew we were in it for real we began to dig an air-raid shelter in the back garden. We lived on the outskirts of Brighton just a few miles along the South Coast from the White Cliffs of Dover and beneath the top soil was the same solid chalk so most of the digging was done with a pick axe.

I remember the first night we spent underground: German aircraft had set the gorse bushes which covered the South Downs on fire and we thought we were going to be bombed for sure so we grabbed our blankets and pillows and took shelter. Nothing happened but it was a cold-drafty night – the first of many.

Blackouts were part of life now. All windows had to be covered with heavy curtains or plywood at night so that the German pilots flying over-head could not see the lights. If a chink of light shone through there would be a knock on the door with the Air Raid Warden telling you 'PUT THAT LIGHT OUT!' and there was a fine if you didn't. Bus windows were dark-ened and had very little light, just enough to find your seat. Car headlights were shielded over the top and just had slits for lights to show through. I remember being hit in the back by a bicycle I couldn't see while crossing a street on my way home from skating one night.

The air-raid shelter at Varndean Secondary School was built in herring-bone fashion. It was about six feet wide with benches along each wall and just long enough between each bench to hold a class; the pattern was to control a blast. When the air-raid sirens sounded we gathered our books, pens and blankets and filed out to the shelters to resume classes there.

Later when the Germans changed their tactics they would fly in low off the sea to miss the radar and then pips would sound to warn us that enemy aircraft were directly overhead. There was no time to head for shelter so we got down on the floor and hid under our desk, hands over heads. We remained there until the all clear was sounded.

Our school was on the top of a hill, a long white building, which looked like a hospital so it was a target for machine guns. Often, looking through the windows we would see our Spitfires fighting the intruders and sometimes a parachute descending from a plane spewing smoke and we would be thankful it was a Messerschmitt and not a Spitfire. The boys in those planes saved us during the Battle of Britain. I know several young men from Canada flew those planes and we were forever thankful to them.

By this time we had graduated from the underground shelter to a Morrison shelter in the house. This was a steel table with steel wire nets around the sides and was where I slept so that I didn't have to get up in the night during air raids. My folks would come under with me if the bombing got bad.

While I was still at school it became law that all teenagers had to take training in one of the armed services. All the young men were off at war and there was no one left to defend us except young people and older men who were in the Home Guard or served as Air Raid Wardens. I joined the Women's Junior Air Corps and we were trained how to shoot by the Home Guard. Almost every street corner had tank traps installed and there were air-raid shelters built every few blocks to protect people caught out on the streets during raids. We had always enjoyed swimming in the English Channel but this came to an end when the beaches were mined and barbed wire entanglements lined the sidewalks.

Because of the arrival of Canadian troops in Brighton a swimming pool had been converted to an ice rink and during my last year of school I learned how to skate. I had a pair of second-hand, black figure skates and took lessons how not to fall down. Little did I know then that this skating rink would change my life.

In England there was a pub on every street corner open from 10 in the morning until 11 p.m. at night and you can imagine what occurred when the Canadians went drinking and then skating on the ice. I was still in school and my mother warned if she ever caught me skating with a Canadian she would burn my skates. She reinforced this by coming to sit in the gallery to watch me. Eventually she put on skates and joined me until she had a fall which finished her skating career.

I had left school in the summer of 1942 and planned to continue with chemistry which was my favourite subject but with the war situation we had to volunteer in one of the armed forces, join the Women's Land Army, or work in munitions. My dad was in the engineering business and during the war they added a factory to make parts for radar. They were in need of a bookkeeper to work in the pay office and I was conscripted. My dreams of becoming a chemist were put on hold.

Skating had become my favourite pastime and during the sessions they would have five minutes speed skating for men, then for ladies, followed by ten minutes pair skating. This mixed up the crowd and one evening a Canadian soldier invited me to skate with him. He asked me how old I was: I said I was seventeen and he told me he was nineteen.

Canadian soldiers could get some things we could not and it took quite a few candy bars sent home from the army canteen before I had nerve enough to invite Les home for supper.

My Dad said, 'Poor beggars, coming over here to fight for us the least we can do is give them fish and chips.' That was the only thing we could get that was not rationed. So Les and his friends would often come home to Patcham for supper after skating.

Les rode his Harley Davidson to visit me but my mother made him park it out of sight and when he left he had to coast down the road so the neighbours would not hear him. Once he arrived with a huge army truck which she insisted he park between the two houses. It would barely fit. I still don't know how he managed to get it in there but he did.

Then one day Les stopped by on one of his dispatch riding excursions and he had his head shaved ready to leave for battle in Europe. Although I didn't know it at the time, that was the last I would see of him for over a year from May 1944 to July 1945.

D-Day came and the sky overhead was black with planes going over in droves hour after hour. Les was with the Service Corps so he did not cross the Channel until the ground troops had secured a beachhead large enough for tanks, big vehicles and supplies to be taken over. For a long time I did not hear from him. I just listened to the news to learn what was going on. Mail was a long time reaching us but we wrote nearly every day so we would feel connected.

The war ended in May but it was July 1945 before Les had any leave. We were sitting on a hillside looking across the Devils Dyke when we became engaged and began making wedding plans for September. Asking my parents was another story. My father was the best bet so Les asked for his approval and left the rest to Dad.

The next step was to get permission to marry from the Army. So many girls had married Canadian soldiers only to find out they already had a wife and family in Canada. When we were interviewed by the preacher, I was not impressed to find out that Les was actually two years older than he had told me the night we met skating. He said later that he didn't think I would skate with him if I knew he was four years older, and he certainly wasn't intending to marry me that night!

Finally, we both had to have blood tests to make sure we were in good health. All being fine we proceeded with arrangements for the wedding, saving ration coupons, begging and borrowing where necessary.

We could get beef tongue off rations so these were cooked and pressed. One of the boys working at the factory arranged for a wedding cake through his father who had a bakery. The bridesmaid's dress was on loan and I had enough clothing coupons for my dress, a plain white dinner gown. My cousin, John Hill, was manager of a shoe store at Haywards Heath and he wangled shoes for us as Les did not want to wear army boots for the wedding.

We were married on 17 September 1945 and after a week's honeymoon Les had to return to Holland where he stayed until he was repatriated to Canada in January 1946 on the *Ile de France*.

I applied to follow Les to Canada and finally in May word came that I was to proceed to a gathering place in London to begin my journey overseas. My parents drove me there and we said our tearful goodbyes on the street. When 300 of us had gathered we went by train to Southampton shipyard where this enormous ship towered above us, The *Ile de France*, the same one that brought Les back to Canada. Wherever we went the band played 'Here Come the Brides' and they piped us on aboard.

We went up on deck to watch as 7,000 Canadian troops also boarded. Guards were placed at all entrances to our quarters and fraternization was forbidden or you would be sent back to England. With so many on board ship there was no place to sit down and having nothing to do we walked the decks stepping over the soldiers who had no place to sit but on the deck.

We could not believe the food on board ship, white bread, even bananas and oranges that we had not even seen for five years. Because there were so many on board we just had two meals a day. We slept on bunks two or three high, and the sheet on my bed had a hole in it. Every time I turned over it would split just a bit more. I remember thinking, 'What am I doing here?' I was homesick already.

When we got to Halifax we were held up by fog and couldn't come in to port. The immigration people came out to the ship to start proceedings and save time. We finally landed at Pier 21 and we picked out our luggage which was arranged alphabetically and soldiers carried it to the train for us.

I had shipped a bicycle and someone had written on it 'Mind My Bike' which was a catchphrase from the BBC radio comedy program *ITMA* starring Tom Handley. Several of the women found their husbands waiting for them and I looked in vain for Les, not realizing I had another 1,200 miles to go by train and car before I reached his home in Burgessville, near Woodstock, Ontario.

It was midnight two days later when I stepped on to a deserted Woodstock station platform – 3,000 miles from home and all alone. I had heard of War Brides arriving and no one showing up to meet them and my first thought was, 'Oh no, not another one!' Pretty soon the Red Cross showed up and they were just going to take me to a hotel for the night when along comes a very apologetic Les – he had fallen asleep while waiting at home.

We had been married in the Church of England and Les had never indicated there were any religious differences between us. He seemed just like me, willing to get along with those around him. When we were in England he always said, 'Tomorrow they might save my life, or me theirs.' I suppose being away from Canada for so long and being in the army had broadened his outlook on life.

So when I arrived and found out that I was in a home of strict Baptists, it was quite a surprise. My father was a Catholic and very open minded about religion. I had been raised in the Church of England but I was allowed to attend other Sunday schools with my friends. My scripture teacher in secondary school was Jewish so we were well grounded in the Old Testament. The only Baptist I had ever heard of was John the Baptist and I found it very hard living in a strict Baptist home. Dealing with this was the hardest part of settling in to Canadian life. I wanted to go back home many times and know of others who felt the same.

I was told Anglicans were the same as Catholics who were despised by this Baptist Church. Dancing was wicked: 'How would you like to see your husband in another woman's arms?'

After a while I had had enough of it and said, 'If I didn't trust him any more than that I wouldn't have married him in the first place!'

It was a good job I didn't smoke, drink, or wear much makeup: my worst sin was I had danced since I was two years old and it was part of my life. It seemed as though I had gone back to the Victorian days. We often talked about going back to England but this was where Les had work to keep us going.

I suppose it was not easy for Les's family either, having a stranger dumped in their midst especially one from a different culture. Language was about the only thing we had in common – and I had an English accent. Les's married brother was working on the farm and lived in a separate part of the same house so there were three families living close together. It took ten months before we were able to move into our own home. My life would have been so much happier if we been there from the start.

We spent a lot of time visiting relatives Les had not seen for four years and chummed around with some cousins who were more liberal minded and knew what we were going through. Since I could drive I was conscripted to work on the farm driving the army truck. This got me out of the house and alongside Les. We also helped load bales onto trucks as they were in the business of baling hay and straw.

That summer several War Brides had arrived in Burgessville. Kay Glover lived next door to us and we helped her out quite a bit as she was also having a really bad time with no help from her Canadian relatives – again because of religious differences. Kay was Catholic and had a little girl Pat. Her husband abandoned them and would not pay the money assigned by the court. After a few years Kay gave up and went back to England.

We finally moved in to our home about the middle of January and our first baby, Brian, was born in February 1947 at a nursing home in Norwich. There was so much snow that Les could not visit us, just four miles away. I remember it was so cold that winter, the milk would rise out of the bottles in the hallway as the pot-bellied stove was not doing a very good job of heating the house.

My parents came over in April to see their first grandchild. I never let on the problems I had been through because my mother would have said, 'I told you so!'

I met them at Woodstock station with Brian in a basket on the seat of a half-ton truck. Typically Canadian.

My dad would not go back to England until he put a bathroom in for us. I remember he called our outhouse 'Adam's House'. We had to hunt around here and there for a tub, toilet and washbasin but I finally got my running water.

We had four more children, two boys and two girls. In 1968 I went home to England for the first time when my father passed away. I tried to persuade my mother to come to Canada but she refused. We took four of the children over for a visit in 1973 and after that I had no desire to go back again. I was homesick for Canada.

Today, when our entire family gets together we number thirty-one. That's not too bad when you consider there were just two of us to start with. We are a happy family, the kids all get along well and are ready to help when needed. All this has been well worth it.

Postscript: On 17 September 2006 Les and Rita Buckrell celebrated their sixty-first wedding anniversary.

She Said She Could Write a Book About Her Life
Margaret (Hill) Bell

Margaret Montgomery (Hill) Bell passed away on 31 October, 1997. She always said that she should write a book about her life and her children are honoured to tell her story.

Margaret Montgomery Hill was born in 1925 in a little town called Rutherglen, south of Glasgow, Scotland. She was the fourth of five children in a very poor family. Margaret's father was a coal seller and her mother was a strict, religious woman who made the family attend church services three times on Sundays. As was the fashion at the time, Mrs Hill dabbled in spiritualism and considered herself a psychic. She held séances in her home where they would contact spirits from beyond.

When Margaret was five years old her father left for Canada saying he would send for the family after he was settled. Mr Hill was never heard from again for many years and he didn't return to his family in Scotland. Margaret's mother was left destitute and any money the older children were able to earn was turned over to her for the family's survival. To make matters worse Margaret's youngest brother James died of spinal meningitis when he was only eleven years old.

Even though they were poor, education was very important to the Hills and the children were encouraged to stay in school as long as they could manage. When war broke out, Margaret and her sisters had to leave school to work in an ammunition factory. Her job at the factory was to rip the tinfoil off the back of cigarette papers. She also worked a second job as an usherette at the Odeon movie theatre in Rutherglen.

Leaving school was a huge disappointment for Margaret as she enjoyed learning and made high marks, but the war and her family's poverty dictated another path to her future.

There was a bomb shelter in the backyard and the Hills were ready to make use of it whenever necessary. One night, as the sirens wailed, Margaret's mother led everyone to the safety of the shelter but on the way she realized she had forgotten to bring the safety deposit box. She ordered her children into the shelter and hurried back to the house to retrieve the box.

On her return, in the pitch black of night she got caught in the clothes line and started screaming, 'The Gerries have me! The Gerries have me!' You can imagine the sight when the children came out and saw their mother thrashing about in a tangled mess.

While the Hill family was surviving bombing raids and the girls were eking out a living in the munitions factory, over in Canada a young man named Harvey Stewart Bell from Sullivan Township, Ontario enlisted in the Canadian Army and was sent overseas in 1942. Before he left, a hired man from another farm told him to look up his family in Scotland if he ever had the chance. The man just so happened to be Margaret's father who had abandoned them many years before.

When Harvey had his first three-week leave, he contacted the Hill family in Scotland. Originally he was supposed to go out with Annie, Margaret's sister, but he happened to go to the Odeon Theatre where Margaret was working and decided she was the one he wanted to date. Apparently he had also been seeing a girl from England at the same time but Margaret won his heart. On his second leave he proposed and plans were set for them to marry.

Margaret's mother was very happy about the upcoming nuptials and she encouraged the marriage because she believed Margaret would have a better life in Canada. The Canadians were highly regarded – although the Scottish men didn't always feel that way, complaining that they were taking all the women.

Margaret and Harvey were wed in the Masonic Hall on 9 October 1943 by the Revd William Wright, the minister at Wardlawhill Church in Rutherglen. On their wedding night eighteen-year-old Margaret was terrified. She was so young and she hardly knew this man she had married. On their first night as husband and wife, Harvey had to sleep in a chair and he affectionately called her 'Frigid Bridget' for a while after that.

When Harvey's leave was over he went back to his service with the Royal Canadian Army Service Corps (RCASC). They only saw each other when he was on leave and when the war ended he was repatriated to Canada. Margaret applied to the Canadian Wives Bureau to join him in Ontario and then the waiting began. They wrote each other many letters and both looked forward to when they would be together again.

Talk of a Scottish War Bride coming to the Bell's farm travelled fast in Sullivan Township. When Margaret's father found out that Harvey had married his daughter and was bringing her over, he high tailed it out of there and moved to Toronto. Margaret never did see him in Canada but many years later her brother Andy found their father and he wanted nothing to do with them. All the children ever had of their father was his obituary in the *Toronto Star*.

Margaret set sail on the *Lady Nelson* on 28 April 1946. She sent a telegram ahead to Harvey notifying him of which ship she would be sailing on and when she would be leaving so that he could ready his plans to meet her in Toronto.

The *Lady Nelson* was a steam liner that had once been used for cruises but due to the war had been turned into a hospital ship bringing back wounded soldiers and War Brides. When Margaret boarded the ship, she took one look around and immediately walked back off. Her mother insisted things would be all right and urged her to get back on the boat. Margaret complied.

It was a very unpleasant journey. Margaret had nothing but a small suitcase and the clothes on her back. All around her were sick and dying men, seasick War Brides and even some with small children who were ill. She wasn't feeling too well herself and for the rest of her life Margaret always hated the water and was terrified to swim.

The *Lady Nelson* finally docked at Pier 21 in Halifax on 7 May but Margaret still had another two-day train ride from Halifax to Toronto. She arrived at the Red Cross centre for War Brides at Toronto's Union station where Harvey and his family were waiting. Ahead was a three-hour car ride to the family farm but the end was in sight.

Yes, she was exhausted, homesick and overwhelmed by her new surroundings but she was also very happy to be reunited with her husband and looking forward to finally being together. Little did she know what awaited her on the Twelfth Concession of Sullivan Township.

What a culture shock Margaret suffered when she set eyes upon her new home! She thought she lived a humble life in Scotland but at least they had indoor plumbing, electricity and running water. Here on the farm they had a pump for gathering water by hand, kerosene lanterns for light and she had to use an outhouse.

This rural way of living took a lot of adjusting. In Scotland neighbours were close by but here in this wide open land your closest neighbour was three farm fields away. The final straw was having no privacy. She and

Harvey lived with her husband's entire family which consisted of six other children and her in-laws. They may have had their own bedroom, but it was at the top of the stairs and everyone had to walk through it to get to their own. It was too much!

Many times over the years Margaret lamented her decision to get back on the *Lady Nelson* and come to this 'Den of Iniquity', as she called it. Harvey's family had a very crude way of living from what she had been accustomed to in Scotland. Here, alcohol was always at the ready with many raucous parties and loose language which Margaret found offensive. She was teased for her accent by her new family and sadly, she corrected her accent and eventually lost it altogether. The only time her children ever heard her Scottish brogue was when she was really angry.

Margaret was quite a beauty, with jet black hair and beautiful dark skin. Harvey's three sisters were teenagers and were jealous of this new woman in the house. They always found ways to make life difficult for Margaret. Once, she bought some chocolates to send to her family in Scotland and the sisters ate every last one. Margaret was expected to do her share of work on the farm which she did, like milking cows, taking in the hay and helping her mother-in-law around the house. After supper the girls were supposed to clean up but they would always seem to come down with a bellyache and head off to the outhouse, leaving all the work for Margaret and their own mother to finish.

Her father-in-law was not fond of Margaret's outspoken nature and on one occasion, when he felt she was being too opinionated, he bluntly asked his son, 'Are you going to hit her or am I?'

Margaret was not one to be told what to do by a man and she responded angrily, 'If you dare hit me, there will be two more hits – one when I hit you and the other when you hit the floor!'

Harvey was a sailor with the Upper Lakes Shipping Company and was away much of the time so Margaret was left to fend for herself with this unusual clan. The one ray of sunshine was her mother-in-law, Elizabeth Bell. Margaret always told her children what a dear women their grandmother was and how kind she had been. Elizabeth appreciated the help around the house and she felt compassion for Margaret's difficult transition to a new life in Canada.

Slowly but surely, Margaret began to adapt to life on the farm. She was pregnant with her first child, Maureen, and was very much looking forward to her mother's first visit to Canada when came the terrible news that her mother had taken ill and passed away in October 1948. The Bell family did not have the financial means to send Margaret home to the funeral and neither did the Hills. Margaret was devastated.

Over the next few months, words of consolation came from Margaret's sister Jeanne, who continued to take part in the séance's that had been a large part of their mother's life. In one letter to her sister, Jeanne wrote that she had received 'comforting' messages from their mother:

> Mammy has been through and given me messages and it is so comforting. I'm beginning to get things for myself now that I am in the private circle, a stranger at the meeting told me that we hadn't to worry as mammy told her to tell us that she had got her passport. I always pray for her progression and that I may see her but Mrs. Orr says I will once she gets stronger as she is still very weak.

Several years later Margaret's brother and sisters did immigrate to Canada but they lived in Toronto and Timmins which were still a long way to visit. At last, Margaret was no longer completely alone in this huge country.

When Margaret was expecting her second child Robbie, named after the bard Robbie Burns, she pleaded with Harvey to get them their own place. He was gone most of the time and she'd had enough of living in such close quarters. Harvey gave in and converted an old garage on the farm into a small cottage. It certainly wasn't much but it was her own.

Things were looking up for Margaret and soon another child, Joni, joined the family. They moved off the farm and purchased a house in the town of Chesley. In 1967 when Margaret was pregnant with Leesa, their fourth child, Harvey died of a massive heart attack. Margaret was left a young widow with three children and one along the way.

Margaret suffered many heartaches and trials during her fifty-one years in Canada. She often said that had she gone back to Scotland when her own mother passed away she probably wouldn't have come back. Her experiences were not always positive but she found joy in her family and although she often wished she never came to Canada, her four children and eleven grandchildren are certainly glad she did.

This article was contributed by Margaret's youngest daughter, Leesa Swigger, with help from her brothers and sisters.

In a Way, I Still Feel English
Gwendolen (Cliburn) Hall

Gwendolen (Cliburn) Hall was born in 1924 in Fulham, London. In September 1939 she was living in Epsom, Surrey with her parents and her older brother Eric.

Then came that awful Sunday, 3 September 1939 when everything changed. It was 11 a.m. when England declared war on Germany. I was only fifteen and attending a commercial college in the town of Sutton. All I could think of was the fact that my brother whom I adored would have to go into the services.

Eric joined the Army in March 1940 which was devastating for me. Then in May came Dunkirk with the evacuation of our troops back to England. Even in Epsom the house was vibrating from the guns on the coast.

Then in late summer air raids started. We were fortunate that we lived where we did and not in London. I remember going to my grandmother's. She lived right by the Thames River on Second Avenue in Mortlake and some of the windows in her house were blown in. It was good to get back to the relative safety of Epsom.

That winter I started working at Messrs J. Sainsbury's in their head office which had been evacuated from Blackfriars in London to Ewell next door to Epsom. I was not old enough to join the services so I took first aid training and did two nights a week at an air-raid shelter in Epsom. It was about a twenty minutes bicycle ride from home. I would go on duty at 7 p.m. until 6 a.m. the next morning, then cycle home, change into my work clothes and cycle to the office by 8.30 a.m.

I used to go to dances with my girlfriends and it was at a dance in Wimbledon at the old town hall on 10 April 1943 that I met Norman. He was a Signalman with the Royal Canadian Corp of Signals (RCCS) and stationed at Weybridge. He was from Kitchener, Ontario and had been in England for one year. He asked me to dance and no sooner had we got on the dance floor then someone tagged me.

A ladies tag dance meant that a lady could tap you on the shoulder and take your partner. So I tagged him back and then someone tagged me again. So I lost him until the end of the dance but we got together again and sat out the rest of the evening talking.

When the dance was over Norman walked with me to Wimbledon Station where I got my train for Epsom and he got his for Weybridge.

He asked if he could call but we didn't have a phone at my parent's home so I gave him my office number.

When he called he didn't get me on the phone and assumed I'd given him a wrong number. As he was walking away from the phone box he realized he had given the operator the wrong number so he rushed back to the phone and this time he got through. We arranged to meet at Wimbledon again that Saturday evening. We had a wonderful evening, didn't dance very much because of the tag dances but found that we just liked being together.

The next day being Sunday we met in London and spent the whole day there until it was time to get our respective trains back to Epsom and Weybridge. I realized I was falling in love with this handsome Canadian soldier and he certainly liked being with me.

Two weeks later we met in Wimbledon again and we walked over to Putney and into Bishops Park. When it was time to go home we discovered that, it being Sunday, Norman's late train didn't run so he couldn't get back to Weybridge.

The ticket collector said, 'Why don't you take him home?', so that's what I did.

My mother and father met Norman at 1 a.m. in the morning and the first thing they did was put the kettle on for a cup of tea. They really liked him and told him he was welcome any time. So from then on we didn't meet in Wimbledon anymore.

Norman got home as often as he could. On Saturday 23 October he had come home for the day and met my brother Eric for the first time. Eric had transferred to the Air Force and had been training in Canada and America as a Lancaster bomber pilot. When it was time for Norman to return to Weybridge I went as far as Raynes Park station with him and that's when he proposed. Of course I said 'Yes'.

The very next day Norman set the wheels in motion by applying to the Army for permission to marry. Then we had a visit from the padre of his unit and eventually permission came through that we could be married on or after 24 February 1944.

Being only nineteen I had to have my father's consent and my father laughingly said, 'If I don't sign this you can't get married.' But my parents really liked Norman and had a lot of faith that he would take care of me.

The night before the wedding we had an air raid. My mother had made the wedding cake and Norman iced it. My dentist fashioned little pedestals out of plaster to hold the top part of the cake as they were impossible to find.

Our beautiful cake was on the dining room table and we were hiding underneath it because of the bombs. I could imagine the cake being blown to bits all over the room but luck was with us and it survived the raid.

We were married the next day in Christ Church, Epsom. My brother was unable to make it to the wedding but he came home four days later for a short leave. That was the last time we saw him. He was reported missing over Germany a month later.

Norman was moved from Weybridge to Deal but he continued to get home to Epsom whenever he could. He was with us on 6 June, D-Day, but we knew he wouldn't be home for long. By that time I was a couple of months pregnant by choice as I wanted something of Norman if he was killed in action. Not a very practical idea but who was being practical in those times?

He went over to France shortly after D-Day and I didn't see him again until March 1945. Our son David was born on 22 December 1944 and that was the only day I didn't write Norman. The other fellows in his unit used to say that if Norman didn't get a letter there was no mail that day.

When Norman came home that March for a seven-day leave from Holland we arranged to have David christened on the Sunday. Then he went right back to Europe and I found it very hard as the fighting was still going on. Letters were so treasured. Every day I would wait for the postman hoping for a letter. Sometimes it was well over a week and my mother would say, 'Well, no news is good news.'

Norman came home safely after the war and was able to have six weeks leave in England before he was sent back to Canada at the end of October 1945. Then came the long wait for me and David. I was up to Canada House in London every month asking how long it would be before I could get a place on a War Bride ship. One of the big concerns was accommodation for War Brides and children in Canada. Norman's dad had passed away before the war ended and his mother had a small apartment in the upstairs of a house. The people who owned the building were willing to let a small child live there so we were very lucky because housing for families was hard to come by.

I received notice at the end of May 1946 that I would be sailing on the *Queen Mary*. One side of me was reluctant to leave and very emotional at the thought of leaving my parents, especially after losing my brother. But the other side of me was so happy at the thought of being reunited with my husband.

On Sunday 9 June I went to Victoria Station with my parents and was met by Red Cross personnel. They had these small buses that were to take

us to a very large house in Portland Square, London where we stayed overnight. Every time a bus came along I said to my parents, 'Oh I'll take the
next one.'

Finally my mother said, 'You have to go. Get on the bus and think of seeing Norman very soon.'

Every girl on the bus was crying and all the parents were crying, not
knowing when we would see each other again. It was very heart wrenching. Travel then was not like it is today. Canada seemed a world away.

The next day we boarded the train for Southampton. I will never forget
the sight of the *Queen Mary* when we got off the train which ran along the
side of the ship. We sailed the next morning and leaving England's shores
was very dramatic for me.

I shared a cabin with two other women who didn't have children so I
didn't see very much of them. On the last day out which was a Friday, I got
deathly seasick and couldn't get off my bunk. David wouldn't go to the dining room with anyone and they wouldn't allow anyone to bring food to the
cabins so he survived the day on Ovaltine Rusks.

We docked at Halifax, Nova Scotia on Saturday morning 14 June and
there was a band there to greet us playing 'Here Comes the Bride'. I don't
think anyone felt very much like a bride at that point. We were processed
through immigration right on the boat and then on to the trains.

I had understood that I would be continuing on my way to Kitchener,
Ontario but when we arrived in Toronto two days later, a Red Cross worker
got on the train and said, 'Your husband is waiting for you.'

I just couldn't believe it. All those months just faded away and there he
was. Our son David didn't know Norman and it took a few hours before
he would go to his father. Norman's mother was with him and I met the
rest of the family later that week.

I had a really wonderful reception, everyone tried to be so helpful. I had
many periods of homesickness which I think was only natural but on the
whole I was very lucky. We stayed in the apartment with Norman's mother
until the following spring when we were able to get one of the little bunga-
lows they were building for returning servicemen.

In September 1947 my mother came over to be with me when our daughter June was born and when she went back in 1948 she talked my father into
immigrating to Canada. My father found work here and fitted in very well.

All in all Canada has been very good to me. Norman and I are very proud
of the fact that both our children graduated from university. I have been in

Canada for more than sixty years now and am a Canadian citizen but I can never forget the country of my birth.

In a way I still feel English. I watch all the English shows on television and I am a big fan of *Coronation Street*. I buy English magazines and of course still have my afternoon tea which I often share with my daughter who lives close by. We have five grandchildren, four are married, and we have two great-grandchildren. We celebrated our sixty-third wedding anniversary in February 2007 and we are just as happy now as when we married in 1944.

A Lancashire Lass at Heart
Elizabeth (Adams) Wasnidge

Elizabeth (Adams) Wasnidge was born in 1918 in Lancaster, Lancashire, the sixth of ten children in a working-class family. She married Carl Wasnidge of Parkhill, Ontario and lived with her mother-in-law who treated her very badly for many years.

England was in the beginning of a Depression as I was growing up and money was scarce. Lucy Street where I lived was in the centre of town right beside the town hall. We were part of a cluster of tiny, wall-to-wall houses so small that if you rapped on the wall the people next door would answer. My four sisters and I had to share one bed. We had no running water in the house, just an outdoor toilet and a communal cold water tap in the backyard. To have a bath we had to bring a tin tub into the house.

We lived in a working-class area with good, honest people always nearby if needed. Times were very tough and jobs were very hard to find. We didn't have many luxuries – even a wall clock was out of the question. We had to go outside and look up at the town hall clock in order to check the time.

Despite all the hardships our family was extremely close and happy. My parents taught us the value of good manners, honesty and respect for our elders. My dad was a veteran of the First World War and he would entertain us for hours with Irish songs and reciting his famous monologues. I can still remember most of the words and this brings back cherished memories.

I started school at four and a half years old. My siblings and I attended St Peter's Catholic School and were taught by the nuns who were very good to us. We must have been considered underprivileged because we were given a hot lunch every day along with most of the neighbourhood children.

Christmas time would have been meagre if not for the generous organizations in our town. One year I remember receiving my first real doll from the Lancaster Police Department. Clothing was never new. My mother would have me go down to the butcher's wife, as they were much better off, and ask if their only daughter had outgrown any clothes. These clothes were then passed down to the girls in my family.

When I was nine we had a terrible tragedy in the family. My eighteen-year-old brother Jack died very suddenly. He was in the Army at the time and had a full military funeral. It was such a sad time for all of us. I remember looking at my mum when she heard the news. She was sitting on the windowsill outside our house with my grandma. The pain in her eyes made her seem so old. My father changed too – his joy was gone. It was many years until I heard my dad sing again.

When I was fourteen I had to leave school and get a job to help the family. This was typical in our area. Financially, it was impossible for me to continue my education. My first job was at the cotton mill in Lancaster. I worked every day from 7.30 a.m. until 5.30 p.m. It was such a noisy place, with heavy machinery that spun the cotton. My full time wages were 7/6 per week, the equivalent of less than £1 each week. It was custom back then to give your parents your pay pack and my mother would then give me a little spending money. I purchased a bicycle which I paid for weekly.

War was declared and it was such a scary time. With fear of the unknown, and one brother already in the Navy, I worried about how this would affect the rest of my family. The daily news reports did nothing to calm us. Everyone was issued an identity card and gas mask. My mother was horrified by these masks and vowed she would never wear one. The town built air-raid shelters every few blocks. Every time the air-raid sirens sounded it was terrifying.

Getting around in the blackout was dangerous and sometimes funny. You could hear people bumping into each other all the time. Every window had to be taped and covered. The Home Guard would bang on your door if any lights were showing.

As if this wasn't enough to contend with, there was severe rationing. Everything was scarce and required coupons. We had to line up just to see if the item was available. We were each allowed about four ounces of meat and two eggs per week, but the eggs were often rotten by the time we got them. They would substitute powdered eggs if real ones weren't available. Bread was dark and flavourless, and margarine tasted like oil. We had very limited tea, sugar, fruits and vegetables. This was the time when many of us started smoking to curb our hunger.

By this time, I was employed as a domestic at the County Mental Hospital. I worked twelve hour shifts, five days a week in the kitchen preparing meals. It was about one and a half miles from our home on Railway Street and I had to walk both ways through a desolate area with a large, walled cemetery on one side. As a young woman, my imagination always ran wild while I was making this journey and in the dark I was terrified.

Mental health hospitals were grim places in those days. Most patients were locked away, but some were put to work with us in the kitchen. They were given menial tasks and were easily identified by their drab clothing. I continued working at the hospital for a couple of years and was growing restless so I decided it was time for a change. This was definitely the wrong thing to do. I was immediately called up for National Service because I fit into the age bracket that was required to serve. I was informed that I would be sent on war work to a munitions factory in Euxton, near Chorley.

This was frightening for me since I had never been away from home. Along with the other women workers, I lived in a hostel and we were bussed to the factory every day. The plant was an enormous building, completely underground so when you arrived you could only see a lovely green field. This was to protect the factory's identity from the German planes that might fly overhead. Upon entering the factory, we had to change our clothes and wear protective suits. We worked with TNT, magnesium, CE powder and other explosives. The TNT turned my hair red, my skin yellow, and I would get frequent nosebleeds and eye infections. The chemicals made our stomachs swell and when we washed out our undergarments the water turned bright red.

You could not wear any jewellery or hair clips as they were considered contraband and we were randomly searched and penalised if we were caught violating this rule. It was very unpleasant working there and then having to go back to our digs after a long night shift to face powdered eggs in the morning for breakfast.

In the meantime, in Lancaster my mother and father were alone and needed help. My four sisters were all married and my remaining four brothers were all in the armed forces. Two were in the Navy, one in the Army and one in the Air Force.

It was on one of my weekend visits home to Lancaster that I met my future husband, Cpl Carl Wasnidge. He was serving with the Royal

Canadian Engineers (RCE) and was stationed at a camp in Halton, just outside of Lancaster.

I had gone to a dance at the Alex Hotel on a Saturday night with a group of my girlfriends. Carl came over and offered me a cigarette, which was quite acceptable back then. Fags were expensive and hard to find so this was a good way for him to get my attention. Impressed by his good looks and manners I agreed to several dances. My first encounter with a handsome Canadian soldier was delightful. Carl was quite charming and a good dancer. At closing time he asked to walk me home but I refused. I promised to meet him at the dance the following weekend.

Although I had doubts during that week I did meet him again. We had a few more dates before he was transferred down to the south of England. We continued our courtship through letters, writing to each other quite often. The next time he came to Lancaster on leave was to meet my parents in late November. He arrived with a kit bag full of goodies, all things that we had not seen for ages. Inside were bottles of liquor, pounds of butter and numerous canned goods that he had managed to get on the black market. My parents thought he was a great guy and he liked them right from the start.

During that visit we got engaged. After asking my father for permission Carl surprised me with a ring that I had seen in a jewellery store window. Although this was sudden, short romances were common during wartime. We decided to get married the following April.

I have many stories about Carl arriving at my house with food that he managed to get for us. One day he went for a walk in the country and arrived back home with several live chickens which he killed and plucked in the yard. With all those feathers flying about, it caused quite an uproar in the neighbourhood. Everyone wondered how we had managed to get fresh chickens.

In early 1944, in an attempt to get me out of the munitions factory and back home to Lancaster to help my parents, my older sister Winnie had to plead to the National Service Board. I was allowed to leave the factory on the condition that I returned to my previous job at the County Mental Hospital. I worked there until the end of that year.

Couples getting married during the war faced a lot of difficulties. The morning of my wedding I had to take a bus to a friend's house to take a bath, since we still had no indoor bathroom at home. Wedding gowns were being borrowed from one bride to another. I was very lucky, my sister-in-law in Canada sent me a new gown to wear on my wedding day. It was beautiful and I was the envy of quite a few girls. Carl and I were married at St Peter's Cathedral on 5 April 1944.

Our wedding went off beautifully with the help of family, friends and neighbours who donated their ration coupons for our small reception at the Castle Hotel. Carl and I managed to go to the Lake District for a few days for our honeymoon, but soon after came D-Day and my new husband was sent overseas.

Carl served in France, Belgium and Holland. In late 1944 he was hurt quite badly in a Jeep accident and he was sent back to England to recover. He was then transferred to the Canadian Treasury based in Lancaster where he continued to serve. Carl and I were able to live with my parents and in 1945 peace was finally declared.

For at least a week there were joyous celebrations in Lancaster and all throughout the country. Although everything was still being rationed we had street parties where neighbours shared whatever they had. For the first time in years the blackout curtains came down and the sun flooded in.

Life started to return to normal. My parents and siblings had survived the war and I was thankful when our first daughter Monica was born at home with the help of a midwife in February 1946. In May Carl was notified that he would be returning to Canada for demobilization. He was uneasy about leaving me and our newborn baby in England but he had no choice. I stayed on with my mum and dad until I got word from the Canadian authorities that I would be leaving for Canada in September.

Now came the time I dreaded the most – having to leave my family. My entire family, friends and neighbours all gathered on Railway Street to say goodbye. It was a day full of sadness, one I will never forget. My dad and one of my brothers-in-law went with me on the train to London where I met the ladies from the Canadian Red Cross. Aside from my brother Jack's funeral, that was the only time I ever saw my dad cry. At that moment, he must have thought he was losing a daughter too.

After seven days at sea on board the *Aquitania* we finally reached Halifax, Nova Scotia. Monica and I boarded a train heading to London, Ontario. We spent two days and nights on the train, enjoying the colourful September landscape. Along the way I watched many other brides reunited with their husbands. When I finally arrived in London I was so relieved to see Carl and I know he felt the same. Throughout my long journey this was the moment I had been waiting for.

Once in London we drove thirty-five miles to my new home in Parkhill where we planned to live with Carl's mother. I was nervous about meeting her but I didn't mind, thinking she would be like my own mum. Nothing could have been further from the truth. It didn't take long to realize that I wouldn't be calling Carl's mother 'mom'. Mrs Wasnidge resented me from the beginning.

Carl had a job in town and he was gone all day. Mrs Wasnidge did not approve of anything I did or said. She would not allow me to invite anyone for tea at *her* house so it was extremely difficult for me to make any friends. I know now that she mentally and verbally abused me for many years. On many occasions she told me she wanted me to go back to where I had come from. I never told Carl what was really going on because Mrs Wasnidge told me that Carl's father had died quite suddenly from a heart attack. She believed that Carl had a bad heart and that the truth might kill him too.

Foolishly, I believed her and loved my husband enough to put up with her sarcasm and cruelty for years.

I was fortunate enough to have two lovely women who made my existence in Parkhill bearable. One was my sister-in-law Grace and the other was an elderly English woman named Mrs Dunning. Although we never talked about Mrs Wasnidge they both seemed to understand what I was going through.

In October 1947 I had my second daughter, Frances. Carl and I were still living with his mother and by this time he had purchased a small restaurant in town. During the day his mother did the cooking and baking at the restaurant while I took care of the children and the household chores. When Carl's mother came home she would put the children to bed and I would work in the restaurant until it closed at 11 p.m.

In November 1949 I had my third daughter, Judith. While I was at the hospital the doctor sent me for X-rays which revealed a shadow on my lungs. That Christmas Eve I was told that I had tuberculosis and would have to go to the sanatorium in London for treatment. I was devastated at the thought of leaving Carl and my three small children. I prayed every day for the strength to cope.

Carl's mother told everyone that I must have had TB before I came to Canada. I know this was not true, due to the very strict medicals that I had before leaving England. The doctor said that I was run down from having three children in a short period of time and trying to work at home and the restaurant.

It was decided that Mrs Wasnidge and my sister-in-law Grace would take care of my children, then aged four, two and six weeks. Carl had to sell the restaurant and take another job in London.

During my fifteen-month stay in hospital, I only saw my children on two occasions, and even then it was only through a window. My husband came every week to see me. Other than him, I had very few visitors during my stay but I made a full recovery and was released from the sanatorium in the spring of 1951.

We moved to London in 1954 but Mrs Wasnidge came with us because Carl's two sisters and brother would not take her in. The next year, against the doctor's advice, I had my fourth and last daughter Kathryn. In 1960 both of my parents passed away within three weeks of each other. All this time, Mrs Wasnidge's nagging, belittling and cruel verbal abuse continued until I became extremely depressed.

Finally I broke down in my doctor's office and told him what had been going on since my arrival in Canada. The doctor called Carl and ordered him to get me away from his mother. This caused quite a riot within the family. Reluctantly, one of Mrs Wasnidge's daughters agreed to take her in. I can't even begin to describe the feeling of freedom I had when she left my house.

I had been a trusting and naive young girl from England. I had come from a loving and caring home, where people were nurtured and respected. It took me a long time to understand what had happened to me over all those years. Today, I am eighty-eight years old and my family is not quite sure how I survived but I know that it was with my strong faith in God, my love for my family here in Canada, and the support from my family back home in England.

I have just celebrated my sixtieth year here in Canada and I have never been prouder to be a Canadian woman, but I'm still a Lancashire lass at heart.

Postscript: Carl died in 1978. Elizabeth has nine grandchildren (one of whom passed away several years ago) and three great-grandchildren. She lives in London, Ontario.

I Lost the Love of My Life
Gladys (Gardiner) Ludwig

Gladys (Gardiner) Ludwig was born in New Cross, London in 1916. Her husband died young, leaving her with four children to raise on her own in Canada.

I met my husband in 1942 when I was working as a cook at an RAF training school in Lewisham, England. Cpl Walter (Wally) J. Ludwig was one of four Canadian soldiers who had been sent to the school for training and we saw each other at meal times. We started talking to each other across the serving trays and before we knew it we were falling in love.

I know it sounds unbelievable, but Wally and the other three Canadians were in Lewisham for a few months before getting notice that they were enrolled at the wrong training school! He was moved to another area but we continued dating and eventually he proposed. We tried to get married in November 1942 but Wally couldn't get permission. After all the paperwork was in order we were married in February 1943 and a year later we had a daughter. I was incredibly happy.

We didn't see each other very often during the war years but we both knew that things would be brighter after the war. In June 1945 my daughter and I came to Canada three months ahead of my husband. He had been overseas for five and a half years.

We sailed from Liverpool on the troopship *Scythia*. The trip was a nightmare. Everyone was horribly sick and they had us War Brides and our babies packed into the rooms like sardines. We were told that soldiers on board had been instructed not to talk or fraternize with any of us; if they did we would be sent right back to England.

My daughter and I went to Kitchener, Ontario where we were met by Wally's sister Helen and his mother. At first, they did everything they could to make me feel welcome, but they were still reeling from the death of Wally's younger brother Roy who had been killed in Normandy. It was a big loss to the family and I felt bad too because I had also known Roy in England through my husband.

I was very homesick but after Wally was repatriated and we started having our family I settled in and grew to like Canada. We had three more children, one of them a son who was adored by his father. Wally went to work at the tire plant in Kitchener but he wasn't happy doing that so he went into the home construction business with a partner. They did well with King and Ludwig Construction and Wally was happy.

In 1954 he was offered a job as manager of a new construction centre in Guelph so we moved there and built a house. Wally worked seven days a week setting up the new business, trying to get a family going, building a new home and landscaping. When we moved there it was out in the country, there were cows in the fields beside the house and at times in the backyard eating the newly planted grass and leaving huge holes in the soil where they stepped. At times they even got into the garden and ate the new vegetables.

We didn't see much of Wally, but we did manage to have one more child. My daughter who was born that year was a true gift. She was the last to leave home and has been a comfort to me over the years.

Shortly after our last child was born Wally became very ill and was diagnosed with a brain tumour. For a long time he was in the hospital in Toronto. David was in grade two and I took him out of school once a week to help me find my way around the city. I don't know what I would have done without David's help because he remembered everywhere that we had to go in Toronto. After two horrible years of suffering, Wally passed away.

After he died the children and I had a horrible time. I became even more homesick and longed for the comfort of my own family back in England but I couldn't afford to return. I spent most days and nights crying uncontrollably. I would leave the house and walk over to the hill by the bush on the other side of the cow pasture and sit there for hours and hours crying myself empty.

Everything that we owned had gone into the business and the new house. The life insurance policy had been cancelled so I was totally destitute. No money, no close friends and none of my own family. My mental health was slipping away fast and I had nobody to turn to. Wally's family was no help at all; in fact, they were icy cold.

The hardships the children and I endured is beyond comprehension. Even the war years with all the bombings and rationing were not as bad as this. I had no choice but to apply for mother's allowance, a precursor of today's welfare. The people at this office treated the children and I like third-class citizens and worse. For some inexplicable reason they took my passport and my birth certificate and I had to fight with them for seven years before they would give them back. I didn't have a criminal record. I was just a War Bride who had married a Canadian serviceman overseas.

We had to account for everything. If we had an extra quarter and they found out about it I had to tell them where it came from. If the woman didn't like the answer she would literally take it back from the pittance that I was getting. We all had to learn how to be penny-pinchers and hide things from the welfare workers or they would take it away.

My son David, who was nine at the time, started doing many odd jobs around the neighbourhood and all the money that he earned was turned over to me to help put bread on the table. He missed his entire childhood in order to help keep the family together and fed. In time my oldest daughter also started working, and she turned over her money to help us survive.

In the years that I have lived in Canada there has been much sorrow and tears. I never remarried or went out with another man. I lost the love of my life in June 1957 and never really recovered. But I've also had joy and laughter. My life became my children: they all received a good education, have good jobs and contribute to society. They, in turn, have raised their own families and I now have ten grandchildren and nine great-grandchildren.

Postscript: After everything Gladys Ludwig went through, she managed to keep the house that Wally built so many years ago. She still lives there and is waiting for the day when they will be reunited. Her son David helped her write this story.

The Girl He Would Marry
Margot (Coombes) Carmichael

Margot (Coombes) Carmichael was one of those lucky War Brides whose mother came to live with her in Canada after the war.

Margot Coombes was still in mourning over the death of her boyfriend – a Canadian airman from Nova Scotia – when she met another Canadian at a dance in Covent Garden in October 1943.

The Italian campaign was in full swing and the Air Force was in the thick of bombing raids over Germany. Every day in the papers were lists of the dead and missing. Naturally, Margot was reluctant to get involved with another airman knowing he too may not survive the war: but nineteen-year-old Ted Carmichael loved to dance and by evening's end he was just as determined that he had met the girl he would marry.

Margot grew up in Earl's Court, London and she graduated from Kensington High School in 1938. Her father was a chemist and the family lived in a flat above his shop at 70 Warwick Road. Canadian servicemen were welcome in the Coombes' home: like most Brits, Margot's parents recognized that Canadians were in England to defend the country – but that didn't mean they wanted their daughter to marry one. Margot's father thought Canada was a 'country of shacks' and he was not very happy about her decision to marry.

When Margot met Ted Carmichael, she was working as the assistant secretary for Thomas R.G. Bennett, the managing director of the Wellcome Foundation. Margot's role was considered an exempt occupation and as such represented her war service. The Wellcome Foundation produced pharmaceutical products considered essential for the war. Not even bombing raids would halt their activity; the Wellcome building on Euston Road had a lookout on the roof to monitor bomb activity and this allowed the staff to work through the sirens.

Ted was a navigator stationed at Metheringham, Lincolnshire with RAF Squadron 106. Between the time he and Margot met in October 1943 to October 1944 they saw each other seven times in London. They escaped the tension of the war by going to see the popular Hollywood movies of the time and dancing in the clubs. When they were apart, which was more often than not, they wrote letters back and forth sharing the frustrations of waiting out bad weather to fly and not knowing when they would see each other again.

By October 1944 Ted had completed thirty-five missions in a Lancaster Bomber over Germany and was fortunate to have many near misses. He was honoured to receive the Distinguished Flying Cross after a major bombing of Stuttgart. The plane was heavily damaged, difficult to navigate and picking the route and altitude home was very challenging. The crew were so late returning to England that they were declared 'Missing in Action.' A telegram indicating he was MIA was actually sent to his family in Windsor, Ontario.

With thirty-five bombing missions under his belt, Ted's tour of duty was over. That October he was on leave at Margot's parents' house in London when he received a telegram saying he was being shipped home. Recognizing that he would have to leave very soon they pulled together their wedding quickly and were married on 14 October.

Ted was only twenty years old and did not have his father's permission to marry so he had to swear an oath that he had his father's approval. The honeymoon was a very brief five days before Ted had to say goodbye.

On 12 December 1944 Margot left Liverpool on board the troopship *Louis Pasteur* zigzagging across the Atlantic to avoid submarines. She endured the long train ride from Halifax to Windsor to start an exciting new life in Canada. Their first child Donna was born in 1946 and a job opportunity took the young family to London, Ontario where Dane arrived in 1951. The Carmichaels were presented with the usual financial challenges but love for each other, their children and some good friends helped them settle into life as a family unit of four.

Everything seemed to be going well for Margot and her little family in Canada, but back in England postwar London was not so easy for her parents. With all four of their own children now gone they had a very unhappy empty nest. As the marriage disintegrated, everything came to a head and Margot's mother was hospitalized for severe depression. As her mother's champion, Margot took the bold step of inviting her to come live in Ontario and in 1953 Ethel Coombes joined the Carmichaels in a new London – this one in Canada. It was the best move Margot ever made, not only for her mother, but for herself and her small family.

Very few British War Brides would have had their mothers living close by. It was a fact of life in 1946 that once a War Bride left Britain she may never see her parents again. So when Ethel came to Canada Margot knew she was a very lucky woman – and so did Ted and the children.

Ted's own mother had died when he was young and in many ways Ethel was the only mother he ever knew. He got her interested in hockey – Canada's national sport – and together he, Ethel and young Dane would watch hockey on television. She became one of the Toronto Maple Leaf's biggest fans, cheering them on to their last four Stanley Cup victories in the 1960s.

The family moved from London to Toronto in 1954 where Ted was offered a new job. Ethel helped balance the family needs so Margot could work, first as an admitting clerk at the Hospital for Sick Children and then as office manager for a group of physicians.

The last twenty years of Ethel's life were special ones for the Carmichaels. Margot, Ted, the children and Ethel comprised a unique family unit that was likely the envy of other War Brides. From the children's perspective, growing up with both their mother's and grandmother's influences was an experience they would never trade: they were lucky, and they know it.

Postscript: Ted passed away in 1998. Margot lives in Windsor, Ontario and is looking forward to a planned visit to England this year with her son Dane, who helped write this story.

The Path That Led Me to This Place
Doris (Sayers) Barr

Doris (Sayers) Barr wrote this story of her life as a War Bride for the Women's Institute of Ontario before she passed away in July 2001. Her daughter Marion and granddaughter Leslie shared it with the people who attended her funeral in Simcoe, Ontario along with her favourite Vera Lynn songs and other wartime music.

Since the end of the war it has been my good fortune to be here in Canada living in a farm area with family, friends and all the things that make for a wonderful life. But this was not always my life and I thought you might like to know a bit about my early years and the path that led me to this place.

I was born in Horsham, Sussex, in 1916. When I was two months old my father was killed in France and it was years before my mother remarried. I don't know why, but for some reason my mother never had much to do with me when I was young.

I was raised by my grandfather, Thomas Whitington, who was a game-keeper at two of England's great estates, first at Findon Manor and then at Leonardslee, in St Leonard's Forest. Leonardslee was especially beautiful, with wallabies running wild through the woods and gardens. My grandfather was very kind to me and I was happy living there.

One of my favourite places was Findon which is still famous for its annual sheep fair. When I was twelve years old I left my grandfather's and went to live with my mother, her new husband and family in a building known as the Wattle House. There were two apartments upstairs and the wattles were stored downstairs for use in penning the sheep. In this new arrangement, I ended up being more of a babysitter than a daughter, which was difficult for me as I yearned for my mother's affection.

We were faced with the Depression in the 1930s and life was often difficult. I married very young and had a baby to support so I worked at the Connaught Theatre in Worthing until the war began. We knew something was happening in Europe which was a scant thirty miles away across the Channel from Dover. Being so close, Sussex was chosen as the launching site for the armed forces which descended on the countryside after 1939 and life was never the same there again.

The Battle of Britain was frightening. It seemed that wherever I moved, the town was the target of bombing. My best friend was my aunt, Rose Whitington: her children were sent to various places in the country where it was thought the children would be safer. It was during that terrible time that the value of having allies like the Canadians was realized and appreciated.

Early in the war two waves of Canadian troops were stationed in Sussex. The towns were inundated with soldiers – good-looking, outgoing, in uniform, with money – and naturally, the local men resented them while they were very popular with the girls. The countryside went from placid farming to training grounds, airfields and military centres. Then the Americans arrived, seeming much brasher with fewer of the social norms we were used to.

The Canadians were often British in background and were part of the Commonwealth – they acted as a bridge, helping us to understand and get along with the others. By the time the Third Division arrived, the Canadians were welcomed and popular with the English people. Much of the war was a waiting game for the troops who were constantly training for the coming invasion of Europe. Meanwhile, Sussex was bombed, supplies and food were short and no one knew what was going to happen.

In 1942 I was living in a place named Cambridge House on College Hill in Steyning, West Sussex. I had my six-year-old boy Peter with me but my marriage had ended and I planned to remain single forever. I worked for a while at a munitions plant in Steyning but I injured my hand so I found other work as a shop assistant.

The Third Division arrived and soon there were social activities such as tea dances going in the local halls. My family insisted I go and one of the Canadians, Sgt Alex (San) Barr, asked me to dance. Next thing I knew Peter called excitedly a few days later saying, 'Mum, there's a Canadian soldier at the door!' Sgt Barr had come to call.

Although he was quiet and pleasant, he wouldn't take no for an answer. My family loved him and fully supported me as I began my path to Canada. We weren't able to get married right away because the military would not give permission before D-Day. However, we did have a few days to travel up to Scotland to visit San's cousins in Lanarkshire and Falkirk.

6 June 1944: finally the day came for which the Canadians had been training. Word came that San was missing in action. Notices went home to his mother in Simcoe, Ontario, and no one knew what had happened. However, his brother Andy located him. Though injured, he had been res-cued by an American ship at Juno Beach and taken back to one of their hospitals in Kent. How lucky we were. San was able to recover enough to rejoin the campaign through France, Belgium, Holland and into Germany.

Our daughter Marion was born in Steyning in November 1944 and a year later the war ended. Now I was going to be a War Bride, one of many thousands. The Canadian government arranged for us to travel on the Cunard liner *Queen Mary* from Southampton. All I recall about that trip was how horribly seasick I was. Fortunately, there were wonderful stewards who helped look after Marion. Peter was in a cabin with another boy and I'm sure I will never know what they got up to. I was told that the steward caught Peter leaning out a porthole window at one point and pulled him back in.

We arrived at Pier 21 in Halifax, Nova Scotia in May 1946. The Red Cross put all the War Brides and children on a train. Two days later we were met by San and his brother Andy at Union Station in Toronto and taken to our new home in Woodhouse Township, Norfolk County. To think I had lived near Arundel Castle, the home of the Duke of Norfolk in England!

There were many other family members to meet and I didn't know what that would be like. San had to spend quite a bit of time in Sunnybrook Hospital in Toronto recovering from war injuries so I was worried about being on my own but everyone welcomed us and helped us adjust to the new life in Canada.

San's family were especially fond of Peter who was just old enough to be excited about all the new things to do in Canada. Over the next years I learned to care for our animals, grow our food, and get to know my new family. My musical knowledge had to expand from brass military bands and popular singers to the pipes, fiddles and pianos so loved by the Barr family with their deep Scottish roots.

I was happy to be in Canada with my husband but of course I missed my friends and family, especially my grandfather who died shortly after we arrived in Canada. It helped to know there were other War Brides in the area and we met in each other's homes frequently. The Women's Institute was very active in this farming area and my sister-in-law and her family soon had me helping with the Lynn Valley Chapter.

Our War Brides' Association did not continue officially but most of us remained close friends for the rest of our lives. The Institute was a wonderful group as we learned things together, got a break from our daily work (no fancy appliances in the early 1950s) and helped wherever we could in the community. There were no big school boards in those days, just local ones, and the people helping run the little country schools were the same people who belonged to the Institute.

I have come a long way from Sussex, England to the Lynn Valley area of Ontario. Many times, there was uncertainty, the tragedies and the joys which make up a life. My husband is gone but we were fortunate to have fifty wonderful years together, to see a lot of countryside and to raise children and grandchildren. I hope that they will have as good a life as I did and will feel proud of the past which led to their life today.

4

Western Canada

War Brides who were destined to points in western Canada had a very long journey ahead of them once they landed in Halifax. Even if they were only going to Manitoba, they were looking at a minimum three-day trip with the constant shrill of the train whistle blowing 'whoo-whoo' at every stop along the way, night and day.

When eastern Canadians say 'out west' they mean everything west of Ontario but for those who make western Canada their home there are the three Prairie provinces of Manitoba, Saskatchewan and Alberta; the Yukon and the Northwest Territories in the north; and British Columbia on the west coast.

To understand how big this part of the country really is, consider that the province of Manitoba alone is two times the size of the entire United Kingdom. Multiply that by four very large provinces and two huge territories and you get an idea of the scale the War Brides were being introduced to when they made their way out west.

Map showing location of Western Canada.

Western Canada begins at Manitoba and the difference in landscape from Ontario would have been immediately noticeable at the first light of day. Flat prairie for as far as the eye could see and wheat fields in every direction were in stark contrast to the lakes, forests and rolling hills of Ontario.

War Bride Peggy MacAuley came to New Brunswick first, but her husband had rejoined the military and was working in Brooks Brook, Yukon, about eighty miles south of Whitehorse. After a short time at his parents' farm in Millstream, NB, she and her one-year-old son Peter went all the way to Whitehorse by rail and air. In her memoirs, called *Surrey Girl: Not Just Another War Bride* she recalls her amazing trip across Canada in 1946:

> Our train journey traversed six provinces; through the woodlands of northern New Brunswick; along the St. Lawrence River to Quebec City; past the quaint farms in rural Quebec and endless miles through northern Ontario where the magnificent vistas alternated from forests to lakes to rock out-croppings of the Cambrian Shield. Then the scenery changed as we reached Winnipeg and proceeded through the great wheat fields of Manitoba and Saskatchewan.

From Saskatoon we journeyed on through the rich farm lands of Alberta to the city of Edmonton. When we arrived in Edmonton I possessed a knowledge of the vastness of Canada that many Canadians would never have the opportunity to experience in their lifetime. It was without doubt a lasting memory, and this was only the start of my pioneering journey through Canada.

The flight north took us most of a day. We touched down at Fort St. John in British Columbia and Watson Lake on the border of BC and the Yukon Territory. As our small aircraft struggled to reach the top of the mountain ranges of the Rockies and Cassiar, the scene below was a desolate wasteland of ice, snow, mountains and forests. I was indeed thankful for the winter clothing as there was minimum heat in the aircraft. In fact, I attempted to eat cold sandwiches with my mitts on. Finally we touched down at Whitehorse. This was now mid-December and the temperature at the airport was minus 45.6°C (-50°F). It was hard to believe that a week had passed since we left New Brunswick. Since arriving in Canada, Peter and I had traveled from the east coast to a remote place in the far northwest – a distance of well over 6,000 kms (3,750 miles).[1]

In 1946 the Prairie provinces were still relatively young compared to Ontario, Quebec and the Maritimes. Manitoba became a province in 1870 but both Saskatchewan and Alberta only joined the Canadian confederation in 1905. Before that, the two provinces were part of what was known as the Northwest Territories – everything west of Manitoba to the Rockies that had formerly been owned by the Hudson's Bay Company.

In 1941, the entire population of the three Prairie provinces was just above two-and-a-half-million people[2], of which the majority (more than one and a half million) were living on farms or in rural areas.[3] British Columbia on the west coast had almost 900,000 people of which less than half were rural.[4] Unbelievably, the huge expanse of the Yukon and Northwest Territories held a combined total of less than 17,000 people.[5]

In these numbers were immigrants from Britain, the United States, Western and Eastern Europe and Scandinavia making it a diverse cultural mix. There were also large Aboriginal populations in all four provinces, from the coastal Indians of the West to those of the plains and the forest, to the Inuit on Hudson Bay.

Considering the vastness of the land compared to Britain, it must have been quite a shock for War Brides who ended up in isolated farms where there may not have been another household for another five, ten, twenty miles or more. There were only five large cities across the entire prairie,

Winnipeg, Manitoba – the coldest city in the country – Regina and Saskatoon in Saskatchewan, and Edmonton and Calgary in Alberta. In British Columbia there were Vancouver and Victoria, BC's capital, on Vancouver Island.

For those who went as far as British Columbia, there was the awe-inspiring beauty of the Rocky Mountains and if they were destined for the Island they found themselves facing the Pacific coast. Victoria was perhaps the most British of cities in Canada, and one where a recently arrived War Bride would feel right at home.

In this description of Vancouver Island from the 1940s, Dorothy Abraham paints a welcoming picture of the 'most English city in the West'.

> Victoria is known as the most English city in the West, or perhaps one should say British, not forgetting the Scottish, the Irish and the Welsh, where as I have already related, you will hear every dialect, and meet the tweeds and the brogues, the top hat and patent boots, the Dowagers and their dogs, and life goes on in peace and tranquility. Meeting an English bride the other day who had recently arrived, she said she felt she had not really left England, it all seemed so delightfully English in Victoria.[6]

Whether it was Victoria on the coast, Lethbridge in Alberta, Moosejaw in Saskatchewan or Portage la Prairie in Manitoba, after nearly a week on board a train rolling across western Canada, the War Brides would have been incredibly happy to see their husbands at the end of the line.

She Lived Happily Ever After
Joan (Fisher) Reichardt

Joan (Fisher) Reichardt was born in Richmond, Surrey. She recalls saying to a friend, 'All these girls marrying Canadians and Americans, that's fine, leaves more English chaps for us.' But marry a Canadian soldier she did, and even followed him to the wide open spaces of Saskatchewan.

It all started on 2 December 1944. I had endured over five years of war, survived the Blitz and the little Blitz, learned to cope with the blackout, the queues, the rationing, the make do and mend. But now the invasion of Europe was going well, I was working in London despite v1s and v2s, and everyone felt the end was not too far away. It was Saturday night and I was off to the regular dance at the Royston!

The Royston was a very small dance hall, no bar, a small live band, and a couple who acted as MC and pianist. I had gone with my two girlfriends, as usual. We were wearing our best utility frocks but most of the young men were in uniform, many from overseas, although no Americans. As we stood watching people come in, my friend commented on a very tall, red-haired Canadian soldier, saying, 'He looks so young.'

The evening proceeded, I danced almost every dance, including the usual array of specials like the Palais Glide, and of course the Paul Jones and the Excuse Me. Then the MC made the announcement that was to change my life; 'The next dance will be a Spot Dance.'

We waited to hear the details and he went on, 'You can all see the tall Canadian.' We looked, but he was not on the floor.

Undaunted, the MC recruited a partner for him and he was up and danc- ing. We were instructed to watch him when the music stopped, and so we did. By now blushing red with embarrassment, this hapless young man was told to 'take four steps this way and ten that way', ending up facing the row of chairs around the hall, at which point the MC told him to turn around and then said, 'There will be a prize for the first lady to kiss him!'

I said to my friend, 'I could do it,' and she said, 'I dare you!' And off I went, across the hall, ahead of the other girls running and jumping up at him, pushed him down onto the chair behind him, sat on his lap and gave him a kiss! There was a great round of applause, and one very shocked young Canadian, wondering who this pushy little English girl was.

The next day our family went for our usual Sunday afternoon walk and who should we meet but my victim of the night before. We stopped and chatted, and he asked if I would be at the dance next week and could he meet me there. I agreed – easy for me, as the Spot Dance prize had been two free tickets for the next dance. Soon after that John and I became a couple. We married on 29 June 1945 and two weeks later I watched as he clattered away, going back to camp and then on to Canada. We didn't see each other again for more than ten months.

I sailed to Halifax on the *Lady Rodney* in May 1946. In my cabin there was a girl named Bette Read who was a member of the Dagenham Girls Pipe Band. As we steamed into Halifax on 24 May we did so with great panache with Betty playing the pipes. There were flags and bands on the dock, which we thought were for us, but were, in fact, for the Canadian Victoria Day holiday weekend.

From Halifax I had another 2,700-mile train trip ahead of me across the continent to Saskatoon, Saskatchewan. The landscape we passed through on that long journey was so different and wild compared to the little patchwork fields of England and, of course, we all crowded to the windows to see who was being met by who whenever the train stopped. A couple of us in my carriage discovered that our food was not as good as that in the adjacent carriage and brought this to the attention of our escorts. It turned out the chap in charge of catering for our end of the train assumed we wouldn't know the difference, so was feeding us on the cheap and pocketing the surplus. That was the end of him. I am still a 'righter of wrongs' and have been all my years in Canada.

On the Sunday we arrived in Montreal and those of us going west were taken on a bus tour of the city. What I remember best is how loud and garish the women's clothing seemed, in contrast to our somber utility garb, and the extraordinary-looking baby carriages, so unlike our English prams. We all agreed we'd have none of those.

Then back on the train and on to Winnipeg, where we lost one girl who nipped out to shop and didn't make it back in time, so we left without her. I remember being shocked by the intense heat and the wind – which I loathed during my years on the prairies – when we got off briefly at some little whistle stop in Manitoba, and also astonished at the flat and featureless landscape we were passing through.

By the time we arrived in Saskatoon it was dark. Having seen some of the strangely garbed characters who had met our fellow travellers as we crossed this endless expanse of land, we were all joking about whether or not we would recognize our husbands in civilian clothing. As I had had the longest wait since I had last seen John, I was delegated to be the first off the train. I remember seeing this young man – not hard to spot since he stood six foot six inches tall and had red hair – and running madly across the station into his arms.

Many years later, I was told by a woman I met in Saskatoon that I nearly knocked her over that night. I don't remember that at all. My lovely expensive hat – a brown felt cartwheel not really suitable wear for the prairies – was knocked off my head and I never wore it again. We got into a cab and as John put his arm around me he stuck his elbow in my eye, which watered profusely. The desk clerk at the Bessborough Hotel probably thought I was in tears. We went up to our room and, anxious to see my new home, I tried to look out the window, only to encounter my first window screen – a heavy duty one at that – which just about knocked me cold.

The next day it was off to meet the in-laws for the first time. I was naturally quite nervous; the family had emigrated from Holland when John was just three years old and I knew that my mother-in-law did not speak

English very well. I don't think they were thrilled that their only son had married an English girl and I was an assertive, empowered woman long before it was acceptable to be that way. I was used to expressing my opinion and can be best described as bossy and outspoken. My poor peace-loving husband knew he would be caught in the middle of course, and I am sure, in retrospect, it was not much fun for him. So as we walked up the long front path his parents and two younger sisters were there to greet me and I tripped on the bottom step and landed – spread-eagled – at their feet!

Despite all this, my mother-in-law and I learned to communicate very well, I grew to appreciate screen windows as a barrier between me and mosquitoes, and John and I stuck together through thick and thin.

It was indeed a shock coming from the south of England where we hardly ever saw snow or freezing temperatures for more than a day or so to a winter that lasted for months on end. I'll never forget the frozen washing, which we felt duty bound to hang out on the line, and the time I snapped one leg off my husband's long johns as I came in the back door.

My husband had tried to explain to me how cold it was in Saskatchewan but it is hard to put into words what fifty below Fahrenheit feels like, so I hadn't a clue. I was well kitted out, with fur coat etc. but still went out wearing a stylish hat instead of a warm scarf or woolly toque because it looked sunny and bright. I froze my nose walking to the bus the first winter and I can still remember the agony as chilled feet and fingers returned to normal.

The first winter we were living with the in-laws and although their house had indoor plumbing there were some across the alley that did not. I was gazing out the kitchen window one bitterly cold day when I saw a horse-drawn wagon coming along the alley. It stopped by what I now knew to be an outside toilet, the driver got down, lifted up the flap and proceeded to use a PICK to dislodge the contents. Believe me, when people talk about s— flying I know what they mean.

Many years later, after the invention of leotards (heavyweight tights), I had to go downtown to do a number of errands and it was very, very cold. Of course, the wind was blowing so I borrowed a pair of tights belonging to one of my daughters. They were a little small but I hauled them up as best I could, put on all my winter gear, including long fur coat, high boots and off I went.

By the time I was walking back from City Hall to get my bus home said tights were rapidly working their way down and the crotch had reached my knees. I crossed the road to the bus stop like a demented penguin, barely able to put one foot in front of the other as my knees were tightly bound to each other. In the privacy of my seat on the bus I managed to hoist them up enough to make it home, but it was still not a pretty sight!

Keeping the house warm was a challenge, especially in the days of coal and wood furnaces. The kids all stayed in bed while dear old Dad ventured down the basement and stoked up the temperamental, octopus-like monstrosity that kept us warm. What a joy it was when we got natural gas. And the frost-laden windows were another one of our winter hazards, as well as frozen pipes, but I truly think the wind was the worst. The icy blast that took your breath away and those little frozen granules of snow that bit into your skin, oh yes, I remember it well.

When we moved from Saskatchewan to British Columbia in 1968 our oldest son was in university, we had two girls in high school, and a girl and a boy in elementary school. Shortly after that I started work with a non-profit society providing in home, community-based services for seniors and the mentally and physically disabled, first on a part-time basis, but later, as the job developed, it became a full-time, senior position.

John was always very involved with the children, more so than many men of his time, and he was extremely supportive of me when I started work. He was proud of my success and when my job-related activities required that I travel all over BC, and later all over Canada, he came with me when he could, but never complained when he was left to fend for himself at home. He was always there at the airport to meet me, with a smile and a kiss, just like in 1946.

As the children grew up and married, we did more and more travelling, spending many wonderful holidays in England, as well as on this side of the Atlantic. We enjoyed the same things and agreed on important issues such as child rearing; I was the disciplinarian and dear old Dad the one they could get around, but we united when it came to the crunch. Despite the fact that we came from two very different worlds and met under such crazy circumstances, we had over fifty years of happy marriage together until John's death in 1996.

Now as I sit alone in my pleasant house, with the view of the lake and the mountains, I still marvel at fate and that Spot Dance. The most remarkable part of this story is that despite the fact that it was a crazy way to start a life together, many War Brides have had good, solid, loving marriages and found it was all worthwhile. If there is a moral to this story it is this: fairytale weddings don't matter, it's the 'lived happily ever after' that counts.

Postscript: Joan Reichardt lives in Nelson, British Columbia. She has five children, seven grandchildren, and one great-grandchild.

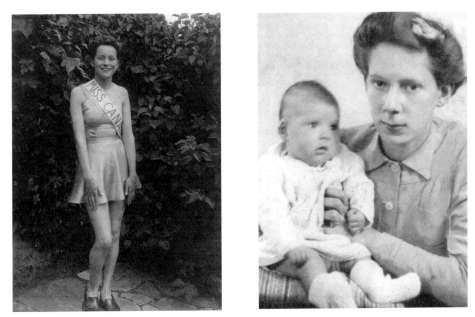

Above left: 1 Betty (Lowthian) Hillman continued to appear with the Isle of Wight Concert Party even after she became engaged. Since she was marrying a Canadian, she appeared as 'Miss Canada' in a pantomime where each dancer represented a different country.

Above right: 2 Jean (Keegan) Paul and baby Christine before they left for Canada in 1946. When Jean and Christine arrived at the train station in McAdam, New Brunswick they were met by her husband Charlie Paul and the Roman Catholic priest who took them by canoe to the Tobique Indian Reserve.

3 Mary (Hardie) and Al Gero's wedding day 12 October 1945 in Edinburgh, Scotland. From left to right: Philip Fontaine, a friend of Al's from the service, flower girl Elizabeth Hardie, Al, Mary, flower girl Helen Hardie and bridesmaid Euphemia Muir, Mary's best friend. Unusual for the time, Mary and Al had a formal sit down dinner for 200 people at the Tollbooth Hall.

Above left: 4 Addison and Elizabeth (Kelly) MacDonald on their wedding day 4 August 1942 in Edinburgh, Scotland. Addison's mother in Canada wrote to Elizabeth and asked her not to marry until the war was over but she and Addison refused and got married anyway.

Above right: 5 Mildred (Young) and Harold Sowers on their wedding day 4 August 1945 in Thornton Heath, England. The story of the unusual events leading to Mildred and Harold's wedding appeared in the newspaper in Canada.

Above left: 6 Mary (Fletcher) Sheppard is shown as a child in Liverpool and in her ambulance driver's uniform from the Second World War. The medals on display include past president of the Ladies Auxiliary, Royal Canadian Legion, and a thirty-five-year service pin. Photo used with permission of CBC.ca and Mary Sheppard.

Above right: 7 Conrad and Joan (Smedley) Landry on their wedding day 19 May 1945 at St John the Evangelist, at Islington, in London, England. Conrad was an Acadian from the Magdalen Islands, Quebec – an isolated chain of islands in the Gulf of St Lawrence where nobody spoke English.

8 Rose (O'Reilly) and Horace Boulay on their wedding day 29 April 1944 at St Agnes Catholic Church in Cricklewood, London. Rose was from Southern Ireland and was working for the war effort in England when she met her Canadian soldier.

Above left: 9 Henrietta Stevens in a studio photo taken before her marriage to Jacques Pronovost. Henrietta's parents disapproved of her marrying a French Canadian but she was in love and married him anyway. Henrietta had fourteen children.

Above right: 10 Joyce (Hilman) and Bob Bezeau on their wedding day in London on 5 February 1945. When Bob came back from war he wasn't the same man Joyce had married.

11 John and Morfydd (Morgan) Gibson on their wedding day 6 September 1944. Morfydd's young nephew insisted on holding John's hand throughout the entire ceremony and was still doing it in the official wedding photo!

Above left: 12 Margaret (Perkins) Bristow Eaton and her two children on arrival in Chatham, Ontario on 13 April 1945. Margaret's husband was captured by the Germans after D-Day and was not liberated until the end of the war.

Above right: 13 Wilson and Martha Stauffer on their wedding day 7 June 1946 in Stirling, Scotland. When Wilson proposed to Martha he said, 'If it's OK with my mom, will you marry me?'

Above left: 14 Les and Rita (Bannister) Buckrell on their wedding day 17 September 1945. Rita loved to dance and she came to a strict Baptist family in Ontario where dancing was frowned upon.

Above right: 15 Margaret (Hill) Bell and her husband on a swing at his family's farm in Ontario. Margaret always said she could write a book about her life.

Above left: 16 Norman and Gwen (Cliburn) Hall in Epsom, Surrey about a week after their wedding. Gwen met Norman at a dance in Wimbledon.

Above right: 17 Elizabeth (Adams) Wasnidge on her wedding day 5 April 1944 in Lancaster, England. She met her husband Carl at a dance at the Alex Hotel.

18 Margot (Coombes) and Ted Carmichael. Margot's father wasn't very happy that his daughter was marrying a Canadian but it all worked out in the end.

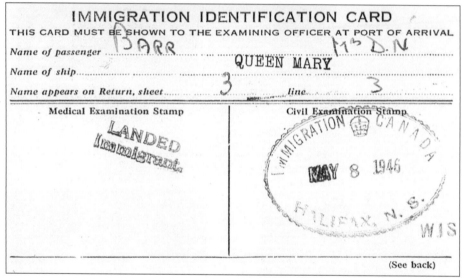

IMMIGRATION IDENTIFICATION CARD

THIS CARD MUST BE SHOWN TO THE EXAMINING OFFICER AT PORT OF ARRIVAL

Name of passenger .... BARR .... M³ D.N

Name of ship........ QUEEN MARY

Name appears on Return, sheet........ 3 .... line........ 3

Medical Examination Stamp	Civil Examination Stamp
LANDED Immigrant	IMMIGRATION CANADA MAY 8 1946 HALIFAX, N.S. WJS

(See back)

19 Doris Barr's immigration ID which was required for processing by Canadian Immigration officials upon landing at Halifax. War Brides who sailed to Canada under the War Bride transportation scheme had one of these Immigration IDs.

TO EXAMINING OFFICIALS:

THE BEARER

MRS. DORIS NELLIE BARR

is travelling to Canada under the Free Passage Scheme of the Canadian Government for the wives, widows and children of members of the Canadian Forces Overseas.

Photograph of Bearer.

Doris N. Barr

Signature of Bearer

| National Registration Code | EMLP | 31 | 6 |

Names of Children (under 16 years of age) accompanying holder.

MARION ISOBEL BARR

PETER RONALD BRAMMAH

20 Canadian Travel Certificate No. 24528 belonging to Mrs. Doris Barr issued by the High Commissioner of Canada in London. 'Valid for a single journey to Canada direct or via the United States of America'.

21 Joan (Fisher) and John Reichardt on their wedding day 29 June 1945 in Richmond, Surrey. They met during a Spot Dance at the Royston Dance Hall.

Above left: 22 Dix and Joni (Jones) Shuttleworth on their wedding day 5 April 1945. Joni ended up in an isolated northern town in Alberta where her nursing background came in handy.

Above right: 23 Doris (Shelton) and Norman Butt outside her family home in Nottingham, England. Doris and Norman's sister had been pen pals since they were children and when Doris and Norman finally met in England, it was love at first sight.

24 John and Peggy (Sayer) Sheffield on their wedding day 5 November 1945 in Bromley, England. Peggy and John met when she working on a farm in Meopham.

25 A family portrait of Dave Keele, son David and Gwen (Harms) Keele Zradicka taken in 1944. Gwen met her husband at a dance in 1939 and they were married when she was just seventeen.

26 Thomas and Barbara (Cornwell) Warriner on their wedding day 5 January 1941 in Northampton, England. Barbara came to a rural farm in Big River, Saskatchewan. The Warriners had twelve children.

27 Betty (Wilmer) Wright poses in front of the family's Studebaker in her brand new fur coat. She thought she was going to town for groceries but instead her husband Jim brought her to the furriers where he surprised her with a coat.

28 Olive (Rayson) and Lloyd Cochrane on their wedding day 8 May 1943 at All Saints' Queensbury Church in Stanmore, Middlesex. Olive kept all of the letters, diaries and photographs from her life as a War Bride.

29 Ralph and Doris (Field) Lloyd in a studio portrait taken before their wedding in December 1941. Doris and her baby daughter Anne came to a small town in north western New Brunswick seven months ahead of her husband who was still fighting in Italy.

30 War Brides and children on board the Arosa Sun in May 1956, on their first return trip to England since arriving in Canada in 1946. Mrs Irene (Parry) Clark of Ottawa organized the travel of these ladies and children through the Canadian Overseas War Bride Association which she co-founded.

31 Pauline (Portsmouth) and Grant Worthylake in their service uniforms in a photo taken before their marriage. Pauline worked in Balloon Command and had many hair-raising experiences during the Blitz.

32 Ron and Dora (Adams) Addison in their service uniforms. Dora met Ron Addison through her Canadian cousin, Jack Adams, when he was stationed in England.

33 Lilian Olson and son Keith on the University of Manitoba campus in Winnipeg. After the war Lilian's husband went to university and the only housing available for returning veterans and their families was a cluster of two-room cabins that were known as 'Veterans Village'.

34 Delice (DeWolf) and Tom Wilby in a wartime studio portrait. Delice was one of the first War Brides to come to Fredericton, New Brunswick. She preceded her husband Tom, who was still behind enemy lines after having escaped from the Germans with the help of the French Resistance.

35 Doug and Edna (Burrows) Simpson on their wedding day 15 November 1947 in Glencoe, Ontario. Edna came to Canada as a fiancée of a Canadian serviceman and lived on a rural farm.

36 After her engagement to Jack Johnston in Fredericton, New Brunswick, Ann (Biles) Lawrence Johnston flew back to Scotland in December, 1946 to visit her parents. The plane (pictured here) was held over in Goose Bay, Labrador for two days due to bad weather.

Above left: 37 Ann and Jack Johnston on their wedding day 28 May 1947 in Fredericton, New Brunswick. Ann came to Canada as a War Widow in May 1946. She was introduced to Jack Johnston by her late husband's family.

Above right: 38 Dewey and Madeline Fitzgerald outside his family home in Tidehead, New Brunswick. Madeline and her sister Sylvia, both War Widows, came to Canada in May 1945. Madeline met Dewey Fitzgerald and they were married within six months.

39 The telegram that Madeline received at her parents' house on 18 June 1944. 'Deeply regret to inform you that your husband C55049 Sgt. Chunn Charles has been reported killed in action 9 / June / 44.'

Right: 40 Phyllis (Head) Grover and baby Haroldene in Fredericton, New Brunswick with Phyllis' father-in-law in 1946-47. Haroldene was named after her father, Harold, who was killed just as the war was ending in April 1945. Phyllis came to Canada in 1946 as a War Widow and she and Haroldene spent a year in Canada with her late husband's family.

Below: 41 Zoe (Blair) Boone (top row, sitting to the left on wing) at the graduation of her Airframe Mechanic class at Millmeece, Staffordshire, HMS *Fledgling*. Zoe's boyfriend was a prisoner of war and she came to Canada as a fiancée because he was repatriated before they could get married in Scotland.

Above left: 42 Mac (MacGregor) Hooker with baby daughter Carole in 1949. Mac met Bill Hooker in England during the war and came to Canada as his fiancée in 1948.

Above right: 43 Margaret and Don Black in a photo taken during one of his leaves in Glasgow. Margaret came to Canada as a fiancée and was married in Cape Breton.

44 The Canadian Wives Bureau helped organize War Brides clubs throughout Britain as a means of introducing War Brides to the Canadian way of life. This club in Croydon was called the Croydon Canucks. Photo courtesy of Susan Willis, daughter of Mildred (Young) Sowers.

Above left: 45 Letter from Canada's Department of Citizenship and Immigration informing Sheila Walshe that she is no longer a Canadian citizen.

Above right: 46 Joseph Taylor Sr., Joe Jr. and mother in a family portrait taken soon after their wedding in May 1945. Joe Taylor Jr. took Canada's Department of Citizenship and Immigration to Federal Court over its refusal to recognize his status as a Canadian citizen. In January 2008 he was given a grant of citizenship in a special ceremony held in Vancouver.

47 Grace (Gibson) and Hugh Clark in a studio portrait. Grace came to Canada at the end of the First World War to live with her husband on a farm in southern Saskatchewan.

48 Dorothy (Allard) Abraham (second row, far right) was a nurse with the Volunteer Aid Detachment in Chirk, Wales when she met her husband Ted. She came to Canada in 1919 and wrote a book about her experiences called *Lone Cone*.

It Reminds Me of Home
Joni (Jones) Shuttleworth

Joni (Jones) Shuttleworth married Dix Shuttleworth in 1945 and came to an isolated outpost in northern Alberta.

I was introduced to my husband, Dix Shuttleworth, in 1942 when I was a student nurse training in Manchester, Lancashire. We were married in April 1945 and I made plans to come to Canada.

My husband was from the small village of Fairview, in northern Alberta. He had signed up with the Army immediately after high school and when I met him he was a signalman with the Canadian Corps of Signals.

His parents had emigrated to Canada from England and they owned a jewellery store in Fairview. When we were engaged, his father sent the wedding rings and along with the package was a cryptic letter from my mother-in-law telling me not to come to Canada. 'English people can't settle in this country,' she warned.

I personally didn't have any qualms about leaving England. I was tired of air raids and rationing and never considered how different it was going to be leaving my family and friends. My parents were very concerned that I knew so little about where I was going and one of my aunts, on hearing I was to marry a Canadian, never spoke to me again. I thought I would be able to come back to England for a visit whenever I wanted, but I didn't return for twenty-three years.

My mother became seriously ill and died the same morning that my husband, who had been on embarkation leave from Europe prior to returning to Canada, was leaving to rejoin his unit. He was refused an extension of his leave. I will never forget Friday the Thirteenth of July 1945. I was devastated. To make it worse, I had just discovered I was pregnant and was not feeling well. It was a very difficult time for us all.

I resigned my position at the hospital and went to live with my father. He was in mourning and since I had no idea how much longer I would be in England I felt I should spend my remaining time with him.

I soon discovered that after Mum died my attitude towards leaving changed. It certainly didn't help that I had been told not to come to Canada by my husband's own mother. I was the only girl in my family and although I had four older brothers, Dad and I had always been very close. When I received a call to go for my medical I was told that I was too far along in my pregnancy to make the trip. I had mixed feelings about this; disappointed that I wouldn't be seeing my husband for some time but pleased that I could spend more time with Dad and that he would get to see his grand-child.

My son was four months old when I got my notice to sail for Canada on 10 June 1946. Ironically, I lived twenty-eight miles from Liverpool but I had to leave from Southampton on the *Queen Mary*. By now I really didn't want to leave as my dad had got so attached to my son. I felt as though I was deserting him.

I don't remember saying goodbye. On the train we were met by the Red Cross and were taken to a hostel in London where we stayed for two days. The hostel left much to be desired. The food was awful and the nappies I washed were stolen.

I was impressed with the *Queen Mary* and with the cabin I was to share with two others. After looking around the ship I felt I was really going to enjoy the trip. Our first meal on board was delicious, the dining room was lovely. We were served turkey and all the trimmings, white rolls, which I hadn't seen for a very long time. But that was the only meal I had, as I became very seasick once we were underway. My son had to be taken to the nursery since I was unable to look after him.

On the third day at sea I didn't care if I ever saw Canada. By day five I was relieved to see Halifax, rather the worse for the wear. It was now 15 June. Ahead of me, lay a 3,000-mile journey by train to Edmonton, Alberta, with a four-month-old baby in tow.

The trip was extremely difficult. We had been assigned an upper berth, the lower one having been given to a girl who was six months pregnant. I don't know how I would have coped without the help of the porters. They just seemed to appear when you needed help.

My son was not well and when we stopped in Regina a doctor came on board to examine him. He was very listless, not at all like the happy baby he was before we started the journey. The doctor felt that the formula change, long trip and all the changes were responsible for his condition.

The train stopped numerous times, seemingly in the middle of nowhere, to let some of the women off. The journey seemed endless – so different. I was surprised to see people in what I learned was native dress, all so colourful and impressive, waiting to greet a War Bride.

After five days on the train, we finally arrived in Edmonton mid-morning and were met by my husband. I hadn't seen him in almost a year and he looked so different in civilian clothes. It was quite a reunion for us, especially as my husband was meeting his little son for the first time.

Our journey wasn't over yet. We spent the night in Edmonton and the next day we had another 350-mile train ride north to Peace River Country. At Rycroft we were met by a taxi and taken on the final leg of our journey across the Peace River by cable ferry, and then on to Fairview, Alberta, population 300. The entire trip had taken two weeks.

In Fairview, I was surprised to see gravel streets, wooden sidewalks, and tall, ugly, wine-coloured buildings which I found out later were called grain elevators. I must say I got used to all these things more quickly than I did to the lack of indoor plumbing and running water. I remember asking where the bathroom was, only to be told 'Just follow the sidewalk, it's out behind.' I had never seen an outside toilet before and when I asked where the taps were, I was told there was a pump!

My next challenge was getting used to a wood stove; I kept forgetting to put wood into it and wondered why my baking didn't turn out. Then there was the laundry. I had to pump the water, heat it on the stove, carry it by the pailful into the basement, and then carry it back up again when I finished the washing. In the winter, the clothes would freeze on the line. Our drinking water, which we stored in barrels on the porch, was brought to us by horse and wagon. The water froze solid and had a most disagreeable taste.

Expecting a warm reception, I found instead that there was some hostility towards me. My mother-in-law wouldn't let me forget the warning she had given me about Canada and I felt very uncomfortable because we had to live with her. There was no housing and we were stuck in that house for a year. I was homesick and feeling guilty about leaving my dad. It was very difficult getting used to this new way of life and living in a small town where everyone seemed to know everyone else's business! I often wished I was back home and I must say I shed quite a few tears.

About six weeks after my arrival, I was approached by the local hospital and asked if I would consider going to work for them. It was my salvation. After my mother-in-law offered to look after our son, I got my nursing credentials from England and went to work at the Fairview Hospital.

In retrospect, I think it was a very good move as I was feeling depressed and sorry for myself. I quickly got used to working in the 28-bed hospital, compared to the 760-bed hospital where I had trained. I continued working at the local hospital intermittently over the next ten years and during this time our second son and a daughter were added to our family.

My husband became Deputy Fire Commissioner for the province of Alberta and after moving from Fairview I nursed in various hospitals where his profession required him to be. We retired to Vancouver Island on the west coast of British Columbia and were glad to leave the cold Alberta winters behind. Since then my brothers and their families have visited us several times and have all loved it here. I made quite a few trips back to England but I just can't think of anywhere else I would rather live. Vancouver Island reminds me of home.

Postscript: Joni Shuttleworth's husband passed away unexpectedly in 2006. She lives in Qualicum Beach, British Columbia.

From Pen Pal to Sister-in-Law
Doris (Shelton) Butt

Doris (Shelton) Butt met her Canadian husband through his sister, who had been her pen pal for many years.

Doris Shelton was eleven years old when she started writing to her Canadian pen pal, a nine-year-old girl named Eva Butt from Cypress River, Manitoba. The year was 1929 and pen pals were a popular way of meeting new friends in distant places. The friendship was especially important to Eva. As a child she had contracted polio and the letters from Doris in the far-off city of Nottingham, England opened up a whole new world for a girl with a severe disability.

As Eva's illness worsened and she became too ill to write, her sister Edna, who was closer to Doris's age, picked up the pen. The girls continued writing through the Depression and the early war years, getting to know each other's families and becoming close friends. So when Edna's two brothers, Alex and Norman, joined the Canadian military in 1941 and were shipped one after the other to England, it was expected that they would make their way to Nottingham to meet their sister's pen pal.

Doris was twenty-one years old and living at home when the war broke out. She had completed her formal education at Nottingham's Mundella High School and was excited to get a job at a shop near the council square in Nottingham. But her father, who was Superintendent Relieving Officer for the City, didn't approve of his daughter working so Doris stayed at 8 Wheatfields Road in Thorneywood to help her mother.

Things changed dramatically as the war escalated in the summer of 1940 with the Battle of Britain. Every ablebodied person was expected to do their part and even Doris's father was pulled into watch duty. So he had little to say when Doris joined the Women's Land Army to work on farms in southern England.

In the diary she kept in 1942 we can see the transition from a relatively easy life, cleaning house in the morning and attending movies in downtown Nottingham – complete with the stars' names and a review – to putting up silage and bringing cows into the barn in Devon.

The farm job in Devon caused Doris some trouble because the farmer took a shine to her and as a result, his wife wasn't too happy with their pretty little Land Army helper. Later she moved closer to home and delivered milk from a dairy near Nottingham. One day, she had to get on the bus carrying her Land Army boots. Thinking there was a rack above her head she absentmindedly put the boots up. Doris soon found out there was no rack and the manure-laden boots came down upon the surprised gentleman next to her. Insult was added to injury because she was laughing so hard she could not stop long enough to apologise.

She describes another time on the bus when a fellow was sitting directly opposite a woman trying to breastfeed her baby. The baby was not complying, so the mother said, 'Go on, tike it ... tike it ... or I shall give it to that man over there.'

The diary is humorous, but it also contains a chilling reminder that in war time death is never far away. During one terrible week in 1942 Doris's best friend, Connie Smith, was killed in an air raid.

Doris and Connie had a pact that if the sirens blew when they were at each others' place, they would stay where they were. If they were in town together, they would each go to their own homes. The women were at the movies when the sirens blew and each scrambled off after saying a hurried goodbye. Connie's house took a direct hit and she was killed that night. Doris' diary entry expressed her numbness, 'I feel dead.'

Soon after Connie was killed Doris met Edna's brother Alex and they became friends. Later, when brother Norman went overseas, Alex encouraged him to go up to Nottingham. 'Why don't you look up Eva and Edna's pen pal?' Alex suggested. 'She's a lovely girl.'

There aren't many cases of love at first sight but the challenges of wartime put a different perspective on things. Six dates later, Norman, then twenty-eight, and Doris, twenty-six, were engaged and plans were made for a wedding. On 4 April 1944 Doris Shelton and Norman Butt were married at Emmanuel Church, Nottingham. A short honeymoon in Scotland followed, and then separation, as Norman went back to his army unit.

With the invasion of Normandy in June 1944 they had only short times together, as leaves were few and far between. Norman, a member of the Royal Winnipeg Rifles' Signal Corps, was on the European continent. Doris was now expecting a baby and lived with her parents in Nottingham. At the end of January 1945 their first child Glenda was born.

Norman was repatriated to Canada after the war ended in 1945 and Doris and Glenda had to wait until July 1946 before they could leave on the War Bride ship *Queen Mary*. George and Rose Shelton must have felt that their world had been torn apart as their only child and granddaughter boarded the huge ocean liner and sailed away to Canada.

When Doris and Glenda arrived at Halifax's Pier 21, they boarded a train for the long journey to Manitoba. 1,600 miles and half a continent later, they arrived in Winnipeg to an enthusiastic welcome from Norman and his family.

In the months since he had been repatriated to Canada, Norman had worked with his brother Nelson at his jewellery store in Carberry, a small town of about 1,200 souls between Winnipeg and Brandon in southern Manitoba. When Doris arrived, Norman got a better paying job as a watch-man at the Carberry airport and Doris often went for the two-mile walk with Glenda in the pushchair to meet Norm as he came off his shift. Not only did British pushchairs have a different name – the Canadians called them 'strollers', but they were bigger and very different looking so Doris and her pushchair sure stood out as she made her way through Carberry streets and along the road to the airport!

Britain continued with rationing in the postwar years so Doris sent care parcels home to England containing the items that were unavailable to her parents. She kept a strict regimen of writing a letter home every Monday and her parents did the same. The children loved to hear those letters that always started with the greeting, 'Dear Doris, Norm and Buttercups,' until both of her parents were gone in 1964.

There were stressful times as the couple started civilian life together but Doris had an advantage over other War Brides who went to an isolated Manitoba farm. Carberry was small but at least it had stores, a theatre and some semblance of urban life. One War Bride Doris met on the train trip out west would come and stay with them in Carberry for short periods of time to get a break from the farm, which could best be described as 'rustic' given that chickens were freely allowed to wander throughout the house!

Doris wasn't on a farm but she had her own adjusting to do in Manitoba, first at Carberry, and later at Darlingford and Manitou, where Norm started his own jewellery business. The cold and dry winters not only straightened her naturally curly hair and froze nappies on the clothesline, but it took some getting accustomed to the reality of a life far less prosperous and with far less amenities than she had been used to in England. As hard as Norm worked at his jewellery and repair business there was not a lot of extra money for their growing family.

Doris's letters to England put the best face on her life in Canada, being careful not to alarm her parents as to how meagre their living was. One thing Doris didn't have to camouflage in her letters was her feelings for the man who had swept her off her feet in Nottingham. She had no regrets for the decision to marry made in the tumult of wartime.

Norm and Doris went on to have two more daughters and in the early 1950s they moved another 1,000 miles west to the small village of Nakusp, British Columbia and a climate that Doris found much to her liking. Their marriage, initiated against the backdrop of war and cultivated by love, commitment and faith, lasted for forty-four years until Norm died in 1986. Doris passed away in 1991.

This story was based on an article written by Doris Butt's daughter, Gloria Mott.

Her Heart and Spirit Belong in Manitoba
Peggy (Sayer) Sheffield

Peggy (Sayer) Sheffield was born in Bromley, Kent in 1921. When she was sixty-three years old she became the second War Bride in Canada to be ordained a priest in the Anglican Church.

Growing up in Bromley, Kent I was entranced by stories of missionaries. I knew in my heart that someday I would dedicate my life to the service of God, but the reality was that my working-class parents could not afford to send me to university.

Instead I attended Bromley Central School which was excellent for those not intending to go on to higher education. I was well equipped to join the army of young women who held down jobs in banks, building societies and other business offices. There was no point telling my parents that my one desire was to be a missionary because it was simply out of my reach.

I found work at the Woolwich Equitable Building Society in Bromley High Street. I would have liked to join my father at the Prudential Insurance Company, but at that time they had a rather snobbish system. Because my paternal grandfather was a painter and decorator, my father, who was a whiz at mathematics, could not hold a clerical position at the Prudential!

From my father I inherited a great love for growing things, especially flowers. My mother, in contrast with my father, who was an extrovert, was a rather shy and private person. It was the holidays we spent in Norfolk when I was a child that opened my eyes to the lure of country living and it was this love of all things rural that propelled me into the Women's Land Army (WLA) in 1942, long before I ever met my future husband at the Kentish farm where I lived and worked. I resolved early on in my WLA career that when the war was over I would find a farmer with sufficient land that he needed someone to keep all his records, and that would be my job.

Fate intervened a few weeks after I had settled in to work on the farm at Meopham, when a Canadian second cousin of the farmer arrived on a forty-eight-hour weekend pass. I first saw John Sheffield sitting at the tea table in the farm kitchen when I dropped in for tea before returning to the barns to finish the end of day chores. Such was the chemistry between us that I knew I would not be returning to Bromley that evening to spend the rest of the weekend with my parents.

When John left the following day we had shared so much of our past, our hopes and dreams that it didn't seem possible we had just met, and that it would be at least three months before there was any chance of another meeting. In wartime hours together were very precious – one just never knew when or if the next meeting would occur.

One amusing story arises out of this weekend encounter. The farmer's sister, a sixty-year-old spinster who kept house for him, was of the old school and watched us like a hawk. On the Monday morning I awoke to raised voices coming from the kitchen area, and heard her say to her brother, 'I'm going to call her mother and tell her what's going on!' I smiled to myself, as my mother refused to have a telephone in the house.

My parents liked John immediately, and while they both realized that if we were to marry I would be leaving England, my mother really agonised over it. She looked ahead to grandchildren they might never see, for in those days it was only the very wealthy who could afford transatlantic travel. In an unguarded moment she once said, 'Life will never be the same again.' That phrase was to haunt me for a very long time, especially when I was very happy, because I felt that my happiness was at the expense of her sadness. When she died in 1963 it still did – and it was only after I talked with my brother after her death that I could in some sense lay that ghost to rest.

John and I wrote to each other every day, as did most other wartime couples. In the three years that we kept up this correspondence there was one period when he received no letters from me for six months. I finally wrote to his padre who immediately wrote telling me that John had been hospitalized twice – once for appendicitis and then for blood poisoning from a leg injury. The padre soon had my letters rerouted and I received a note from John telling me that he was partly through 170 letters!

The war ended and John was back in England in time for our wedding on 5 November 1945. He returned to Canada just before Christmas, and in mid-June 1946 I received word that I should be ready to leave for Canada at forty-eight hours notice. The last week before I left was very bittersweet. I remember on the last day when my mother and I were eating lunch, my cat sat watching me as though he knew something was up. I was totally torn between excitement and profound sadness, but felt helpless to do anything about it.

My mother and I took the train from Bromley to London. When we arrived at Victoria Station we were met by my father and my Aunt Sallie. Once all the War Brides boarded the bus, reality hit hard and most of the women were in tears. My family were very brave, smiling their goodbyes as the bus pulled out of the station. It was seventeen years before I again set eyes on Victoria Station and by that time my mother had died.

My journey to Canada aboard the *Queen Mary* was memorable for a few reasons. I did not have children, the food was wonderful after six years of rationing, and on the second day out, the office staff called for volunteers who could use a typewriter. Having nothing better to do I volunteered but after one day listening to the constant messages, changes in travel arrange- ments, etc. I was exhausted. The next day, I only registered for a half day.

We arrived in Halifax on 1 July, Canada's national holiday, and then began the 2,200-mile-long train journey to Winnipeg. The heat was stifling, and as we were travelling in carriages with no air conditioning we proceeded to open the windows only to close them rapidly as the soot from the engine blew through the window screens. Very soon after we left Halifax a doctor and nurse went through the train ordering mothers to strip their children to the waist. Some protested, whereupon the doctor said it was an order, to avoid an outbreak of dysentery.

After three days of listening to the 'whoo-whoo' of the train whistle as it went through small settlements and towns, and dropping off War Brides along the way, we finally reached Winnipeg. For the last half-hour of the journey those of us scheduled to get off in Winnipeg stood silently in the aisles. Standing up as we were, we couldn't see too much of the countryside through which we were passing, At that point we really were not interested. This was the end of our great journey to a new country and the beginning of the rest of our lives – our post-England lives. The excitement and tension put an end to all the chattering. Each of us was deep in our own thoughts – our own experience – something very difficult to portray in words, and we just did not have the words at that time.

The train drew into the station in Winnipeg and there was John standing with a group of other husbands – the only one carrying a box of flowers. After two days in Winnipeg, we left for the 100-mile drive to Swan Lake. It poured rain all the way, and at times the windshield wipers couldn't clear the window fast enough for us to see where we were going. We had been driving on a perfectly straight road for quite some time when I innocently asked John when we would turn a corner. He laughed, and said that was something I would have to get used to in Manitoba – the long, straight roads with no hedges on either side.

When we finally arrived at his mother's farmhouse, the family were waiting up for us, sitting around the oilcloth-covered kitchen table with an oil lamp placed in the centre for light. Oil lamps were no strangers to me as my two aunts who lived in Norfolk used the same form of lighting. My new relatives also had outdoor toilet facilities, which I had also encountered in Norfolk, and as I had been told about these things ahead of time I did not have the rude awakening that some other War Brides did.

John found work on farms in the Swan Lake area, then in April 1947 he was offered a bookkeeping and parts manager position in the Swan Lake Garage. He was a born mathematician and mechanic and he enjoyed the work so in 1958 he purchased the business.

My parents did come to visit us in Canada. The first time was in 1953, when they stayed for five months, so my mother did see my two eldest children. My father was never able to persuade my mother to travel again, but after her death he did return a few times and met all of our five children before he passed away in 1978. He enjoyed his visits here very much, as he was a very gregarious person who soon knew more of the townsfolk than I did.

My dear husband John died of cancer in 1974 at the age of fifty-five. It was the only time in my life that I felt the future had suddenly been snuffed out; in fact it was quite a long time before I could contemplate a future.

But 'life goes on and love is all, in spite of grief and pain, and deep within my heart, I know that we will meet again.' I don't know who wrote those words, but they are very true.

John had been a lay reader in the Somerset Parish of St Barnabas Anglican Church in Swan Lake for twenty-two years and the congregation wanted me to follow in his footsteps. Out of the ashes of the old life rose a new, and so I agreed to become a lay reader.

After some forty years I was able to answer the call in a way which I could never have dreamed of so long ago in England. During my years at Somerset, I was approached by lay friends, clergy and the bishop concerning ordination. It was 1983 before I gave it any serious consideration. I valued my lay status and had absolutely no desire to give it up, but I was so thoroughly entrenched in parish and diocesan work that I began to realize that I was masquerading under the title of lay reader. In 1984 I was ordained a deacon of the Anglican Church and the following year, I became the second War Bride in Canada to become an ordained priest in the Anglican Church.

Although I am not as active as I used to be I still read the lessons in the church, which is important to me because I believe the lessons should be read in such a way that they transmit a message – and I'm not above using a version of the Bible in contemporary language if that's the only way to get the message across.

I have made several trips back to England – the first in 1963 and the last in November 2005 for a family wedding. I love going back to England for a visit, but my heart is now in Manitoba. Each time I return back to Canada and step outside the airport in Winnipeg I see that huge expanse of sky and prairie and I know that this is where I belong.

Postscript: Peggy has five children, eleven grandchildren and three great-grandchildren. She still lives in Swan Lake.

I Can't Imagine Living Anywhere Else
Gwen (Harms) Keele Zradicka

Gwen Harms was born in Thornton Heath, Surrey in 1922. Her husband was an RCMP officer in civilian life and they lived all over western Canada.

When my mother was very young her mother died and she was taken in by a cousin, Ellen Fennell and her husband Will, of Thornton Heath.

The Fennels never officially adopted my mother but they raised her as though she was their own daughter. They were my true grandparents and I loved them very much. My mother was given the best education and was very involved in music. She played first violin with the Croydon Symphony Orchestra, one of south London's leading amateur orchestras. She went to Pitmans Business School and worked as a stenographer until she married my father after the First World War. They settled in at 59 Norbury Avenue in Thornton Heath and that's where my sister and I were born.

When I was seven my parents built a bungalow in Kenley, Surrey. I was sent to the local Church of England School and from age ten to fourteen I attended Roke Central School. In ordinary circumstances, I may have gone on to high school, but the only way to get a higher education was if your parents had money.

In those days, my father was very involved with making instruments that were used in laying the cable from England to America. He worked a lot of overtime. During this same period my paternal grandfather died and my father had a nervous breakdown. As part of his recovery, the doctor advised him to take a glass of port wine before each meal. One drink led to another and my father became an alcoholic. Those were very unhappy days for us. My father eventually lost his job and we lost our home. My father sold everything of value to pay for his drinking, including my mother's engagement ring, other jewellery and silverware. That was the end of my parents' marriage.

By tragic coincidence, around the same time we lost our home both Mr and Mrs Fennel passed away and in the will they gave their fully furnished home on 20 Trafford Road to my mother. It was a bittersweet gift from the only parents my mother ever knew. My mother, sister and I moved into her childhood home and were able to make a new start without my father in our lives. I finished school and went to work as a girl probationer in a government office in London. I worked my way up to filing clerk and later I applied for a similar job with Crane Ltd. During this time the war broke out.

How well I remember sitting and listening to Neville Chamberlain saying 'We are at war.' We had no idea what was in store for us. One day we heard the planes overhead and went and stood out in the garden and watched, in amazement and horror, as a dogfight took place between our Spitfires and the German fighters. We watched our fliers bail out of the planes when they were hit and as they parachuted down, the German planes machine gunned them and killed them.

During the Battle of Britain it was a nightly task to try and get home from work in London and into the Anderson air-raid shelter in our back garden. In 1941 our house and the surrounding houses on Trafford Lane were demolished when two bombs were dropped, one across the road at the front and one behind. As these were row houses, all joined together, the entire house didn't collapse but the inside of the house was completely demolished. We lost everything, all buried under a pile of rubble. Our house was condemned and we had to move to 122 Warwick Road, Thornton Heath, an empty house that had been confiscated by the government.

One Saturday night in 1939 I met my husband at Grandisons Dance Hall. I was sixteen years old and like a lot of young girls, I loved to dance. He was a Mountie (Royal Canadian Mounted Police, or RCMP) and had joined the Provost Corps so that he could go overseas. He took a shine to me and we started going out together. He was twenty-six years old, tall and good looking and I guess I was flattered. Six months later he proposed.

We were married on 21 June 1941 in the same church and by the same minister who had married my parents. That should have told me something about what I could expect out of my own marriage but I was seventeen years old and had no cares in the world.

At first we rented a small bedroom in a house near the base in Farnborough, Hampshire. But by early 1943 I was pregnant with my son David so I returned to my mother's place in Thornton Heath to await his birth. David was born on 24 October 1943, and when he was about eight months old the buzz bombs started to attack us. These were unmanned missiles with a limited range and when the engines stopped we all held our breath, waiting to see if we were the unlucky ones to be blown to bits.

After all I had been through already, my husband wasn't taking any chances with our little baby. He sought special permission to send us to stay with his parents in Canada until the war was over.

In July 1944 I received notice that I was to leave for Canada. I remember one of the soldiers told me that I should take a good look at the trees in England because in Saskatchewan it was so flat that you could see a train three days before it got to you and that if I stepped off the sidewalk in Winnipeg, the Indians would scalp me.

David and I went down to London where we were put on an overnight train to Scotland. We arrived in Gourock the next morning and were ceremoniously piped by kilted bagpipers on board the ship. The crossing was a nightmare. The ship took a zigzag course across the Atlantic to avoid U-boats. When we were off the coast of Newfoundland the engines were shut down and we had to be very quiet as we were told there was a U-boat in the area. After a harrowing journey we finally arrived at Pier 21 in Halifax, Nova Scotia on 1 August.

I took the train to meet my husband's parents 2,200 miles west in Winnipeg, Manitoba, where they were vacationing. After two weeks in the city we arrived in Wadena, which is located in east central Saskatchewan on the shore of the Quill Lakes. All I knew about Saskatchewan was what that soldier had told me before I left and that it was where wheat came from.

Arriving in Wadena was truly a culture shock. My in-laws had no running water, no telephone or electric lights. The toilet was down the backyard and the Eaton's Department Store catalogue was our toilet paper. At least you could sit there and look at all the nice merchandise.

My husband's parents didn't make me feel very welcome. They told me the only reason they accepted me was because I had produced a son to carry on the family name. I had a very unhappy year waiting for my husband to come home. Then the battle began. My sisters-in-law told me after two days that I had had my husband for long enough and now it was their turn. He went along with their wishes. The outcome was that I left Wadena, leaving my husband and son behind.

I went to Winnipeg, Manitoba and ironically, I got a job with Eaton's Department Store. Then another British War Bride from Wadena came to Winnipeg and got in touch with me. She had received much the same treatment and just couldn't take it. We found out that there was a new practical nursing course being started at St Joseph's Hospital in the north end and decided to apply. We were both accepted and went into residence there for our training.

In the meantime, my husband had come back to Winnipeg RCMP headquarters and we began to see each other again. I missed my son very much and when my husband was sent to the detachment at The Pas, Manitoba, we decided to get back together so I moved to The Pas and finished the practical end of my nursing course at the local hospital.

In late 1949 my husband was transferred to Wabowden, Manitoba, a very isolated little village north of The Pas and below Churchill, Manitoba, the polar bear capital of the world! There were no roads in to Wabowden. The only way out was either by the once-weekly passenger train to Churchill, a way freight train (also once a week), or by plane, which had skis in the winter and pontoons in the summer for take off and landing on the lake.

Our daughter Shelly was born at the end of the year and in January 1950 the four of us went to live in Wabowden. We arrived very late at night in

-50°F temperature and had to walk up the snow-covered railway tracks to the detachment house, toting a six-week-old baby and a very tired six-year-old. The house was very isolated, had no running water, lights or telephone but it had a wood stove and wood-burning furnace. The only way to get water was to have one of the Native Indians chop a hole in the ice on the lake and haul it up to the house where there was a huge tank in the bathroom. All the water had to be boiled of course.

I was in charge of the Indian Department drugs and the natives would come banging on my door, at any time, wanting drugs. They mostly wanted cough medicine, because of its alcoholic content. Sometimes, they would come and fetch me by dog sled to go to their shacks to see an ill relative. I then had to make a decision whether or not the sick person needed to go to the hospital in The Pas.

In 1951 I contracted tuberculosis, which is not surprising given that TB is extremely contagious and the natives I came into contact with through my work had a high rate of infection. Originally, I thought I had pneumonia so I took the weekly train to The Pas and was admitted to the hospital. X-rays showed that I had contracted tuberculosis. I was very ill and spent the next three months in a special clinic in Winnipeg. My son went back to Wadena and my daughter was cared for by friends in The Pas.

Due to my illness, my husband got a compassionate transfer to Dauphin, Manitoba. When I was released from the clinic, I went to Dauphin and we finally got the family back together again. I went to work at the local hospital and for the next six years life went on. Our marriage was showing many signs of trouble by then, and when my husband was transferred to Portage La Prairie in 1956 it was obvious to both of us that we wouldn't be together much longer.

My husband retired from the RCMP in 1961 and he moved to work in security in Fort William, Ontario. The children and I followed him there a few months later but our marriage didn't improve so I left my husband for the last time and took the children with me back to Winnipeg. I found a job and over the next seven years we all moved forward with our lives. After my husband and I were divorced, I married Harry Zadricka, a lovely man whom I had met when we lived in Dauphin.

Harry and I lived in Richmond, BC and were very happy for thirty-five years until he was diagnosed with Alzheimer's disease and died in 2003.

I am now eighty-three years old and still live in my own home, enjoy good health and volunteer at the nursing home where Harry died. I cannot imagine living anywhere else but where I am now.

Canada Is My Adopted Home
Barbara (Cornwell) Warriner

Barbara (Cornwell) Warriner came to a farm in Big River, Saskatchewan. She had twelve children.

Barbara Cornwell was born in Northampton, England in 1922. Her father was an English bobby and although he was overprotective of his two daughters, there was little he could do when a Canadian soldier named Thomas Warriner was billeted next door to their house at 24 Hunter Street.

Thomas Warriner was born in England but his parents and sisters immigrated to Canada in 1927 settling in the Tantallon district of southern Saskatchewan. After seven years of battling drought and dust storms in the South, they packed their belongings and followed the drifting top soil north to Big River. They eventually settled in the West Cowan District, west of Big River, where they operated a mixed farm with a few cattle, chickens and horses which were used for farming and transportation.

When war was declared Tom was among the first to join up and he was sent to England with the First Canadian Division, arriving in Greenock, Scotland, on 17 December 1939. Canadians were normally stationed at Camp Aldershot, but his division was billeted in private homes in Northampton since there were no barracks for them in the area.

Tom was assigned to a room at 22 Hunter Street and it didn't take long before he met Barbara Cornwell next door. Their courtship started over an English garden fence. This final obstacle was soon crossed and while the rest of the division speculated that they had been brought to England to 'clean the bluebird droppings off the White Cliffs of Dover', the happy couple was planning their wedding.

Barbara and Tom Warriner were married on 5 January 1941. They had two daughters in England, Judy and Linda, and when the war was over Tom was repatriated to Canada where he resumed farming in Saskatchewan. Meantime, Barbara had to wait for her turn to come to Canada on the War Bride ships. On 7 January 1946 Barbara and the two girls boarded the *Stavangerfjord*. The ride was rough, they were all seasick and Barbara was thankful to have both feet on land again. Later, she said it didn't matter which land, but she was glad they said it was Canada!

Barbara and the girls spent a week on the train before arriving in Saskatoon, 2,700 miles west of Halifax, on 21 January. There they were met by Tom, whom she described as 'unrecognizable' because it was the first time that she had seen him in civilian clothes. After spending two nights in the relative comfort of Saskatoon, it was time to head for her final destination, Big River, a place she would call home for the rest of her life.

Big River is called the Gateway to the North, and for a good reason: it marks the transition from the southern, more populated areas, to the northern, mostly wilderness areas of Saskatchewan. During the 1930s and 1940s, Big River's population was never more than 1,000 people.

Barbara, Tom and the girls caught the train for Prince Albert and were met by a dear old lady, Mrs Mary Lamb, a volunteer who met every train carrying War Brides. Before leaving on the Muskeg Express for Big River, Mrs Lamb presented them with goody bags of books, chocolate bars and fruit to while away the hours on the last leg of their journey.

The family finally arrived in Big River on 26 January at 1:30 a.m. on the coldest night of the year. At the train station they were met by Tom's mother and a team of horses laden down with every blanket in the Warriner household. As they departed for the last leg of their trip across Cowan Lake, Barbara and the children huddled under the blankets and were warned not to lift their heads for fear their inexperienced English noses would freeze from the cold weather. She had heard of the expression 'freeze the you know what' off a brass monkey but never believed it until now.

Over the next eight years, Barbara learned to cope with her fears and the loneliness of being so far away from her own family in England. She settled into farming and helped as much as she could. They moved a few times in the area, always looking for a better place for their growing family, which now numbered eight children.

In 1954 after hearing word that her mother was coming for a visit, it was decided to build a more modern house to accommodate the entire family. This one had two bedrooms with wall to wall beds, a kitchen and living room. The night Barbara's mother arrived from England, they still had no back door on the house so a horse blanket was used to keep out the blood-sucking mosquitoes.

Barbara's mother came and left, and was no doubt a bit concerned over the family's living conditions. Tom and Barbara took a long hard look at their financial situation; they'd had three bad years in a row, with drought and disease in all their cattle. She was pregnant again and they realized that the money had to come from somewhere else. Tom took a job with Waite Fisheries in Big River, leaving Barbara behind to tend to the needs of everyone and everything on the farm.

It was a lot of hard work for one adult and all those children. What they didn't have they made or went without. Saturday was shopping day and Barbara either walked the six miles to town or else caught a ride and then came home with her husband in the evening after he got off work.

Barbara never had a driver's licence and with Tom in Big River during the day it became increasingly difficult to cope with the needs of her large family, which by this time had grown to eleven children. So in 1960 they moved into Big River to an old mission house which still had the cross on the roof. Another child was born two years later, making Barbara the very proud mother of twelve.

When the last of the children had left the nest, Barbara joined the Saskatchewan War Brides Association, Canada's first official War Bride organization which was established in 1975. The Saskatchewan group led the way for all the other War Bride Associations in Canada and it still exists today.

Over the years Barbara attended sixteen War Bride reunions and what fun the ladies had. She loved every minute of the time she spent with her War Bride friends; reminiscing about the past made things feel so real once again.

Barbara passed away suddenly on 14 September 1991 shortly after she and Tom celebrated their fiftieth wedding anniversary. Before she died, Barbara was interviewed by a local newspaper about her life as a War Bride. When asked about her decision to come to Canada, she said it was 'the right one' but she still had fond memories of the old boot and shoe town of Northampton, of the Saturday night dances at the salon and the drill hall.

'I still love England,' she said, 'and I've enjoyed the trips back for a visit, but would not like to return there to live. Canada is my adopted home and I love it.'

Based on an article contributed by Kathy Panter, Barbara Warriner's daughter.

Don't Learn How to Milk the Cows
Betty (Wilmer) Wright

Betty (Wilmer) Wright was born in 1927 in Sydenham, London. She went to a farm in Tisdale, Saskatchewan.

I met my husband Jim Wright when he was recuperating from severe injuries suffered in the liberation of northern Holland. He was in England prior to going home to Canada on a medical discharge and we just happened to meet in Worthing where I was on a week's holiday before joining the WRNS. We decided to get married, and since we were still minors, for the next three months Jim avoided being sent home while we got all the paperwork in order.

On 24 November 1945, the day after my eighteenth birthday, we were married in Lewisham. Having run out of excuses, Jim was scheduled to be on board ship to Canada the next day. Instead, we went to Dorking and avoided military police for a week's honeymoon!

I returned to Gosport WRNS station and my husband returned to Canada. I enjoyed my military service but was also fretting as it took nine months before my demob papers and passage to Canada were arranged.

My father, a man of few words, had this to say before I boarded the *Aquitania*; 'You don't know what you are going to, but make of it what you will and do well my girl.'

I was sad to be leaving my parents but also excited to be reunited with Jim. I arrived in Halifax, Nova Scotia in August 1946. A returning Canadian soldier asked me where I was going and I replied, 'To Tisdale, Saskatchewan.'

His response was, 'Oh hell, honey, get back on the boat!'

Luckily for me, his advice was not in line with my experience. My father-in-law, Percy Wright was a Member of Parliament in Ottawa, Ontario, where he represented the constituency of Melfort-Tisdale-McKenzie from 1940 to 1954. He was a veteran of the First World War and had received the Military Medal at Paschendale. He arranged to meet me on the station platform in Montreal, Quebec. It was a special event as he brought a big basket of fresh fruit which I handed to another bride on the train. I don't recall what was left of the basket when I returned from that short visit.

I didn't realize how big Canada was and it was another two days and nights on the train before Jim met me in Winnipeg, Manitoba, 2,200 miles west of Halifax. We spent a few days reacquainting, as they say, before leaving for the last leg of my journey, a 420-mile drive by car to Jim's farm at Tisdale, Saskatchewan.

My mother-in-law and Jim's sister were there to greet us. I have nothing but praise for the way I was welcomed, not only by Jim's family, but by the community which was to be our home for the next ten years.

I had many things to learn, but the first good piece of advice I got was when Jim's mother told me, 'Don't learn how to milk the cows or you will be stuck with that forever.'

Cooking on a wood-burning stove for my husband and farmhands was a frightening experience and I often called neighbours for help after I mastered the rural telephone. I had to take driving lessons on the three-ton truck in case I needed to take myself to the hospital for our first baby!

My Jim always seemed to be out in the field when calves or pigs were born. One time, Jim was on the tractor seeding wheat and he asked me to keep watch on a huge sow that we expected would drop her piglets any day. Sure enough, she circled the pen and after twenty minutes had eleven newborns. Jim had fixed up a shelter with a heat lamp, so I followed her around, gathering the piglets up and putting them out of harm's way. The last one to arrive looked pretty weak, so I took it to the warm oven in my kitchen and had it sucking on a bottle of warm milk when the men came in for dinner.

Another time, Jim was off on a three-day meeting in Regina, which was 200 miles away. It was early in the winter but there was a coat of ice on the pond beside the well house. Jim had asked a neighbour's son to come and help with the chores at the barn. He left the gate open by the pond and four market steers found their way onto the ice. When they broke through, he called for help. I sent him running home for his dad and tried to keep them alive until they returned. With a rope found in the pump house, standing on the icy and wet bank, I tried in turn to keep them up against the icy bank, hoping they could get footing to climb out.

The neighbour arrived and with an axe he chopped away the ice so we could help them out of the icy water. We chased them to the barn and rubbed them down with sacking. It was afterward, when I realized how close I had come to joining those steers in the pond, that I cried and shook with fear.

It wasn't all work. Jim and I loved to dance, so one time after the harvest we set out with friends to find a dance. After a forty-mile drive crammed in the seat of a half-ton truck, we arrived at a hall lit by lamps with the orchestra consisting of an accordion and a fiddle.

Jim's friend Leo asked me for a dance and when Jim asked how we got along, he said: 'She's a great dancer, but she talked all the time and I never understood a word she said.'

Jim coached me to slow down my speech and change my wording to avoid embarrassing mistakes, like the time I asked the hired man if he would like me to knock him up in the morning. In Canada, asking someone to 'knock you up' meant to get pregnant and the hired man sure wasn't expecting that proposition from the boss's wife!

My mother and father came to Canada a few years later and lived in a separate house on our farm. Dad looked after the yard and garden and my mother passed on her cooking skills and helped with our four girls. Meanwhile Jim had gone back to university to study agriculture, but his health could not stand up to active farming so he moved on to work at an agriculture cooperative.

My sister Barbara was also a War Bride. She lived in Nova Scotia but the marriage didn't last, so she came out west to visit us all at the farm. Barbara met a railway engineer and they fell in love and married, settling in Transcona, Manitoba. By this time, we had been on the farm for ten years and were contemplating a change, so my parents moved to the city of Winnipeg to be close to where Barbara was living. We took the family to Moosomin, Saskatchewan, where our son was born – a change of water I was told!

Eventually we settled in the capital city, Regina, where Jim had a management position with the Saskatchewan Wheat Pool. My days and nights were fully occupied raising our five children, with the support of my husband, whose job took him all over Saskatchewan, to parts of Canada and even overseas.

As our family matured I was able to travel with Jim to the UK, Europe, Asia, Africa, the USA and all across Canada. During my years in Regina I enjoyed several activities, including a fitness program at the YMCA, singing with the church choir and the ladies Regina Choir. I got involved in a programme called Meals on Wheels delivering to shut-ins and helped nurses to care for sick children and babies in a program called Tender Loving Care. On warm sunny days I would invite Jim from his office to share lunch with me in Wascana Park by the lake in front of the Legislative building.

Our family had all moved on to university or to work when we decided to retire and move to Vancouver Island, British Columbia, on Canada's west coast. We stay involved with golfing, curling, senior's dances and keep in touch with our five families which now consist of thirteen grandchildren and one great-grandchild. All in all we have been blessed with a good family, good friends and good health.

I have enjoyed several visits back to the beautiful countryside of England, but never regretted chatting up that farm boy with red hair on that August day in Worthing.

Postscript: Betty and Jim Wright live in Cobble Hill, BC.

Close to the Heart
Olive (Rayson) Cochrane

Olive (Rayson) Cochrane came to Vancouver, British Columbia and eventually settled in Saskatoon, Saskatchewan. Olive kept a treasure trove of memorabilia from her life as a War Bride.

Olive Rayson was born in 1921 and brought up in Edgeware, England where she lived on Lawrence Crescent in the Stag Lane Aerodrome Estate. She started working at eighteen when her uncle, a British Major, found her a clerical job with the military. As the war progressed she worked at various telephone exchanges including Colindale and Grimsdyke.

Olive was always reticent to state exactly where she worked, as many of the sites were amongst those secreted below London. Even after she was married her husband was only allowed to approach within a pre-set radius of blocks to meet her after work. Her relatives believed she was involved with the Bletchley Park projects such as Enigma but we'll probably never know.

In 1942 Olive's brother Trevor convinced her to attend a dance at the Lyceum Theatre in London. Olive was beautiful – 5ft 7in tall, dark hair, blue eyes, the classic English complexion. She had several admirers and was engaged to an RAF pilot but he did not survive the Battle of Britain. She had been in mourning over the death of her young English flyer for some time and Trevor was trying to get her out of the house to have fun with other young people.

At the dance Olive was introduced to a young Canadian named Lloyd Cochrane. Lloyd was an only child whose mother died of tuberculosis when he was just four years old. Fearing a custody battle, his father cut all ties with his deceased wife's family and raised Lloyd as best he could, moving from place to place in Western Canada throughout the Depression. Lloyd was seventeen years old and living in Vancouver, British Columbia when war was declared. He was already in the militia so he lied about his age and was mobilized in October, joining the 58th Heavy Battery of the Royal Canadian Artillery in Vancouver. He was sent to England with the Second Canadian Division and had been in England for over a year when he met Olive that night at the Lyceum.

Lloyd was smitten with this beautiful English woman, but it took him most of the evening to gather the courage to ask her to dance. When it was time to leave the trains were no longer running so Lloyd and his friend walked miles in seeing Olive and her friend home to Edgeware and then back to where they were staying.

From then on, Lloyd and another friend, Bob Payne, became frequent visitors to the house on Lawrence Crescent. By the end of six weeks he proposed to Olive. Despite all the reasons not to – including a proposal from a British soldier – and concerns about her marrying a Canadian, she said yes. Apparently his 5ft 11in of charm, intelligence, sandy hair, and the blue-green eyes that always betrayed his feelings were enough to sway her. They were passionately in love – something that would never change.

It took several tries for the wedding to take place. The initial plan was revised when Olive learned she was three months older than Lloyd and, since he was under twenty-one, he needed written permission from his father to get married.

Then, early in 1942, while stationed on the south coast of England, Lloyd was badly injured by a parachute bomb. He spent most of the next year in hospital undergoing reconstructive surgery. The surgeons did marvellous work and, even though he always had a long, deep scar on the side of his neck, his looks were not affected. Interestingly, throughout his entire recuperation he never saw what he looked like, as most reflective surfaces were denied him. Even the water was coloured so as not to reflect his image.

During this period Lloyd's division took part in the tragic raid on Dieppe. It was a painful episode for him and Olive had to console his sense of guilt at not being with his buddies while at the same time exulting that he had not been able to take part. When it was over there weren't many survivors from amongst those Lloyd had enlisted with in Vancouver.

Once Lloyd was completely recuperated they planned to marry in early April but Olive's emergency appendectomy caused another delay. They were finally married on 8 May 1943 at All Saints' Queensbury Church in Stanmore, Middlesex. With all the delays, family and neighbours had ample time to save ration coupons for Olive to have a church wedding complete with white gown, veil, bouquets, and wedding cake.

1944 was an eventful year for several reasons. Olive found out she was expecting their first child and was very happy, but it was not an easy pregnancy and she nearly lost the baby a couple of times. In February there had been many raids and Olive was on fire watch. On one occasion the damage was particularly heavy and the next night she was working by candlelight. Lloyd had at least one or two days leave most months to come to London. The first week of March they enjoyed a seven-day leave together, but in her little diary for 1944 it is evident from her cryptic notes of 'No Letter' that any time too many days went by without hearing from Lloyd caused her great concern. By this time she realized the pregnancy was not going well, particularly at the end of May and beginning of June. On 3 June Lloyd unexpectedly showed up for a few hours. He would have known what lay ahead and was probably just coming to say his goodbyes but he was absent without leave and before he returned Olive had a row with him which she regretted and wrote to him immediately.

Then on D-Day, 6 June, she noted in large, bold, capital letters that the invasion of Europe had started. She wrote to Lloyd that day, expressing her love and belief in him. He carried that letter in his soldier's service and pay book until the end of the war, and it was still there when it was found in his bedside drawer after he died in May 1996 – as always close to his heart.

> 6 June, 1944 2 pm. My darling Lloyd. This is just a short note to wish you 'god speed' … I heard the news at 1 p.m. and if you are not already fighting I guess it won't be long before you are … take care of yourself and I pray you will be with me Safe & Sound. I love you my darling with all my heart & soul …

Lloyd served throughout northwest Europe as a gunner, dispatch rider, and signaller. He was repatriated to Canada and discharged from the service in Vancouver in August 1945. He was fortunate to find employment with a hardware firm in the city but his heart wasn't in it. When Olive arrived in Halifax nearly nine months later with their one-and-a-half-year-old son Paul, Lloyd decided to join the Air Force, hoping for better opportunities in the military than civilian life.

He was immediately sent off for training and Olive was on her own with a toddler in a strange city without family or financial resources. Like many veterans, Lloyd had spent his entire adult life as a dependent of the Canadian Army and he didn't understand that he had to provide housing and food for his wife and child.

Olive contacted her parents for assistance and they sent her what they were allowed by the British government and offered to pay her passage back to England. She declined, and instead she contacted the Red Cross. They set her up with some food and financial assistance and contacted Lloyd, making him understand the necessity of sending her a percentage of his pay.

Lloyd's initial posting was to Vancouver where their second child, Trevor, was born in 1948. Olive learned from her neighbours and new friends how to preserve vegetables, fruit, salmon and meat. She was an accomplished seamstress and knitter and she made clothes for herself and the boys. It was during this time that Lloyd completed his high school by correspondence. He also enrolled in the Air Force Administrative School which lead to him becoming an Administrative Supervisor and eventually a Sergeant. In September 1950 he was transferred to Fort Nelson, BC.

In a pattern that would continue for most of the fifteen years he served in the Air Force, Lloyd was sent on ahead and Olive followed later with all their belongings and two small boys. Among the highlights was being introduced to the -50°F temperatures and snow drifts of northern BC in winter.

In the mid-1950s they returned to Europe and lived in Trier, Germany. Lloyd was assigned to NATO's Fourth Allied Tactical Air Force and as the first Canadians on station their billet was a suite in Hotel Luxemburgerhof. As there was no school for the boys to attend, Olive had to arrange for schoolwork to be sent from Canada by correspondence. She was also able to see her family in England a few more times – something which would happen rarely once they settled back in Canada.

After two lovely years in Europe, they were transferred to the RCAF base in Saskatoon, Saskatchewan. It was definitely a change from Europe to the small prairie city and took some getting used to but Saskatoon turned out to be Lloyd's last posting. With a new baby girl in the family, Lloyd left the military and found civilian employment as an office manager for a commercial laundry company. A year later, he began a decade of working for a Moving and Storage Company. Over the course of the next twenty-five years he worked in remote northern mining camps and would spend more time away then he did at home but it was good money and more than he could dream of making in the city.

Olive understood that this was the way it was going to be and made the best of her life in Canada. She liked to host afternoon tea once a week for the neighbourhood ladies and at least once a month she invited two of the families with whom they were closest to supper. She would set up the kitchen table with her best linen, trying very hard to create gentility in the life around her.

She encouraged her children to read, to ask questions, and research the answers. She believed that her deep faith in God was best demonstrated by living it and she performed many acts of charity – most anonymously. She baked, canned, and cooked for her family. It was a family joke to say that you would never be without food at the Cochrane's but you might starve while choosing what to eat. On Saturdays, after *Hockey Night in Canada* ended, Olive would join the family to watch a variety show while sitting on Dad's lap in his big armchair.

Olive and Lloyd had a happy life together until his first stroke when he was fifty-seven years old. Over the next seventeen years, Lloyd would have several medical emergencies – strokes, blood clots, and double bypass surgery through which Olive would nurse him. In May 1996, six days after their fifty-third anniversary, Lloyd made it home from the library just long enough to tell Olive he loved her and then his heart stopped. In the drawer beside his bed were his soldier's service and pay book with the letter Olive had written to him on D-Day tucked away in the folds.

Olive passed away in April 1999.

This story was contributed by Michelle Rusk, Olive and Lloyd Cochrane's daughter. Michelle has all her parents' memorabilia, including photos, love letters, diaries, and telegrams as well as correspondence and archival documents that were sent to her mother by the Canadian Wives Bureau prior to her departure to Canada in 1946.

5

Military Service

British Women and Work During the Second World War

- Some 7.5 million British women in total were mobilized during the Second World War.
- Of these 450,000 were conscripted into the armed forces.
- By 1943, 375,000 women were in the Civil Defence comprising a quarter of its strength, while 36,000 drove ambulances and 73,000 were in the Auxiliary and National Fire Services.
- Some 80,000 women were in the Women's Land Army by 1944.
- The vast majority were engaged on essential war work and fire-watching.

Source: Women and War – Imperial War Museum (www.iwm.org.uk)

The Second World War marked the first time in history that British women were conscripted for service in the armed forces and on the home front.[1]

Whether they served in uniform or toiled away in munitions factories, worked in the Women's Land Army or drove ambulances, the wartime work experiences of British women who married Canadian servicemen and then came to Canada as War Brides is an inextricable part of who they are and how Canadians perceive them today.

While Canadian women were no strangers to war work themselves, it was under entirely different circumstances and nowhere near the numbers that transpired in Britain. At the height of the war effort in 1943 seven-and-a-half million British women were mobilized.[2] Of these, 450,000 were conscripted into the three branches of the armed forces, including the Auxiliary Territorial Services (ATS), the Women's Royal Naval Services (WRNS), and the Women's Auxiliary Air Force (WAAF).[3]

In addition to those who signed up for military service, British women did all manner of work under all types of conditions, day and night, in every type of employment requiring the lowest to the highest skill set: in banks and offices, in chemical and munitions factories, transportation and agriculture, health and communications, chemical and vehicle building, in every workplace where a man could be released to join the military you could find a woman who was trained to do his job, and she was doing it well.

Exceptions were made for married women and those with children at home, who were caring for the elderly and infirm and even conscientious objectors. But in the main, the number of British women involved in the war effort increased over the course of the war years as the needs of a country fighting for its very survival evolved.

At the beginning of the war and even into 1941 and 1942 the Ministry of Labour's efforts to have all eligible women voluntarily register for work did not have the results the government was looking for. Recruitment drives in 1941 and '42 emphasised the need for women to register and volunteer for war work. But a review of registration in August 1941 found that of two million women registered, only 500,000 had been interviewed and of these, only 87,000 had been put to work in the Women's Auxiliary Services or munitions.[4] There was resistance from those who were caught between contributing to the war effort and traditional role expectations of girls and women which kept them in the domestic sphere.

In the 1940s it was generally expected that unmarried women would live at home until marriage. Depending on the circumstances in the home, the family's social condition or class and the number of children, most girls over fourteen who were finished with their schooling would enter the work-force and contribute their earnings to the family's upkeep.

The kinds of jobs they had varied; women from middle- and upper-class families who had gone to school beyond age fourteen may have had the option to work or not, but most girls after age fourteen had to work and found employment in the traditionally female sector, such as an apprentice in a clothing shop or bakery, as a domestic servant or some other form of work that was easily recognizable as belonging to the women's sphere.

In addition to paid work, most girls performed unpaid household work such as taking care of younger siblings and shopping, which in wartime Britain meant standing in line for hours in queues that only grew in size as rationing increased.

In the case of married women without children or elderly relatives to care for, the Ministry of Labour made it difficult to refuse work and even denied unemployment benefits to those who defied the rules. For some women, reluctant fathers and husbands – many who were in the service themselves – fed the fear that home life would disintegrate if wives and daughters left the protection of the family home.

Nonetheless, pressure on single and married women to volunteer for registration mounted and in the end, the needs of industry and the military for workers predominated over the personal wishes of women and the men in their lives.[5]

At the time, it may have seemed a huge sacrifice for single young women to leave their parents and siblings for military service or essential work in factories, but for those who took the leap – and the majority did – the rewards have lasted a lifetime.

Doris (Field) Lloyd of Halifax, Yorkshire, was seventeen years old and 'green as grass' when she joined the WAAF in January 1940. Her story of the transition from a comfortable middle-class home to surviving one of the biggest air raids of the Battle of Britain is typical of many War Brides who were in the military when they met their Canadian husbands.

In this chapter we will meet several women whose military service is one of the uniquely British experiences that is part of their Canadian identity today. More than sixty years later, they are extremely proud of their work in the armed forces, and so too are their Canadian children and grandchildren who take great pride in knowing the War Bride in their family made a contribution to winning the Second World War.

She Went Ahead and Did it Anyway
Doris (Field) Lloyd

Doris (Field) Lloyd was born in Halifax, Yorkshire in 1922. She and her daughter came to Plaster Rock, New Brunswick in November, 1944 while her husband was still fighting in Italy.

In the summer of 1940 German bombers rained devastation on southern England, targeting air bases that formed the nucleus of Britain's air defence. Doris Field of Halifax, Yorkshire joined the WAAF in January 1940 when she was just seventeen years old. She was at the Kenley Air Force Base south of London when it was attacked on 18 August 1940.

> It was a gorgeous day. I remember because it was so hot with our uniforms on. We had just started lunch and they were suddenly on top of us. We ran to find cover. I remember looking into the sky and seeing so many bombers, the sky was black. They came in waves and the German fighters would come down low and machine-gun anyone who was running. We managed to get into safety. When they let us out the whole place was on fire. It was an awful sight. The next day the Germans started all over again. We got bombed every night for months after that as the Germans made their way to London and to other airfields in cities throughout England.

Doris was raised in Halifax, Yorkshire and graduated from Battinson Road School at age fourteen. Her mother wanted her to learn how to sew so she arranged for Doris to get a job making dresses and aprons in a little shop close by.

'It didn't appeal to me at all,' says Doris. 'After three months of making button holes I had enough of that!' She found another job as a grocery clerk at Redmands Grocery that was located in an arcade in the centre of town. She was much happier working with the public and stayed with Redmands until January 1940 when she volunteered to join the WAAF.

Doris and a friend at Redmands Grocery wanted to do something more exciting than selling fruit and vegetables so they decided to join the Air Force. Her friend was nineteen years old so she could do what she wanted but Doris was only seventeen and you were supposed to be eighteen to join up. Doris was determined so she went ahead and did it anyways – her mother figured they would send Doris back home so she didn't do anything to stop her; besides, the Phony War was on and it wasn't like Doris's life was in danger.

As it turned out, Doris passed the examination with flying colours – but her friend failed – so when the time came for basic training Doris was all alone for the first time in her life. How things were to change in the next eight months.

Doris joined a group of twenty-five women at the Uxbridge training centre outside of London. The first order of the day was to outfit the new recruits in uniform – bra, knickers (which were jokingly referred to as 'blackouts'), shoes, stockings, dress, hat, shirt, greatcoat, and tie. Everything that could be worn had to be military issue. Next they were ordered to parcel the clothes they had arrived with and send it back home. Then the young women were sent back to barracks and Doris says she can always remember sitting on her bed in the barracks that day: 'Everybody was busy changing and this girl was sitting on the cot next to mine and she had nothing on the top. I was embarrassed. I'd never seen a woman with no clothes on before!'

The next day the female recruits had to learn how to march. Doris says the Drill Sergeant was a bully who spared nobody's feelings, but she figures he must have known what he was doing. The first thing he said was, 'If anybody feels faint, step out because if you faint you lay where you fall.' That's when Doris started wishing she was home with her mother, but it was too late to start crying for mommy now. One week later she had blisters on top of blisters but she sure knew how to march!

At the end of a grand total of one week's training the recruits were divided up and sent to different places where they were needed. Doris and six others ended up at Kenley Air Force Base where she stayed for two years. They were billeted in private homes in the area that had been taken over by the military. Some of the billets were huge, beautiful homes with tennis courts and swimming pools – with no water of course – but they didn't stay long in any one place and were moved around a lot.

During her first three months at Kenley, Doris met a young British airman named David Foster who was putting in time at the pay office. David was her first real boyfriend but he was transferred to another facility and although they continued to correspond with each other, he was killed in action in the early stages of the Battle of Britain. Soon, Doris had her own harrowing experience with German air power when Kenley was bombed that August and she barely escaped with her life.

At one point early in 1941 Doris's mother and her four-year-old sister Pauline came to Caterham to visit for a few days and they stayed with a family there. Doris was used to the bombing and didn't really think much of it but her mother and Pauline spent most of the time under a table in the dining room and it was quite an ordeal for them.

'Night after night and even during the daytime, you'd see a German plane up in the sky and one of our fellows chasing it,' Doris explains, 'but my mother up in Yorkshire, she hadn't really experienced the bombing and they were really frightened.'

In 1941 the Canadians arrived next door in Caterham and Doris's life quickly changed. 'There were West Novies, the Carleton York, a French outfit, another one from Saskatchewan and others from Ontario,' Doris recalls.

> They were billeted in these beautiful homes in Caterham and I became friends with one soldier who was from Halifax, Nova Scotia. He wasn't my boyfriend or anything like that, but he really wanted to see Halifax, Yorkshire, so I invited him to stay at my parents' house where he was made most welcome.

The Canadians Doris met were different from British soldiers: 'They weren't afraid to ask you out,' says Doris. 'When they were doing route marches they would whistle and call out to you and we would giggle.'

Doris met Sgt Ralph Lloyd of the Carleton York Regiment at a dance in Caterham in July 1941. He asked her to dance and after it was over walked her home. Ralph was born in England and had emigrated to Canada with his family in 1919 when he was just a baby. He was from a small village called Plaster Rock, New Brunswick where he lived with his widowed mother, two sisters and a brother who was also stationed overseas. Ralph was musical and he played the saxophone. He and Doris hit it off and were together for nearly five months when he proposed.

Doris wrote to her mother to tell her that she was going to get engaged. At the time, you couldn't get married until you were twenty-one without your parents' permission so Doris's mother came back to Caterham to meet Ralph and she spent another week 'hiding under the table', Doris says with a laugh.

After all the permissions were obtained and the forms filled out, Doris and Ralph were married on 11 December 1941 in Caterham, four days after the bombing of Pearl Harbour. They spent their honeymoon in London with a friend. 'I suppose we didn't have enough bombing so we had to go to London,' Doris says.

Doris stayed in the WAAF and they were both moved to different places, she to Andover for a couple of months and then on to Cornwall, and Ralph all over the countryside training. They only saw each other infrequently when they both managed to get a leave at the same time.

In January 1943 Doris found out she was pregnant so she was released from her WAAF duties. Ralph was in Seaford teaching in a school for British officers so he rented a place and she joined him there. In March 1943 when she was six months pregnant, the regiment was moved to Scotland in preparation for the invasion of Sicily so Doris had to return to her family in Halifax. Ralph couldn't get away from Scotland to see her before the baby was born but he phoned her every night. On 17 June 1943 Doris's mother sent Ralph a telegram announcing the birth of a healthy baby girl, Anne. Shortly thereafter he was shipped to Sicily and it was two years before he saw his wife and little girl.

Doris travelled by ship with her sixteen-month-old daughter Anne on the *Ile de France* in November 1944, arriving in Canada seven long months before Ralph was repatriated. The ocean journey was frightening as German U-boats were prowling the ocean waters and they had to zigzag to avoid detection. Compared to future transports of Canadian War Brides there was little or no help with the children from any organization such as the Red Cross so the War Brides were on their own, seasick or not.

Doris couldn't have arrived in Plaster Rock, New Brunswick at a worse time of the year. The winter was just beginning to settle in and the dirt roads were covered with snow and slush. In the spring the roads turned to a sea of mud. The cold was bone-chilling and there wouldn't have been much to do other than visit with relatives and neighbours.

Plaster Rock was a small lumber town of 1,200 people in an isolated part of northwestern New Brunswick without theatres or a library. Besides the shock of adapting to rural life where outdoor toilets and wood stoves were the norm, Doris had to get used to the fact that Ralph's mother and two sisters had moved into a very small, two-bedroom house during the war with no room for another adult and child. After three months of living in these crowded conditions, Doris moved up the road to her brother-in-law and his wife's house where she and Anne stayed until Ralph returned to Canada by hospital ship in July 1945.

When Doris saw her husband again after more than two years of separation, he wasn't the same man she knew in England. His nerves were shattered and the Military Cross he earned in Italy for 'gallant and distinguished service in action' didn't make life any easier as she tried to adjust to life in a small town where everyone knew her business.

Ralph had nightmares and recurring bouts with malaria over the years. There was no help for Second World War veterans like there is today so they just had to cope on their own. Instead, he sought the fraternity of his army buddies at the Legion and spent more time there than he did at home with his wife and daughter. For most of their married life Ralph only had seasonal employment as a Fisheries Officer from May to November so Doris made her own work. She bought a small restaurant and when that closed she worked for several years at the local grocery store and later at the Liquor Commission.

By the mid-1970s, their daughter Anne was married and raising her own two children in Saint John. Doris heard about a group of War Brides in Saskatchewan who had organized themselves into an association, the first one in Canada. She contacted Gloria Brock, one of the group's leaders, and went about establishing the New Brunswick War Brides Association, becoming its founding president. The War Brides organization played a big part in Doris's life over the past twenty-five years. She has attended reunions all over the country and even one of Overseas War Brides in England in 1986.

Ralph died in 1997 and at age eighty-five. Doris stays closer to home these days but the memories of her life in England are as vivid today as they were more than sixty years ago. It took some adjusting to her new life in Canada and she certainly had her share of disappointments, but would she do it again?

'Definitely,' she says. 'It's the best country in the world to live in and I wouldn't want to be anywhere else.'

Postscript: Doris Lloyd still lives in Plaster Rock.

Six Weeks and Sixty-Four Years
Irene (Parry) Clark

Irene (Parry) Clark was born in Ashington, Northumberland. In 1941, although in a reserved occupation, she joined the WAAF as she had two brothers in the Army in North Africa and another brother in the RAF. Little did Irene know that in just over a year, she would meet a handsome Canadian and get married!

I was posted to RAF Station Cranwell, Lincolnshire with the WAAF and worked in the Dominion Sergeants' Mess. I really enjoyed myself and found that if you did your assigned duties without a fuss, you got on well with the higher authorities and stayed out of trouble.

I came from a large, close-knit family so my service at Cranwell opened a new and exciting world for me. Social affairs were very well organized at the station, with a cinema and dances. I was in daily contact with NCOs from England, Canada, Australia, New Zealand, the West Indies, and other Commonwealth countries, France, Poland and even Turkey. One of the French NCOs was a French Count. We also had a single Chinese sailor training as a wireless operator.

When I had been there for over one year, two Canadians arrived for Wireless Operator (Air) training. One of them was John Clark. Within a very short time of meeting John he proposed to me and we began to talk about a late summer wedding. His commission caught up with him just then. He was granted leave immediately and we decided to get married. The Flight Sergeant in the Orderly Room was a bit of a romantic and she spoke to the CO on my behalf so I got five days' leave to coincide with John's.

The race was on. We were issued ration coupons, travel vouchers and new uniforms – one a Pilot Officer's uniform from the camp tailor shop which someone else had ordered, but not picked up. It fitted John perfectly. When we set out from Cranwell to catch the train to Newcastle-on-Tyne, I suddenly remembered I hadn't even told my parents about John, let alone that I was engaged.

As soon as we got off the train at Grantham, I sent a telegram to them: 'Coming home to be married.' I would have liked to have seen the look on their faces when that telegram arrived!

Later, I asked Mum, 'What did Dad say?' She replied, 'He said, whose heart is she going to break now?' Once they caught their breath however, they prepared for our arrival.

We had to get a marriage licence and arrange for the church. We met with Father Smith, a young Roman Catholic priest who was assisting the elderly parish priest. He needed to get permission from the Bishop to perform the ceremony for three reasons: 1) we were the first couple he would marry, 2) John was a Catholic from another country and didn't belong to his parish, and 3) I was an Anglican.

While the priest was doing what he had to do, my mother raised the question, 'What are you going to do about a white dress?' Right then our plan of me wearing my uniform was blown out of John's mind. He wanted me in white with a veil. Then came the scramble for a dress, which was arranged with the help of a family friend who always knew how to get coupons.

Meanwhile, Dad booked taxis for the wedding day. Because it was war-time we could only cater for fifty guests and the wedding cake wasn't iced due to sugar rationing. Dad also ordered wine and other beverages, got a pianist to play for us and another friend with a beautiful tenor voice to sing. My cousin's wife, Jean Parry, was my matron of honour, my little sister Lillian was my bridesmaid and our next door neighbor and friend, Tommy Hetherington, was John's best man. Our family friend who helped get my dress handed me a gift and said she would like me to wear it when I got married as it was special to her. It was a lovely silver necklace of maple leaves; John and I were very touched.

At the reception there was a knock on the door and when my Dad answered he said, 'Well, you better come in.' A group of small children who lived nearby entered and sang 'O Canada'. It was such a lovely touch but we had no idea where they learned the song; everyone was deeply moved. The reception and ceilidh went on until three in the morning. John still says he never had so much fun at a wedding as he did at ours.

I was discharged on compassionate grounds from the Royal Air Force in May 1943. John was posted to an Operational Unit shortly afterwards and I returned to my parents' home for the duration of the war. At the end of the year our first child was born. Peter was much loved and spoiled by his granddad who took him out in the pram for his daily walks. It was a good time for all of us, as my mum was able to teach me a lot about taking care of babies and young children, which stood me in good stead when the others arrived.

In early 1945 I received notice that my name had come up for transport to Canada. John was headed to Canada for a one-month leave and he felt Peter and I should go as we had no idea how much longer the war would last. So in February, Peter and I sailed for Canada on the RMS *Aquitania*.

The ship docked early on the morning of 12 February at Pier 21 in Halifax, Nova Scotia. We disembarked the next day and Peter and I boarded a train for the 800-mile journey to Montreal, Quebec. It was a long train ride but I have few memories of it as I was so tired from the sea voyage. John met us in Montreal and we took the train to Ottawa, Ontario where I met his widowed mother and large family. John had to return to England to his new posting four days later so Peter and I settled into life in Ottawa. Over the next seven months John and I wrote to each other frequently and I sent him pictures of Peter as he grew up with his cousins. Time passed very slowly as I missed John and my family.

In September John returned to Ottawa, was discharged and we restarted our life together as a family. He returned to the civil service and life proceeded as it did for most married couples: work, our first house, bringing up children and handling day to day life. By 1951 we had four children; Peter, Anne, Ian and Christine.

My father had died before our last child was born and at that time I was unable to go to his funeral. Five more years passed and I decided it was about time my children saw their family in England. After some discussion with other British War Brides, I decided to organize a group charter to England. I looked into all matters related to organizing these trips and contacted local radio stations and newspapers. I was inundated with phone calls from War Brides.

The Canadian Overseas War Brides Association was born and I was elected founding President. Joyce Lalonde, our Club Secretary, was a legal secretary with the largest law firm in Ottawa and she assisted me in the legal matters and other issues that arose from time to time for the organization. Through her efforts we were able to receive a Dominion Charter for the Association. With the close support and time spent together, Joyce and I became firm friends for the rest of our lives.

We negotiated with the Arosa Line for two boat charters and were also able to obtain a charter from Flying Tigers Airlines. In May 1956 over 200 women and their children went to Britain, including several War Brides from the First World War. My four children and I went to England on the *Arosa Sun* and about mid-voyage, we passed one of our sister ships, the *Arosa Star*. There were whistles blowing and shouts from the passengers greeting each other.

We landed at Southampton after a seven-day voyage. It was a thrill to see England again. Several of the War Brides said, 'Let Mrs Clark and her children disembark first.'

As we disembarked, an old lady hugged me and said 'God bless you because if it wasn't for what you did, I would never have seen my daughter again.'

My sister Ethel, my mother and I stayed up all night drinking pots of tea and talking. Ethel's husband Fred tried to keep up with us but couldn't. When he awoke at 7 a.m. he said, 'Are you lot still up?' We talked all the next day and night as there was so much to catch up on that couldn't always be said in letters.

In September, after our full and happy visit, we embarked at Southampton and sailed for Quebec. Nearing Newfoundland, we saw a huge iceberg and later that night, we witnessed the most spectacular display of the Northern

Lights I have ever seen or heard; the colours were just like a rainbow and the atmosphere was crackling with the noise. John met us in Quebec and we were all happy to see him after four months apart.

By 1966 the children were grown up and I started to think about what I could do. I had always wanted to be a nurse from my childhood, but the opportunity had always evaded me. One day I saw an ad in the Ottawa newspaper for a Registered Nursing Assistants course. My husband said to me, 'Here is your chance to fulfill your dream, so go for it and I'll help however I can.'

I started my training at the Ottawa Civic Hospital School in early January, 1967. Out of a class of forty-six students, forty-one had just graduated from high school. After I finished the course I worked at the hospital for a number of years and enjoyed the experience very much.

From the early 1970s until just recently, John and I volunteered a lot of our time with the prison ministries in Ottawa, visiting the Kingston area prisons. Lately I've been spending time researching my genealogy on the Internet and travelling. I am also getting involved again in War Bride activities which I enjoy very much as I am writing my memoirs.

John and I celebrated our sixty-fourth wedding anniversary this year. We have four wonderful, successful children, eleven grandchildren and eight great-grandchildren. We only knew each other for six weeks when we married, and we have weathered many storms, but we've come through just fine.

Postscript: In 2004, Irene received the Queen's Golden Jubilee Medal in recognition of her work with the Canadian Overseas War Brides Association and her 30 years in Prison Ministry. On Remembrance Day 2006, she was invited to place a wreath at Canada's National War Memorial in honour of all War Brides.

I Never Dreamed I Would Leave England
Pauline (Portsmouth) Worthylake

Pauline (Portsmouth) Worthylake was born in 1923 in North London, England. She joined the WAAF and worked with balloon command.

In 1942 I decided to help the war effort by joining the Women's Auxiliary Air Force (WAAF). My father was wounded during the First World War and believed that the services were no place for his daughter. When he joined up at sixteen they never checked his age, but I was eighteen and didn't need my parents' approval.

There were only certain trades open to women at that time. I didn't want to spend my time behind a desk so I volunteered for balloon command, knowing this was an outdoor job. Up until that time men had serviced the balloon sites, but now they were needed elsewhere.

These ungainly hydrogen-filled gas bags were 620 feet long and 25 feet in diameter. They had a maximum effective altitude of 5,000 feet and were dotted randomly over targets to be defended, such as armament factories and important shipping. The balloons were intended as a deterrent against low-flying air craft and to prevent dive bombers pressing their attacks to low altitudes.

If an aircraft struck the cable, which was very rarely, explosive cutters severed the wire at the top and the bottom, allowing the bomber to carry the cable away. Attached to either end of the cable was an eight-foot-diameter drogue parachute. When fully opened, it exerted a combined drag of 7 tons at 200 miles per hour, sufficient to stop an aircraft in its tracks and send it spinning out of control.

The main balloon-defended areas were in south east England. The first three months I was sent up north for training. Then my first real posting was in the East End of London where the Blitz was really on. Our crew numbered about twenty women housed in an almost empty house. We were up every night raising the balloon when expecting German planes that were bombing every night, and lowering the balloon when our own aircraft came chasing them. We slept during the day. Our beds consisted of three straw-filled biscuits – mattresses – which were hard and uncomfortable but we were all so tired that we slept anyway.

My next posting was near Bristol, protecting a large suspension bridge which connected the city with the outlying areas. It was quieter in Bristol and by this time I had attained the rank of sergeant, in charge of the whole unit of twenty or so girls and a corporal. I was only twenty years old.

My next move was to Glasgow in Scotland where we worked at balloon sites to protect shipping. One winter was enough – it was very cold. By this time, the enemy were able to bomb successfully from any height so balloons were no longer needed. I was sent to a practice bombing range in Brancaster, Norfolk on the West Coast.

An old ship which had ended up on the rocks was used as a target for American pilots to practice bombing skills. Two quadrants on land, one on the left and one on the right, each manned by a WAAF, took readings each time a bomb was dropped. The results were sent to the pilots noting how close they were to the target.

Norfolk is also where I met my Canadian. Grant was on a rest period. He had just finished one tour of operations as a navigator. He was one of the officers in charge of our group, which is how we met. He was an officer and I was a non-commissioned sergeant so we saw each other whenever we could, although we were actually forbidden to do so.

I never dreamed I would leave England, although I did think I would marry sometime. Grant, in turn, had been asked by friends before he left Canada if he was going to find an English girl like his father did. His reply: 'A Canadian girl is good enough for me.'

We were engaged and decided to wait and get married in Canada, but then the war ended and Grant was being repatriated in two weeks so we changed our minds. We were married within forty-eight hours in a church, both of us in uniform. We went to St Ives in Cornwall for our honeymoon, a sleepy little fishing village on the West Coast.

Grant left right away. I had to wait nine months before I could get on a ship and since I was no longer in the service I found a job as a cashier in a shop. While I waited to come to Canada, Grant's mother and his sisters wrote and explained all about the part of Nova Scotia where I would be living. Grant's mother had been an English War Bride at the end of the First World War. Her mother was still living in Essex and she had two aunts near London so it was comforting to meet some of Grant's relatives. Later those aunts visited us in Nova Scotia so we renewed our friendship with them.

I finally got a spot on the ship the *Ile de France*, leaving Southampton in March and arriving in Halifax on 5 April. The ship was filled with wives and children, and members of the Army. We slept in three-tier bunks; it was really crowded. I don't remember a thing about the food. It was so rough that the china slid off the tables. Lots of people got seasick, including me.

I remember talking with a soldier and he asked where I was going. He didn't think Nova Scotia was such a great place; he must have been from out west!

I will never forget my first sight of Nova Scotia, straggly trees and snow, and oh, so cold. All I had with me were clothes fit for spring. We docked in Halifax and finally I saw Grant and his sister Juanita. I remember seeing Juanita joking with Grant, pointing at the ugliest girls and saying, 'Is that her? Is that her?' When I came down the gang plank he met me halfway and hugged me so tightly that I felt both of my underslip straps break.

We stayed at the Nova Scotian hotel for three days, getting to know one another again. I could not help noticing how large the cars were in comparison to the ones in England; they seemed huge. Then we were off to New Glasgow to meet all the family. Their house looked so big compared to the house I had grown up in. It was such a warm welcome. The family had a shower and a wedding cake to make up for the one that we didn't have when we were married. There was also a shower by the neighbours. I had never heard of wedding showers before. These were parties with presents for the bride that usually take place before the wedding. We received so many towels that it was a long time before I bought any.

Grant had left school and was working when war broke out. He was a good student, but his father was unemployed so Grant had to help support the family. With government assistance for veterans after the war, Grant went back to school and took grade eleven and then grade twelve by mail.

Over the years I grew to love cooking and I think that I am a fairly good at it. However, I remember my first attempts. Grant was in school and his mother had returned to England to visit her family. I was left to look after Grant's father, his younger sister Mavis and a boarder. I remember making baked beans without a recipe and the beans turned out black and hard – no soaking and too much molasses.

At Christmas time I roasted a turkey in a wood stove. When I pulled it from the oven to baste it, the turkey landed on the floor that I had just scrubbed. I picked it up and popped it back in the pan, swearing Grant's family to secrecy. By the time my mother-in-law came back – eight months later – I was a much better cook and Grant's father loved my wholewheat biscuits. Mrs Worthylake hardly got into the house before she asked me if the fat on the ceiling was where I had dropped the turkey. Grant's dad had told her the story!

Grant successfully completed high school and he was awarded an entrance scholarship into Dalhousie University in Halifax. Later he received a scholarship for medicine. We lived in a small trailer at the end of Barrington and Duffus Street on land that Dalhousie rented for its students. Grant's cousin built the trailer for $500 (Cdn). It was only eleven feet long and seven feet wide.

We had our first baby in 1950 and made room in the trailer. Then in 1952, expecting another child, we moved into cockroach-infested apartments in the same area. Every few months all students had to vacate the apartments while the apartments were sprayed with obnoxious fumes and an oily liquid which was all to be cleaned afterwards by us.

Neither of us had families with money so I remember we ate a lot of soup. Grant was in the habit of picking up groceries for me on the way home from the university. One day he arrived with a huge soup bone. When I asked about it he said he got it at the usual place. I made stock out of the bone but it would not gel. I made the soup but somehow it did not taste as good as usual. We were eating dinner at our tiny table and I was trying to eat the soup. Finally I told Grant the soup was just not right. He nearly choked as he admitted that it was a horse bone.

When we finally left those apartments we shook everything twice before packing; we were so scared in case we took a cockroach with us.

By 1954 Grant had graduated with an MD and I was expecting again. We had not yet decided where we wanted to live, although we were sure we would get a job, so Grant covered a practice in Kennetcook, a picturesque little town outside of Halifax, for a year to help out a friend who was graduating.

Grant always loved the Annapolis Valley of Nova Scotia so when we heard of a practice opening up in Kentville we came to live here very happily. We brought up six lovely children and I learned to do so many things that I am sure I would not have done had I continued to live in England. Today, I am involved with volunteer organizations like the Historical Society and I have been painting for many years – something that I would never have done in England. I paint with acrylics, mainly flowers and nature scenes, and have even exhibited my artwork and sold a few pieces.

Nova Scotia has been good to me. I had a very happy marriage and a wonderful husband. We were married fifty-seven years and I only wish it could have been more.

Postscript: Pauline Worthylake has eight grandchildren. She still lives in Kentville, Nova Scotia.

Remember Me to Dora
Dora (Adams) Addison

Dora Adams was born in Peckham, London in the closing days of the First World War. In 1942 she joined the WAAF and became a Leading Aircraftswoman (LACW).

Dora Adams was twenty-one years old when the Second World War began. She and her widowed mother lived in the upstairs of a house in London but bomb damage forced them out and they finally settled into a flat near Victoria Station which had a two-tiered shelter.

Victoria Station was a prime target so there were many nights of bombing. Being so close to the station, they knew when an alarm would be sounded before it happened because they could see and hear the big gun coming down the track. Dora spent months sleeping in the shelters: some were equipped with bunks, others, you brought your mattress down and slept, all lined up, a toilet at the end. Although the shelter wasn't one hundred percent safe, it protected people from the fires of the incendiary bombs.

Dora remembers the first night London received so many of these fire bombs that the city could be seen from the coast. One night a whole building came down except for one wall. In the morning, amongst the rubble, the mantle was still standing and a dress was hanging on a hanger. Another night, a fire truck had been sent to the station. All that was left was the truck ladder leaning against the building: the truck was completely burned up.

In December 1941 the National Service Act was passed to allow for conscription of British women between the ages of nineteen and thirty-one. Dora was working at a ladies clothing store and her employer argued that she was needed but it was no use. Within a month, she was conscripted and the department store had to find another employee.

Once called up you could choose where you wanted to serve. At first Dora thought she would like the Women's Land Army, but she decided on the Women's Auxiliary Air Force (WAAF). She was sent to Innsworth, Gloucester where she was outfitted and deloused, then it was on to Morecambe Bay, Lancaster where they listened to lectures and learned how to march properly. Dora trained as an equipment assistant and had to know everything from nails and airplanes to how to fill out forms and keep track of inventory. She graduated as a Leading Aircraftswoman (LACW).

As it so happens, Dora had a Canadian cousin from Toronto named Jack Adams who was in England with the Canadian Army. While Dora was training in Yorkshire, Jack had been bringing his three friends to see the family in London. On one trip home in 1943, Dora opened the door to see a Canadian named Ron Addison in her mother's flat. Ron was from Carberry, Manitoba and he had joined the Canadian Army in November 1941. Ron's training took him to Kitchener, Ontario where he met a whole new set of friends: one of them was Jack Adams.

Jack, Ron and his friends brought plenty of excitement to the Adams household. On one leave, Dora and her mother found the sink full of flowers.

They were afraid that the Canadians stole the flowers from the church but they learned that it was a neighbour's garden which had been raided. When the neighbour found out it was Canadians, he forgave them, knowing full well what lay ahead for these soldiers: 'They don't know what they're in for,' he said.

In July 1943 Jack and Ron went to Sicily where the invasion of Italy began. Jack and Dora wrote to each other and Dora would ask Jack to 'Say "hello" to Ron.' When Jack wrote back, Ron would say, 'Remember me to Dora.'

Finally Jack got fed up and told them both, 'Write your own letters!'

Letters were the only mode of communication and four months went by without a word from Ron. She assumed he lost interest until she received word from Ron's parents in Carberry, Manitoba. Had she heard from him? Dora was very worried until one day Ron just showed up on her doorstep. The reason he hadn't written? All letters were censored and he wasn't going to write knowing someone else would read it!

Shortly thereafter Ron asked Dora to marry and come with him to Canada.

'What about Mother?' she asked.

'She'll have to come, too,' was his reply.

Even though Dora was twenty-seven years old, she had to get her mother's permission and that of her top officer. Her letter of recommendation from Squadron Leader Kenneth Parkinson, Chaplain RAF, Air Ministry Unit, read:

> Dora has an 'excellent record in the WAAF and is admirably suited to be the wife of a Canadian, and is the right kind of girl to emigrate to Canada from the United Kingdom.'

In October 1945 Ron found out he was being shipped home. Dora quickly arranged a wedding for 8 November. The day arrived and two of Ron's friends showed up but Ron couldn't come because there was an outbreak of scabies at the camp. Everyone was called to say the wedding was postponed. Two hours later, Ron showed up and the wedding was back on. The newlyweds had a few days' leave before Ron went back to his unit and by Christmas he was back home in Manitoba.

It was June 1946 before Dora received notice that she could come to Canada. The good news was offset by the fact that her mother would not be allowed to travel on the War Bride ship. Dora was very upset and when she went to plead their case, the policy had been changed. Her mother could come.

In two weeks they sold everything in preparation for their trip to Canada. The *Queen Mary* brought a shipload of War Brides to Pier 21 in Halifax, Nova Scotia but instead of a cheery welcome, the first person they saw was a drunk on the dock in Halifax saying, 'Go home you brides, we don't need you here!'

The women going to the Maritimes got off first, and since Dora and her mother were headed out west they would be among the last to disembark. Dora remembers telling her mother, 'They sure must be religious here, the church bells are going all the time.' The next day, when it came time to board the train, she realized it was train bells she had been hearing.

On the *Queen Mary* they had been given very light rations, much as they were used to in wartime England. On the train they fed them full meals: 'As much meat in one meal as we'd had in a week in England, then cream pies with whipped cream for dessert,' says Dora. Their stomachs couldn't take it and many were violently sick, including Dora's mother who couldn't look at tomato juice for six months afterward.

Dora often wonders what happened to some of the women that she met on the train. The wife whose husband was shell shocked and did not want her to come. She was going to Saskatchewan by special request of the Red Cross in hopes that it might help him. Then there was the woman who never left her berth without being 'painted up to the nines'. She was going to a farm. Then, there was the very pregnant wife who was going to be dropped off in the middle of nowhere. She didn't know if anyone would be there to meet her.

Their trip on the *Queen Mary* had prepared them for life in Canada with lectures, geographical information, lessons on how the money system worked and differences in language. So when Dora and her mother got off the train in Winnipeg and were met by Ron's mother, they started putting that information into practice, asking questions about all that was new and interesting around them.

At first they rented rooms in a house in downtown Carberry. Then their first child, Tom, came along in 1948 so they bought their own home where their second child Shirley was born in 1949. In the summer Ron worked on cattle ranches and grain farms nearby, and in the winter he drew coal. In 1952 he found a full-time job with the Town of Carberry which kept him busy until he retired. Dora stayed home raising the children and their house was often full to the brim: besides her mother, whom they looked after almost to the time of her death, they also cared for Ron's father and for a period of time, his Aunt Flora.

Dora went back to England twice: in 1959 she had a summer-long visit with her mother and the two children, and once again with Ron many years later. In the fall of 2001, Ron and Dora Addison died within two weeks of each other. Their funeral cards showed them both in their service uniforms.

This article was based on a story by Gloria Mott, Ron and Dora Addison's niece.

She Preferred the Colour Blue
Lilian (Gibson) Olson

Lilian (Gibson) Olson was an only child, born in Dover, England, in 1922. She met her husband when she was based with the WAAF at Pershore.

Lilian Gibson finished school when she was fourteen so by the time the Second World War broke out she had been working as a nanny for several years. She decided to join the WAAF on the spur of the moment when she and her mother happened upon an RAF recruiting office while out shopping in Dover. She didn't fancy being a Land Army girl with their khaki uniforms, and since she was approaching the age of call up for home service, she decided to join the WAAF. She also preferred the colour blue.

The RAF said they needed cooks, so Lilian was immediately accepted and sent for training. She ended up at Pershore, near Stratford-upon-Avon, at an Operational Training Unit (OTU). The station trained bomber crews which often required late-night meals for nighttime bombing runs. Her main work was in the Airman's Mess which served up to 1,000 men, hence it was a big operation with a lot of shift work.

During this time she recognized that there were a small number of Canadian airmen with the RAF. These were radar mechanics recruited for the RAF but at the time were only identified as 'radio' men, as radar was highly secret during this period. Julien Olson, an Alberta-born son of Norwegian immigrants, was one of these Canadians.

Julien saw Lilian frequently when she was on server duty and he wanted to get acquainted with this particular WAAF but there seemed to be no opportunity – even though he got a nice smile when the line passed quickly by her food serving station. He considered himself a shy country boy at the time but that situation soon changed.

On Christmas Eve 1943, when operations ceased for the day, a party was organized in the Mess Hall. Four of the Canadians thought a better time would be had biking to the Red Heart Pub. On the way back to the station the group decided to drop in to the Mess Hall to see how the party was going. Being near curfew time most were leaving but the Canadians recognized some of the WAAF who were chatting so they went over to introduce themselves. One chap noticed some mistletoe hanging with other decorations and challenged Julien to kiss Lilian. It must have been the pub drinks, because before he knew it, he had her in his arms. After that, the two would greet each other whenever she served him meals. After a while, Julien got the courage to invite Lilian to go to the movies in Worcester.

As things happen in the military, they barely got to know each other when on 1 March 1944 Julien was posted to a Pathfinder Squadron near Bedford. They corresponded and an occasional forty-eight-hour pass allowed them to meet in London – or preferably Oxford, as London was then being bombarded by v1 and v2 rockets.

Julien faced a dilemma when Lilian asked him to meet her parents in York. He realized parental acceptance of the relationship was taking place and some sort of commitment would likely be expected if he accepted the invitation. He wanted Lilian to fully understand what she was getting herself into. He outlined the huge undertaking she would face and the hardships ahead as he planned to complete his education when discharged from the service. She was willing to take a chance on her Canadian radio man and they were married on 15 September 1945.

Shortly after the wedding, Julien received notice he would be repatriated to Canada in October. By then Lilian had obtained her discharge and she was able to see her husband off at Torquay on the South Coast where the troops were assembled for repatriation.

After he left, Lilian found out she was pregnant so she was given priority passage and sailed to Canada on the reconverted hospital ship *Letitia*, arriving in Halifax on 3 April 1946. Once in Halifax she boarded a War Bride train that dispersed passengers all across Canada. Lilian was one of fifteen War Brides heading 3,000 miles west to Calgary so she saw a lot of reunions en route. She left her small group in Winnipeg, however, because Julien was studying architecture at the University of Manitoba and she was able to get permission to detrain there for a couple of days.

Staying for any length in Winnipeg at that time was impossible as family accommodation was non-existent. Lilian continued westward to Calgary and was glad to be met by her two sisters-in-law, but the journey was not over yet. She was put on a local train and travelled to a small town called Carstairs, about one hour north of Calgary. There she was picked up by car and driven about ten miles west on country dirt roads. Spring thaw had taken place and a bridge was washed out, preventing the car from reaching the family farm which was a further five miles west. At this juncture Julien's father met her with a team of horses and a wagon to ford the creek and finish the trip.

Poor Lilian. She had to introduce herself to her in-laws but fortunately had no problems as they were happy to welcome her into the family. She took over her husband's empty bedroom and one thing that stayed with her was the soothing sound of the west breeze coming through the screened windows. It helped her to fall asleep. Alberta farms in 1946 were still quite primitive – no electricity, outdoor toilets, wood-burning stoves and lots of chores. But the food was plentiful, which was a great improvement over wartime military rations.

Lilian enjoyed helping out on the farm, especially feeding orphaned lambs that had arrived in the spring. It wasn't long before she was feeding her own child, a son Keith, who was born in early June. Baby bottles were kept cool in a container inside a spring-fed well which was the farm's only refrigerator. The night time feedings meant a nervous walk in the dark to retrieve a bottle. What made it even scarier was that her father-in-law warned her to watch out for bears. It was a while before she realized she was being teased. Even so, for a city girl, the night walk with strange country sounds must have been frightening.

In the autumn of 1946 Veteran's Affairs started constructing two-room cabins on the University of Manitoba campus which were available to rent by Canadian war veterans with families. Over the next three years a veteran's village grew up on the university grounds. Conditions were still primitive as the cabins were not insulated and were each heated with one small coal-burning stove that had a small oven on the side. You had to ensure your stove was properly supplied with coal at night, otherwise in the winter the water bucket would be iced over in the morning. Cooking was done on a two plate propane-fed burner and water was brought in from the ablutions building in the centre of the village.

For women like Lilian with military experience, life in the 'Circles', as the cabins were called, was easy to adjust to but for others it would have been a challenge. The single entrance doors were a disaster for keeping the cabins warm so the students used leftover lumber to build entrance porches which helped considerably. These porches were built large enough to hold a baby carriage and all the infants spent their afternoon naps in them in the frigid Winnipeg weather.

Graduation in 1949 saw the breakup of the veteran's village. Employment in western Canada had not yet built up steam so most students moved east, many to Ottawa, Ontario where the Federal government was greatly expanding its programmes to overcome prewar and wartime constraints. Julien found a job in Ottawa but since housing was still in short supply Lilian remained behind in Winnipeg with an aunt for a few months. This also allowed her to recover from giving birth to their second child, Dianne, in June 1949.

In September, Lilian and the two children joined Julien in Ottawa. A new life commenced, looking after the family and developing new friendships. It was an hour's ride from their home into downtown Ottawa by streetcar to the market. She enjoyed doing this on Saturday afternoons when Julien finished work at noon. She would spend that time ordering a week's supply of food and browse around the shops, then return home when the shops closed to find her supplies had been delivered and supper being readied.

In 1950 Lilian had another child Christine, and in March 1954 she went back to England for the first time since the war, taking her youngest for a one-month visit.

Lilian was never homesick in Canada. She found life a pleasant challenge and made friends easily. She never worked outside the home, was content to raise her children and get involved in her community. Having lived through the upheaval, bombing and rationing of the Second World War, she overcame minor difficulties as she met them and could manage with limited resources. And she coped with the loss of her mother and father even though she could not be with them at the end.

Lilian lost her eyesight in her sixties but she and Julien were still able to make a number of trips to England to visit cousins as well as trips to Norway to visit his relatives. When Julien retired the two of them would spend a month or more each year in Alberta to visit family. In May 1994 they had planned a trip to England but two months before departure she became ill and the overseas trip was cancelled. After medical testing it was found that she had liver cancer and on 25 June 1994 Lilian passed away.

Contributed by Lilian's daughter, Christine (Olson) Trankalis, with help from her father, Julien, who was happy to recall the series of events that brought Miss Lilian Gibson into his life.

She Took A Chance On Love
Delice (deWolf) Wilby

Delice (deWolf) Wilby joined the ATS in 1940. She arrived in Fredericton, New Brunswick four months ahead of her husband who was behind enemy lines with the French Resistance.

Delice Wilby has the heart of an adventurer. She dreamed of a life of travel as a girl growing up in London. Little did she know that eventually, destiny would bring her into the life of Tom Wilby and a new home in Fredericton, New Brunswick.

She was the baby of three girls in Emanuel and Marie deWolf's home. When she was in school, she was awarded a scholarship but she refused it.

'Because it meant I would have had to stay in school until I was sixteen and I wasn't going to have any of that so I left at fourteen,' says Wilby.

She worked as a hairdresser's apprentice but quickly grew bored and quit. Next, she worked in her sister's dressmaking shop. That didn't hold her attention for long, either.

When the war broke out, she signed on with the army. The twenty-year-old was stationed in the heart of London working with top secret military documents. After work, like many young women and men, she wanted to have a good time. There were thousands of young soldiers in the city and the beautiful brunette could have dated any of them.

'I had my pick of them and that was the one that I married and had children with,' she remembers.

Delice deWolf met Tom Wilby in 1942. He was a tall, dark, handsome man who was training to be a pilot. The attraction was immediate and intense.

She could hardly resist his charm. He took her dancing at the *Palais de Danse* on their first date. He was an excellent dancer, she recalls.

'I was a bit of a klutz myself,' she says.

Tom Wilby was Lebanese. The next night he took her to a Lebanese restaurant so she could try this cuisine. When the meal was over, he asked her back to his hotel where they enjoyed a beverage at the bar.

I can still see it. We were sitting at a little table and he said: 'What would you say if I was to ask you if you would like to get married?' And I said 'Are you crazy?' And he said 'What would you say if I asked you?' And I said 'Well I guess I'd say yes.' And he said 'Do you mean it?' And I said, 'Yes.'

Ten days later, on 6 June 1942, they were married in a civil ceremony. She took a chance on love and the gamble paid off. They had a long and happy life together.

But it wasn't always easy, especially in the beginning.

At first both families weren't pleased with the union. Both had been engaged to others. She'd already agreed to marry an American and Tom was promised to a girl back home. Soon after they were married, she brought Tom Wilby home to meet her folks. Immediately they liked him.

The war pulled the newlyweds apart for months. But when they did get together there were, as she describes it, fireworks.

It wasn't long before she discovered she was going to have their first child. She told her husband the happy news. He asked her to take a train from London to York so he could see her. But when she arrived, a senior officer met her at the train station instead.

'He said: "Tom went off on operations last night and didn't return." He was missing in action.'

He was a gunner on a mission over France. On the return flight there was trouble with the plane so the pilot gave the order for everyone to bail out. Wilby managed to get out of the plane; the others didn't. But instead of crashing the plane regained altitude and continued the flight home.

Wilby landed in a tree with a broken leg. He managed to cut himself free of the parachute and he dropped to the ground. Next he crawled to a farmhouse. When the farmer realized he was a Canadian he allowed him in and called a doctor. But the physician turned him over to the Germans.

'They took him away and made him walk on his leg.'

Even though he was repeatedly told he was going to be executed, he was taken to a hospital where French nurses treated him well. Thanks to the French Resistance, he managed to escape. It took eight arduous months before he arrived home.

Weeks turned to months and there was no word of whether he was dead or alive.

Because of the danger in London, Delice Wilby's new brother-in-law convinced her to board a ship for Canada so she could live with Tom's family in Fredericton while she waited to have the baby. She was desperately homesick, she recalls. Six months pregnant, in a new city with no friends or family. Her in-laws weren't happy to have her there. Despite it all, she tried to make the best of things.

Over time, her in-laws warmed to her. The arrival of their first grandchild helped immensely, she recalls. Christopher was born in June 1943. While she was in the hospital, she received a phone call. It was Tom Wilby.

'He said: "I'm in Moncton and I'm on my way home."'

As a former prisoner of war, his service was over and he was free to come home to his wife and new son.

She remembers their reunion as through it were yesterday.

'The first thing he did was look at me and then he looked at his son. He said, "He's cute."'

'He wanted to have seven sons. I'd never held a baby in my arms before.'

They did have seven children, but their sixth was a girl. They couldn't have been more pleased. Tom Jr. arrived in 1944. Next, Ed was born in 1946. In 1950, Joseph arrived followed by Dan in 1953. Their girl, Anna, was born in 1956. And the baby of the family, Louis, was born in 1958.

Theirs was a very busy life. With the end of the war, he took over his family's business, The Imperial Restaurant. She would help run the cash register over the noon hour rush.

They continued to run the business until they decided to retire in the mid-1980s.

With the children grown and on their own, they had time to relax and enjoy their time together. She's always had a passion for travel. While he would agree to go with her on shorter trips, he didn't care for long-haul journeys.

Tom Wilby passed away three years ago. She misses the loving, caring and loyal man terribly.

But she says her children, grandkids, and great-grandchildren are a comfort to her. So are her many friends she's gotten to know over the last sixty-four years in this city. Many of her pals are War Brides, too.

She joined the War Brides club in 1944. It was wonderful to get together for coffee parties where they could boost one another's morale.

Time has passed quickly, she says. Life didn't turn out anything the way she expected. Even though she was married with seven kids, she still managed to see much of the world.

She's travelled to Africa four times to visit her sisters who married British soldiers who were posted there.

She's also been to Brazil, Italy, France, Spain, Bermuda, Florida, and England. But the trips back home seemed less important over time. Now when she thinks of home, it's Fredericton that comes to mind.

Delice Wilby is a young-looking eighty-six-year-old. She enjoys asking people if they can guess her age. Often, she says, many mistake her for a much younger woman. She has a young spirit as well.

She's continuing to travel. Recently she returned from a trip to Florida where she visited two of her sons and their families who live there. When she's home, she enjoys going on outings with her friends and family. Often her children who live here call to invite her out to dinner.

But Wilby is an excellent cook who enjoys preparing Lebanese food. She grows fresh mint on her balcony to include in many of those dishes.

When she settles down to relax, there's nothing any better than a good book. She enjoys staying up to date with popular authors and their novels.

Wilby likes her life mostly, she says, because of her loving family.

'If I didn't have them, I'd go crazy.'

This article was used with permission of the Fredericton Daily Gleaner *and* Laverne Stewart.

6

War Widows

We don't know how many War Brides were widowed during the Second
World War but they certainly must have numbered in the hundreds. More
than 40,000 Canadian servicemen lost their lives in the conflict, representing
nearly ten per cent of the total number of Canadians who served. Based on
those figures, an estimate of 400 to 500 widows is probably not too far off.

In the Canadian newspaper coverage of the War Bride transport during
1946 one sees references to these 'War Widows' who were coming to Canada
to meet their husband's relatives – pathetic reminders of marriages that were
contracted in happier times, but for whom no future ever came.

> In one eight-bunk cabin was Mrs Vera Price, who husband, Donald, was killed
> 12 days after the birth of Diane, 2, whom she is taking to Halifax.[1]

Why a young woman would decide to travel to Canada knowing full well her
husband would never meet her was an entirely personal decision rooted in a
sense of duty to a dead husband whose life in Canada was a mystery to her:
Who were his parents? Where did he come from? How did he grow up?

We know that some War Brides had promised to go to Canada and meet
her husband's family if anything ever happened to him: for these widows, the

journey became a pilgrimage in fulfillment of that vow. When a child was involved, the sense of duty was ever stronger. Others simply wanted to bury a ghost, and only those who have ever lost a loved one can truly understand the reasons why.

War Widows were technically still 'War Brides' so they were allowed the same opportunity to come to Canada. They were given one-way passage on the War Bride ships, their journey was organized and prepared for by the Canadian Wives Bureau and they also had to undergo the same rigorous application process – including investigation of settlement arrangements – to make sure the place they were destined to in Canada was 'satisfactory' according to the Immigration Branch.

Like other War Brides, widows could choose to stay in Canada or return to the UK, but a widow's pension wasn't much to live on, especially if there were children, so it's likely that personal finances would have made the decision for them.

Some widows never even made the trip because there was no family in Canada to visit: others because an ill parent in Britain couldn't be left alone. In the 'Unwilling to Proceed' file of the Canadian Wives Bureau are lists of women who have rejected the Canadian government's offer of a free trip to Canada, and among them is this small sample:

Mrs M. Allard, 'Widow – Not proceeding to Canada'
Mrs R. Andrew 'Widow – Remaining in UK with mother'
Mrs E. Artress 'Widow – Remaining in UK'
Mrs C. Bouchard, 'Widow, not proceeding yet'
Mrs R. Bridges, 'Wife Widow – Proceeding later'[2]

Although their stories are inherently sad, there is also joy to be found in their experience: some War Widows found new love in Canada and ended up staying. In these women's lives there is a sense of optimism that out of tragedy can come hope, and out of love lost, can come the wonder of love anew. For others, the trip to Canada was never meant to be any more than a few months or maybe a year at the most. When it was over, they packed their bags and went back to Britain, enriched by the experience and satisfied that they had fulfilled their husband's last wish.

Witness to History
Ann (Biles) Lawrence Johnston

Ann (Biles) Lawrence Johnston was born in 1922 in Glasgow, Scotland. When war was declared, she joined the nursing sisters where she did her training at Mearnskirk, near Glasgow. On 10 May 1941 she had an unexpected encounter with Rudolf Hess – Hitler's right-hand man – that made her a witness to history. But it was her experience coming to Canada as a War Widow of a Canadian serviceman that defined her War Bride experience.

When the war started, it was suddenly like 'boom' – everything changed. Every house had to have blackout curtains. No lights could be seen anywhere. The headlights on cars were the size of a quarter. Part of our rock garden was torn out and made into an air-raid shelter. My parents spent every night there during the war and one night the bombing was so close that every window in the house was blown out.

I had just finished high school so I was automatically conscripted. There was no teenage life for us. I had a choice of the Army, Navy, Air Force or nursing. If you couldn't decide, it was off to the munitions factory for you, so I chose nursing.

Andrew, my brother, was exempt, since he was an engineer working in my dad's factory making invasion barges and other things pertaining to the war. Alastair, my other brother had just graduated from Agricultural College and my dad had bought him a farm so he was also exempt. At that point, my little brother Jock was too young.

I started my training at a hospital called Mearnskirk in Renfrewshire, Scotland, about three-quarters of an hour away from home. Mearnskirk was built in 1930 as a tuberculosis hospital for children but during the war it assumed a new role as an emergency service hospital and was taken over by the Navy. Every ward was a separate pavilion. Nursing quarters were also there. I was placed in Pavilion Four which was all naval officers. I really enjoyed my course, but such sad sights. One grew up quickly.

I was a part-time ambulance driver at Greenock, about an hour's drive from Glasgow. They would bring the wounded there, most of them so young, without legs, arms, some with beriberi since they had been prisoners in Africa. They were just like skeletons and some were very confused and angry. They would steal food and we would have to be very careful just giving drinks of water or Jello until their stomachs were ready. One night an old school friend of mine from Glasgow, Jimmy Stuart Monteith, arrived. He had been on lookout duty with binoculars and was shot right through the lens. He lost his right eye and hand.

I was on duty at Mearnskirk the night of 10 May 1941 when we received a call about a German plane with one person in it landing in a farmer's field. My buddy and I went out with the ambulance and found this man on the ground, the farmer standing over him with a pitch fork. It turned out to be Rudolf Hess, Hitler's deputy. Hess was looking for the Duke of Hamilton, thinking he might be able to stop the war. Apparently this was all done in secret without Hitler's permission and when Hitler was informed of what Hess did, he declared Hess a psychopath and removed him from the Nazi Party.

That night we brought Hess to Mearnskirk with a broken ankle. He had that fixed and then was sent to a castle in Scotland where he stayed until the war ended. We knew that if he stayed in Mearnskirk spies would find out and the hospital might be bombed.

I met my first husband, Ralph Lawrence, when he was a patient at Mearnskirk. Ralph was from Nashwaaksis, New Brunswick, and he was First Lieutenant in the Royal Canadian Navy of the Tribal Class Destroyer HMCS *Athabaskan*. Some of the patients on the medical ward were mobile and able to go out so on my day off, I'd take them to my home to meet my parents. Ralph was one of them. Before he returned to the ship, we were engaged.

Ralph did not want to get married until the assigned tasks for the *Athabaskan* were less risky. At the time we were engaged, *Athabaskan* was on convoy escort duty from Murmansk to Scapa Floe, in the Orkney Islands. In 1944 *Athabaskan* was assigned to what was believed to be the less risky English Channel. He received a forty-eight-hour leave and we were married in my church on 17 April 1944.

Ralph had mentioned another Canadian named Jack Johnston. He said Jack was his brother's best friend in Nashwaaksis. Since Jack was stationed in England with the RAF, Ralph asked him to be the best man at our wedding. Jack was not able to get leave from his duties, however, so my brother Andrew did the job.

Ralph returned to his ship and twelve days later, on 29 April 1944, during a night battle off the French coast, the *Athabaskan* was torpedoed and sunk. There were some survivors but Ralph went down with the ship. I just could not return to Mearnskirk afterward, so I was transferred to a rehabilitation hospital in southern Scotland.

I had never met Jack, but he started writing to me. One time, he was on leave and stayed several days at my home with my parents. He wanted to meet me.

On my day off that week, he came by train to Barr Hill where I was work-ing and we spent the day together. That was the only time I ever saw him until my visit to Canada after the war ended.

As the widow of a Canadian serviceman I was entitled to one-way trans-portation to Canada just as were other War Brides. I didn't plan to stay in Canada but thought it would be a good opportunity to meet Ralph's fam-ily. I had been invited by the Canadian Navy to assist in the launching of the second HMCS *Athabaskan* in Halifax, Nova Scotia so in late April 1946 I sailed from Southampton, England on the *Aquitania* travelling as a War Bride and arrived in time to be part of the launch ceremonies on 4 May.

The commander of the ship met me in Halifax and I stayed a week at his home. I then travelled by train from Halifax to Fredericton, New Brunswick to meet Ralph's parents. They were wonderful people and I spent eight months with them. Unknown to me, they actually brought Jack Johnston and me together. They insisted that Jack show me around, even taking me to the Encaenia (end of the term) dance at the University of New Brunswick in Fredericton where Jack had started taking his forestry degree after the war. I stayed with Ralph's folks until December, as I wanted to go to Scotland for Christmas. Jack and I became engaged before I left.

Jack wanted to come with me to Scotland and marry there but travelling so soon after the war was unpredictable and he couldn't miss his courses at UNB which were due to start again in January. My parents knew that I was coming back home and my dad insisted that I not return by plane. Nevertheless, that is exactly what I did and I ended up stranded for a few days in Goose Bay, Labrador due to poor weather. After getting all my affairs in order in Scotland I returned to Canada on 28 May 1947. Jack met me in Montreal and we took the first flight back to Fredericton, arrived at noon and were married at 2 p.m. Paul Lawrence, my first husband's brother, was best man.

After Jack graduated from UNB Forestry Engineering in 1948 we moved to Bridgewater, Nova Scotia where he had a job waiting. I lost my first two children, twin boys, when they were born prematurely in 1948. My own mother passed away soon after and I wasn't allowed to travel because of my health so I couldn't attend her funeral.

We raised three children in Bridgewater and in 1965 we eagerly returned to Fredericton when Jack accepted a position with the Federal Department of Forestry. I was kept busy with the children but after they finished school I went to work at York Manor, a home for senior citizens, where my income helped put the kids through university. When the children were all gone, I was able to indulge in my own hobbies; painting, knitting, sewing and flower arranging.

Jack and I lived a good life, we enjoyed our home and family, travelled and belonged to several organizations in the community. Then, in 1990, he was diagnosed with Alzheimers and after a period of declining health he was admitted to the Veterans Health Facility in Fredericton in 2001. I visited Jack every day for three years, even big snowstorms couldn't stop me. I would call a taxi and walk out to the main road if I had to.

On 13 October 2004, at the age of eighty, Jack passed away.

Postscript: Ann Johnston was never the same after her husband's death. She tried to keep herself busy so she embarked on a project to write her family history. She even made beautiful scrapbooks for her three children that documented her life in photographs. But she desperately missed Jack, and her spirit was gone. Ann had been diagnosed with leukemia in 1997 and her own illness combined with worsening arthritis prevented her from doing the hobbies she loved, so the time was long for her. As the winter of 2006 turned to spring and summer, she became weaker and after a fall in early July she was hospitalized. The week before she died, she told her oldest daughter Sandra how sorry she was to put her through this, that she knew how hard it would be because of her own experience losing loved ones, her husbands, her parents, her twin boys at birth, her brothers – it's hard to imagine the losses and still go on. Ann died on 22 July 2006. Even though she didn't live to see her granddaughter's wedding, the flowers she had arranged for the ceremony were there to remind everyone of the love she left behind.

She Found Love in Canada
Madeline (Rusbridge) Chunn Fitzgerald

Madeline (Rusbridge) Chunn Fitzgerald was born in Richmond, Surrey, England, one of six children of Reginald and Elsie Rusbridge. She joined the Women's Land Army and met her Canadian husband at Siddelsham.

Madeline Rusbridge graduated from Central School for Girls in Richmond when she was fifteen years old. Her father had retired from the antiques business and since her older brother Jack had found a good job at Lockwoods Department Store in Worthing, the whole family moved to Worthing.

Their new home at 16 Navarino Road was idyllic: Madeline remembers it was so close to the ocean that you could walk right out the front gate and be on the beach in moments. Madeline was a sporty type who was into horseback riding and gymnastics so she loved their new place because she could put on her swimsuit one minute and be out swimming the next.

Madeline was working in a confectioner's shop when war was declared, but it was obvious for quite some time that war preparations were underway; living so close to the coastline she couldn't help but notice the large cement blocks 'as big as a house' that were placed like a barricade along the shoreline. The blocks were lined with barbed wire and booby trapped with mines to protect Britain from an expected German invasion. There would be no more swimming or walking along the beach in Worthing. Rumour had it that dogs would go sniffing around the beach and be blown to bits after stepping on a mine.

The first thing that happened in the Rusbridge family was that Madeline's oldest brother, twenty-two-year-old Jack, joined the RAF and became a mechanic. Nineteen-year-old Royston had a pilot's licence so he volunteered with the RAF as a night fighter flying Beaufighters out of Cornwall. The RAF had taken over a hotel in Cornwall and Royston was billeted there. He was a talented musician and soon earned a reputation for livening up everyone's spirits by playing the piano in the hotel lobby.

On 19 October 1941 Madeline's parents received the devastating news that Royston had been shot down and killed. His body was never recovered. The black-edged telegram was delivered to their door and the shock was so great that Madeline's father had a stroke. Her parents never got over Royston's death. 'It crushed them,' she said.

Madeline had tried to join the women's services but at eighty pounds and four feet ten inches she was rejected for her size. Instead, she joined the Women's Land Army and worked on a poultry farm in Godalming where her contribution to the war effort included feeding chickens, collecting eggs, and cleaning out the chicken coop. After Royston's death she felt that she needed a change so she transferred to Siddelsham, to a huge farm development for displaced Welsh coal miners that was run by the government. The miners' homes were built around a twenty-acre field which had to be plowed and maintained. There Madeline ran a tractor and ploughed acres and acres of land, hoeing and seeding wheat, corn and potatoes. Every weekend she would come home to be with her parents in Worthing.

Close by to the farms were empty houses that had been taken over by the army and Canadian troops were billeted there. Madeline was staying with the family of her friend Mary, who was also working in Siddlesham. The two women wouldn't have anything to do with the soldiers because they'd heard bad things about the Régiment de la Chaudièrs, a French-speaking outfit from Quebec. But they couldn't ignore the Canadians forever: a friend suddenly announced she was going to marry a Canadian and one day, Madeline met Sgt Charlie Chunn, a young, good-looking Canadian from the Stormont, Dundas and Glengarry Highlanders.

She was carrying a 100 weight of potatoes when Charlie came over to her and said, 'You're too small to be carrying that!'

After helping Madeline with the potatoes, he told his friend, 'There's a little redhead over there and I'm going to marry her.' The next thing Madeline knew, Charlie showed up uninvited at the house she shared with her friend Mary.

The two of them started going out and when Charlie was moved up to Arundel Castle he would visit Madeline every weekend at her parents' house in Worthing. Madeline's parents really liked Charlie. After her father's stroke it was good to have a man around to help take care of his personal needs: Charlie was very good to Mr Rusbridge, bathing him and even taking him out to the pub for a drink. Charlie officially became part of the family on 25 November 1942 when Madeline and he were married. At the wedding, Madeline's younger sister Sylvia met Merle (Bud) Dickson, another Glengarry who was invited to the ceremony. They too fell in love and were married.

As 1943 turned into 1944, there was talk about a new front opening up but no one knew when or where it might be. The men realized that eventually they would be heading to Europe and they may not come back alive. Before he left for France, Bud confided in Madeline and made her promise that if anything happened to him she would accompany Sylvia to his hometown in Tide Head, New Brunswick and see that she was settled in.

Both Charlie and Bud took part in the D-Day invasion on 6 June 1944. Two weeks later, Madeline and Sylvia were at their parents' home and just settling in for a cup of tea when they looked out the window and saw a telegraph boy come up the lane, get off his bike and lean it up against the low garden wall in front of their house. Then came a knock on the door. Sylvia and Madeline knew instinctively that the telegram had to be for one of them. Sylvia, then pregnant with her second child, begged Madeline to answer the door.

The message was for Madeline. Charlie was dead.

'I was hoping it would just say he was wounded,' Madeline said. But there in black and white were the words she had been dreading.

Deeply regret to inform you that your husband C55049 Sgt. Chunn Charles has been reported killed in action 9/June/44.

Madeline still has the telegram, now faded and yellowed with age. She remembers the last time she saw Charlie as if it was yesterday: 'He was in the back of the bus waving goodbye.'

One month later, Sylvia received her own telegram. Bud was killed on 8 July. Now there were two widows in the Rusbridge family.

In April 1945 Madeline fulfilled her promise to Bud Dickson and came to Tide Head, New Brunswick with her sister and the two children to meet Bud's family. They travelled on the *Athlone Castle*, arriving in Halifax on 12 May, just a few days after the European war ended. Charlie had only one brother in Peterborough, Ontario so there was no point in Madeleine going any further west. Her plan was to stay with Sylvia in Tide Head long enough to see her settled in and then return to England.

The two widows were big news in this small village in northeastern New Brunswick, close to Quebec. They were welcomed in every home and strangers would stop to greet them on the street. Madeline and Sylvie stayed with the Dicksons and over the next few weeks Madeline became friends with a local woman named Trudy Fitzgerald who had invited her to dinner at the family home.

Trudy had a brother named James (Dew) who had been severely wounded in Italy. Dew was hospitalized in Italy and England – eventually undergoing a risky experimental bone transplant in a successful attempt to save his arm. He ended up in the hospital in Halifax, Nova Scotia and was sent home in a body cast to recuperate in Tide Head.

Madeline was introduced to Dew and to everyone's delight, they fell in love. The two of them wasted no time; six months later, with Dew still in a body cast, they were married in Tide Head. Meantime, Sylvia fell for Bud's brother Wallace and before too long wedding bells were ringing for them.

Sylvia and Wallace eventually moved to Campbellton and had four children together. They are both gone now. Madeline and Dew stayed in Tide Head where they raised two daughters and a son. When Dew retired, their oldest daughter was living in England so he and Madeline moved to Riverview to be closer to their other children. Dew died in 1998, making Madeline a widow for the second time.

Postscript: Madeline Fitzgerald still lives in Riverview, New Brunswick. Her daughter Lynne helped write this story.

Born on the 13th at Number 13
Phyllis (Head) Grover

Phyllis Rose Head was born on 13 July 1922 at 13 St James Street, Lewes, East
Sussex, England. 'Born on the thirteenth at number thirteen – what do you
expect?' she would often say when bad luck befell her. Except for one year in
Canada after the war, Phyllis lived on St James Street her entire life.

Phyllis Head was the only child of Ethel and William Head. She was
born and grew up on St James Street in Lewes and in 1936, when she
was fourteen years old, she left school to start her first job as an assistant
at Morrishes, a department store in town. She had been working there
for three years when the Second World War was declared.

William Head had served in the First World War and knew only too
well what lay ahead for his family. Due to his age and a respiratory
condition caused by many months in the gas-filled trenches of France,
he became a reserve member of the local Home Guard. He had a small
allotment garden at the rear of their home and he built an air-raid shelter for his family to take cover should enemy aircraft attack the town.
Blackout curtains, rationing and gas masks became a necessary part
of life.

One of the first positive things to happen because of the war, as far as
Phyllis was concerned, was the arrival of Annie, a young evacuee from
London. Annie was one of these poor unfortunates who, with no family
outside of London's vulnerable streets and rooftops, was put on a train
with many others like her and sent to the relative safety of strangers in
Sussex. Phyllis quickly took her under her wing, looking after her as an
older sister would.

At this time public buildings and commercial premises were taken over
by the military to house servicemen stationed in the town. Southover
Manor School, situated only a short distance from St James Street, had
been given over to the Canadian military. It was here that a young man,
Gunner Harold Russell Grover of the Royal Canadian Artillery (RCA),
was stationed.

Harold Grover was from Fredericton, New Brunswick. During the
Depression he found work in the woods and lived at home with his
parents and two younger brothers, twins Edwin (Ed) and Elwin (Pete).
Their father Herbert was serving as a corporal with the Signal Corps

in nearby Saint John so Harold followed his father into the Army in 1938 and started service with the RCA. He was sent overseas and landed in Gourock, Scotland on 4 September 1940, eventually making his way to the Canadian headquarters at Borden, Hampshire.

In 1941 Harold was sent to join the 6th Field Regiment of the RCA at the converted Southover Manor School in Lewes. As there was no space for him there, he was billeted for a week in the home of the recently appointed Verger of Southover Church, Mrs Ethel Head.

Harold's arrival at St James Street marked the second positive thing to come out of the Second World War for Phyllis. A very polite, friendly and good-looking Canadian fellow had come to live at her home!

The next week a room became available at the Manor School so Harold packed his bags for the relocation. Harold was usually given sentry duty and Phyllis would often walk the family dog past and stop to chat. From these meetings a few dates to the local public house, The Bell, and the town cinema took place and romance blossomed very quickly for the couple. They had quite a lengthy courtship, mainly due to Harold being moved around the country and sometimes being sent overseas.

Harold was well liked by Phyllis's parents and it was no surprise to them when he asked for their daughter's hand in marriage. As parents would, they worried about Harold making it through the war without serious injury or death and also the likelihood of Phyllis moving away to Canada as a War Bride. Nonetheless, they gave their blessing and arrangements were soon underway for the wedding.

The first thing Harold had to do, once he had written to his family back home in New Brunswick with the news, was to apply for permission from his commanding officer to marry Phyllis. Harold bemoaned the fact that he had to ask so many times for her hand; first – and most important – Phyllis herself, then her father and then his CO.

Harold and Phyllis were married on 14 March 1944 in Southover Church, Lewes. William Head was proud to give away his only daughter, who was dressed in a beautiful silk wedding gown – the rather extravagant and expensive dress for wartime rationing was the result of material sold by Phyllis's employers being passed into the able hands of Phyllis's aunt, who was a skilled seamstress. Harold wore his RCA Gunner's uniform – with a slightly modified regimental badge on the cap. As a mark of respect to Phyllis he had made a spare RCA badge bear an English coin in place of the wheel of the gun carriage to reflect his joining an English family.

After their honeymoon in Edinburgh, Harold and Phyllis returned to Lewes where she started a new position in the Needlemakers, a factory which produced hypodermic needles. One day a bomb was dropped on the town with the factory as the likely target. Less than 100 yards away from the factory stood The Stag, a local public house and hotel. Harold used to sit on a bench outside The Stag and wait for Phyllis to finish work. Late one afternoon the air-raid siren sounded and everyone immediately took cover wherever they could.

Phyllis was working in the factory at the time and she felt the ground shake and heard windows breaking all around her as the bomb wrought havoc close by. The factory filled with dust so she could scarcely see a thing and long after the sound of the initial explosion had passed she could hear things falling and breaking. Then there was shouting and crying out – mostly because people couldn't see where they were or who was nearby and were calling out for some sense of direction in the mess. When the air cleared well enough for them to see, the workers were confronted with a factory floor of broken glass, upturned tables and needles – a sea of stainless steel still shining under the layers of dust lay before them.

Meantime, someone had come with the news that The Stag had been razed to the ground by the bomb. Panic and confusion hit Phyllis all at once; had Harold been meeting her? Was he on leave today? Could he have been on duty and parked his jeep or motorcycle in the usual place, waiting for her? It transpired her fears were groundless as Harold was at the manor barracks at the time, though he wasted no time in racing to the bomb site. It was a very near miss for both of them and they felt a great sense of relief amidst the sadness of the losses of others in the disaster.

Harold was posted overseas a number of times, something Phyllis found difficult to cope with due to the slow communication and consequent fears for her husband's safety. He was promoted to the rank of Bombardier and in February 1945 was granted nine days' leave.

The couple spent every minute of those nine days together and when his leave was over Phyllis waved a tearful goodbye to Harold on Platform One of Brighton Railway station. It was the last time she saw her husband and the memory of that moment remained etched in her mind for the rest of her life.

On 16 April in Germany, the good fortune travelling with Harold Grover throughout the war turned on its heels, packed its bags and deserted him. His motorcycle was knocked down and run over by an armoured personnel carrier. He was seriously injured and was consequently taken to a field hospital for treatment where he remained on the critical list for three days before he died.

Slow communications from the battlefield played a cruel trick on Phyllis. She received a telegram on 23 April saying Harold had been injured and taken to a field hospital, followed by a letter a few days later to say he had been placed on the critical list. More days passed until Phyllis finally received word that Harold had died on 19 April and was buried in the Canadian War Cemetery in the village of Holten, Holland.

An unhappy communication with her in-laws in New Brunswick, Canada, followed for Phyllis. She was able to give them some good news, overshadowed as it was by Harold's death; she was carrying his child. On 15 November 1945 Phyllis gave birth to a baby girl whom she named Haroldene in memory of her husband. Years later, Haroldene named her own son Russell, her father's middle name.

Phyllis decided to take advantage of the free War Bride transportation offered to war widows to visit Harold's family in Canada as soon as she and the baby were able to travel. The plan was to stay for one year only. On 27 August 1946 Phyllis and Haroldene boarded the *Queen Mary* at Southampton and departed for Canada. On board ship War Brides were comparing stories and photographs and those travelling to be reunited with their husbands were expressing their sorrow and feelings of guilt to widows who had lost theirs. Some had heard from other brides who preceded them to Canada and were relating tales of mixed fortunes upon arriving at their new homes. This kind of talk set many of them worrying about what sort of life they might expect when they met their new families.

Phyllis was obviously as nervous about her situation as the others but was greatly relieved upon meeting her mother-in-law Margaret and Harold's brothers, Pete and Ed, who had travelled to Halifax, Nova Scotia to meet her at Pier 21. Together they took the train back to Fredericton, New Brunswick about six hours away.

Phyllis and Harold's family hit it off immediately and by the time they had arrived at the family home in Fredericton, Phyllis felt she had known them for years. The house was cosy and welcoming with a room specially decorated and prepared with a cot for Haroldene and a comfortable bed for Phyllis. They quickly became the centre of attention for the family, neighbours and friends who all wanted to meet them. Phyllis used to send letters and photographs back home to her parents to assure them that she was enjoying her stay and was being well cared for by the Grover family. Haroldene had her first birthday in New Brunswick and was treated to a party at her Aunt Mary's farm where she was showered with gifts from the family and friends, as well as those sent over from England.

Phyllis got on well with Harold's younger brothers who loved to look after her and the baby, often competing for the task of pushing the pram or carrying Haroldene whenever they went out. Harold's father, Herbert, was still in the Signal Corps in Saint John and was often stationed there in barracks but would come home whenever he could to spend time with them.

The first winter brought with it the first experience of heavy snowfall for Phyllis and she remembered marvelling at the sight of it all. She had skates fitted to Haroldene's pram and was able to push her across the frozen Saint John River. She was the butt of good-natured teasing about her English accent and Pete and Ed used to play tricks on her when they were out walking in the woods at the farm by shouting 'moose!' or 'bear!' and running to hide from the imaginary beast whilst she was trying to keep up with them.

Phyllis's Canadian experience was very positive and she found it difficult to leave when the twelve months came to an end. Everyone tried their best to get her to stay in New Brunswick permanently but Phyllis felt that without Harold she should return to her family and friends in England. So it was that another tearful farewell followed as they boarded the *Aquitania* in Halifax for the return journey home.

The year before Phyllis arrived in Canada, Harold's brother Pete had been involved in a train wreck and as a result of his injuries had contracted tuberculosis. He had fallen ill just before Phyllis and Haroldene had left for England and died while they were sailing home. More sad news for Phyllis to receive when she got home and another lost son for Herbert and Margaret Grover.

Phyllis never remarried and always wore the ring Harold put on her finger on their wedding day. She was proud that she had never taken it off and it wasn't until it wore so thin with age and broke that she ever did.

Phyllis kept in touch with the Grovers in Canada, exchanging letters and photographs regularly. There was the gradual passing of the family members but Harold's surviving brother, Ed, married and had a family of two boys, Tom and Laurie and a girl, Anne Marie. Unfortunately, after the death of Margaret Grover in the early 1960s Phyllis lost touch with Ed and his family as they moved around Canada and she herself moved down the street to 4 St James Street in Lewes.

In 2001 Phyllis's grandson Russell traced Ed's family in Canada through the Internet. Since then, Russell has visited his aunt and cousins in New

Brunswick every year and in the summer of 2004 they came over to England to meet Aunt Phyllis and cousin Haroldene.

It was a timely visit as Phyllis was diagnosed with cancer later in the year and after a mercifully short illness died on 7 February 2005 at the age of eighty-two. Her cremated remains are buried at Southover Church in Lewes, opposite St James Street where she had continued to live until her death. Russell kept a portion of his grandmother's ashes and he and his mother made the trip to the Canadian War Cemetery in Holland to place them on Harold's grave, reuniting the War Bride and Groom for eternity.

Postscript: Harold Russell Grover is commemorated in Lewes on a memorial plaque in Southover Church where he and Phyllis were married and also on the War Memorial in Lewes town centre. This article was contributed by their grandson, Russell Weller, who immigrated to Canada in 2008. He now lives in New Brunswick, not far from Fredericton where his grandfather grew up.

7

War Fiancées

Love letters straight from your heart
Keep us so near while apart
I'm not alone in the night
When I can have all the love you write

I memorize every line
Then I kiss the name that you sign
And darling then I read again
Right from the start[1]

Not every British woman who came to Canada under the War Bride transportation scheme was married to her husband when she arrived. For some
very good reasons, many women couldn't get married before their fiancés were
repatriated to Canada.

Some women only met their Canadian servicemen late in the war
and marriage wasn't something they were willing to discuss before he
left. Long-distance love affairs cultivated by mail turned into propos-
als for marriage and eventually the two decided they couldn't be apart
any longer. Some men even made their way back to Britain to see for

themselves if the love letters were real and if they were, a proposal soon followed.

Other women's boyfriends were prisoners of war and when these men were released from captivity the government was more concerned about shipping them back home than it was in sorting out their personal affairs. Knowing how complicated and time-consuming the process of applying for permission to marry was, getting medical inspections etc., he was often long gone before the paperwork could be completed. Meantime, back in Canada, long-lost sons would arrive to a hero's welcome from relatives and friends and then the waiting game began.

As the men were being repatriated in large numbers in 1945 the issue of War Fiancées came up frequently. In a 1946 memorandum to the Deputy Minister (Army) it was noted that there were 550 applications for fiancées to enter Canada, of which 438 were from Britain and that more were coming forward at a rate of 20 a week.[2] By April 1946, that number had climbed to 1,000.[3]

Simply put, fiancées were not a priority. In 1945 and 1946 especially, the Immigration Branch, the Army and the Canadian Wives Bureau had enough on their hands trying to organize the transportation of married women and children to Canada. Fiancées had to wait until shipping was available and in the meantime, their boyfriends in Canada had a lot of paperwork to fill out, including a 'Statutory Declaration of Intention to Marry'.[4]

A young woman planning to marry a Canadian could travel on the War Bride ships if space was available, and the Army would help get her documentation in order but she was a 'visitor' and she had to pay her own way. Upon arrival she had a certain amount of days to make up her mind and marry or return to her home country. In the files of the Immigration Branch there is one form that says she had thirty days but we know of some women who had ninety days and another who had six months.

A few women got fed up with waiting and they flew to Canada, but they would have been rare. Airline travel was expensive and it wasn't like it is today. Bea Surgeson flew to Canada in 1948 and in this excerpt from her memoirs she describes the experience:

> We didn't know that it was going to take almost two years for me to get a passage to Canada. Norman was no longer in the Air Force; he had been de-mobilised as soon as he got back so the Canadian government had no responsibility to bring me over as a War Bride. It was up to us to pay our own way and make arrangements for travel.

I was totally naïve about travelling and thought that I could go to Thomas Cook's and buy a ticket to Canada. Not so. All the Atlantic shipping was concentrated on getting Europe and Britain back to normal. Norman tried to get a passage for me from here; no luck. Immigration rules were also much different to what they are now and I had to make my own application to the Canadian Consulate in England to come for the purpose of marrying a Canadian citizen. I wasn't allowed to book my passage until my application was granted.

The Immigration Department then had to contact Norman to see if this was indeed what he intended AND to inform him that he would be held responsible for my good behaviour and that he would have to see that I would not become a liability of the Canadian government. These were the days of all communication being done by mail, add this to the speedy service given by government departments. If accepted, I would be allowed to try to get a passage.

My application was accepted after a medical and all kinds of form-filling and red tape. There was no credit applied in view of all Norman's efforts on my behalf whilst he was in the service so I had to start from scratch. This status allowed me to stay in Canada for six months from the date I arrived, and if I wasn't married by then I would have to go back to England. I would not be allowed to work in Canada during this time and I had no status except as a visitor.

Trying to travel by sea was hopeless, so Norman decided that we should try for an airline ticket. This was more expensive, but easier to obtain. Commercial flights were very rare and at that time most civilians did not relish the thought of flying. I think the staff at Thomas Cook's Travel was glad to get a ticket for me with TCA (Trans Canada Airlines) if only to get me off their back.[5]

There is some disagreement among the War Bride community whether fiancées even qualify as true Canadian War Brides. It has been said that those women who didn't get married overseas during the war or immediately after, up to the end of 1946, and if they had to pay their own way, aren't War Brides.

The fact is that the Canadian government recognised that some weddings could not take place overseas and allowed for these unusual circumstances by assisting with the transportation of fiancées. The important factor to consider is that the love affair was rooted in their mutual wartime experience. A more inclusive definition of who is a genuine War Bride therefore includes women who met their Canadian husbands overseas during the war when he was in the service of his country (or in the immediate aftermath up to his repatriation back to Canada).

The story of the War Fiancées could take up an entire book and space doesn't permit. We know that relationships that were formed during the war years continued to result in marriages as late as 1948 and probably for many years after. Although this group of women may not have shared the quintessential War Bride experience of marrying in wartime Britain, coming to Canada on the government organized ships and travelling in a group across Canada by train, they are still War Brides and nobody can take that away from them.

She Got What She Wanted
Zoe (Blair) Boone

Zoe (Blair) Boone's marriage to her wartime sweetheart was delayed when he was taken prisoner of war. She came to Canada on a *Trans-Canada Airlines* flight in December 1946.

If it hadn't been for the Second World War seventeen-year-old Isobel (Zoe) Blair of Aberdeen, Scotland would have followed in her mother's footsteps and attended fashion school in Paris to study hat design. Her mother was Hilda LeFevre, a well-known milliner who ran a popular women's hat store at 212 Union Street in Aberdeen.

Instead Zoe ended up at the Fleet Air Arm Base in Macrahanish, Scotland where she worked as an Aircraft Mechanic Airframes with the WRNS, and when the war was over she flew to Canada at the height of winter to marry her fiancé, a soldier who had spent two years as a German prisoner of war.

Zoe Blair was born in 1922 in Muchalls, Kincardineshire, Scotland. Her father was a Customs and Excise Officer and her mother was a successful businesswoman whose shop bore her own name 'Hilda LeFevre'. Their house, which still stands today, was located on 9 Ashley Road and from the back garden there was a beautiful view of the Holburn West Church.

Zoe attended Albyn School for Girls in Aberdeen. At age sixteen she decided she had had enough of school so she went to work at DM Brown department store in Dundee where she learned the basics of the trade in the millinery department.

At the time Zoe didn't really know what she wanted to do. 'I was just filling in time,' she recalls. But when war was declared everything came into sharp focus. She returned to Aberdeen and immediately signed up with the Women's Land Army. After a year at Craibstone Agricultural College outside of Aberdeen she worked on a farm in Strachan where she was responsible for twenty-seven head of beef cattle, cleaning out the barn and haying.

Zoe was a small woman and it was rough going so she transferred to a potato farm in Perwinnes, Dyce where her small frame was not an issue. She loved it there; her co-workers were fun and the fresh air was invigorating. But Zoe was no match for the adult form of the measles which she contracted from one of the farm children and she took very ill. In August 1941 she was sent home to recuperate and never did go back.

That same year Zoe met Marshall Boone, a twenty-four-year-old Canadian serviceman from Rowena, New Brunswick. Marshall just happened to be in Aberdeen on the fifth day of a seven-day leave from his camp in Aldershot, England where he was stationed with the Carleton York Regiment.

'I remember it was a Monday evening and I was out with two girlfriends on our way to the pictures,' says Zoe.

> It was the middle of a blackout and I stopped to put a letter in the post box to my (then) boyfriend, who was in the RAF near Dollar. As my friends continued walking along without me I shouted out ahead to them, 'What movie are we going to see?' Out of the darkness came a male voice that said 'Go see Johnny Apollo!'

The girls had no idea who the voice belonged to but, as Zoe says, 'We were young and adventurous and so my friend replied back, "OK, we'll go," and the next thing I knew we were on the way to the cinema with these two Canadian soldiers, Marshall Boone and Rowan Bauer of New Brunswick.'

Zoe says she didn't want to sit next to the soldiers so she made her two girlfriends sit in between. After the movie the third girlfriend departed for home, leaving Zoe and Phyllis with Marshall and Rowan. The four young people stopped at Herds Cafe on Bridge Street for a cup of tea. 'They seemed like nice fellows so my friend Phyllis and I asked them to come over to my house to meet my mother.'

From such inauspicious beginnings grew a long-lasting love between Zoe Blair and Marshall Boone. They knew they were destined for each other but the reality was that Marshall had a mother and a disabled father back in Canada who depended on him for financial support. Every month, half his pay went to help his parents back in Rowena.

Zoe and Marshall agreed they would marry after the war was over so they put off marriage for the time being. This allowed Marshall to continue to support his parents financially with the monthly contribution from his army pay which would have normally gone to Zoe had they married.

Zoe remembers Marshall's last leave before he went to Sicily. 'It was April 1943 and he knew something was in the air but he couldn't say,' she recalls. 'He didn't want to return to Crieff, where they were taking mountain warfare training. "I shouldn't go back," he said.'

Zoe had a hard time convincing him that he had to return to Crieff. '"You won't get leave again if you don't go back," I said, not realizing that he knew a lot more than I did about the plans that were being laid for the invasion of Sicily.'

The last time Zoe saw Marshall was as he left that April morning to go back to Crieff. It was too early in the day for public transport so he headed down the Great Western Road with a little bag over his shoulder intending to hitchhike to the railway station.

Zoe found out later that the first car to stop was a hearse and the driver shouted out to Marshall, 'Sorry Sonny boy, you're not ready for me yet.'

On 10 July 1943 Marshall took part in the Allied invasion of Sicily with the First Canadian Infantry Division, part of General Montgomery's famed British Eighth Army. Twelve days later Marshall was taken prisoner and later transported to Germany where he was moved around from one prison camp to another until he was liberated in May 1945. Over the course of the next twenty-two months Marshall was allowed to write one letter a month, so he would alternate between his mother one month and Zoe the next.

Zoe still has all eleven of his letters and the secret diary he kept of his day-to-day existence in the POW camps.

But in the spring of 1943 Zoe had no idea what the future held for her and Marshall. Soon after he walked out that door in April she was called up for the WRNS. Then Marshall was taken prisoner and in September she began her training to become an aircraft mechanic at HMS Fledgling in Mill Meece, Staffordshire, England.

The WRNS kept her busy and was a good distraction from the depressing news about Marshall. She trained to be an aircraft checker at Worthy Down and shared a room at Mill Meece with three other trainees, Margaret Garbutt from Yorkshire, Joan A.A. Storey from Dagenham and Jean Birkdale from South Shields, Durham. They were good roommates, thoughtful and sensitive to what Zoe was going through.

The young women were proud to be part of the Fledgling project which marked the beginning of training for women in the Fleet Air Arm. They wore distinctive sailor rig; blue bell bottoms, white square neck tops (called gunshirts) and blue uniform jackets. After her training was completed, Zoe was stationed at the Royal Naval Air station at Machrihanish on the tip of the Mull of Kintyre where she and a team led by an RAF Sergeant repaired Barracudas, Spitfires, Swordfish and Avengers. Later she worked at an airfield in Evanton, near Inverness and lived in a cabin at Novar House which was part of the Novar Estate.

Zoe's claim to fame was that she worked on the modification of torpedo tubes on the Barracudas that bombed the German battleship *Tirpitz* on 3 April 1944.

'My hands were small so I could get my fingers into the narrow space along the inside of the delivery tube to hold the nut that the screw went in,' she explained. 'We worked day and night for two days and we didn't know until after it happened that we had played a part in bombing the *Tirpitz*.'

Zoe was stationed at Evanton when the war ended. A few days later, she was sitting in her cabin at Novar House when someone came down from the telephone room to say her mother was calling from Aberdeen.

When Zoe picked up the phone, her mother said, 'There's someone here who wants to speak to you.' It was Marshall.

Zoe had to find a way to get back to Aberdeen immediately but the problem was that she and Marshall were not actually engaged. If Zoe's Commanding Officer wanted to be a stickler she could refuse the leave to Aberdeen.

So Zoe went back to the cabin and told her roommates what had happened. 'What am I going to do?' she asked. One of the women had just become engaged so she pulled off her ring, gave it to Zoe and said, 'Go and plead your case.'

The ruse worked. To Zoe's relief the CO was most sympathetic. She said 'Oh how wonderful,' and then 'Are you going to be married?' Zoe replied: 'I don't know, I haven't seen him in two years.'

So with the CO's blessing Zoe took the first train to Inverness and got a bus down to Aberdeen where Marshall met her at the station. By coincidence on his way down to the bus Marshall met his friend from Canada, Rowan Bauer, whom he hadn't seen since Sicily. As Zoe disembarked, there to meet her were Marshall and Rowan, completing a circle of friendship that had begun in a blackout nearly four years before.

That night Zoe and Marshall talked about everything that had happened in the past two years and when the sun broke over the horizon they agreed they still loved each other and would 'give it a try'. They hoped to spend some time together before Marshall went back to Canada but since he had been a prisoner of war he had priority in shipping and was almost immediately repatriated.

In their short time together Zoe and Marshall didn't even have time to think about getting all the paperwork together to get married. As a result, she had absolutely no priority when it came to the War Brides shipping because fiancées were at the very bottom of the list.

By November 1946 Zoe's patience had run out. She was tired of waiting for the war to end, tired of waiting for Marshall to be liberated, and tired of waiting to come to Canada. So when the Canadian Wives Bureau informed Zoe that the earliest she could come to Canada was on the War Bride ship *Aquitania* in February 1947 she took matters into her own hands. On Tuesday 15 December 1946 she phoned a travel agent and on Thursday 17 December she boarded a *Trans-Canada Airlines* plane in Prestwick destined for Montreal. Two days later, after a detour in the Azores, she landed in Quebec in 'twelve feet of snow'. Marshall met her at the train station in McAdam, New Brunswick and the two travelled along the Tobique River in a 1939 Ford to Perth and then to Rowena, population 100.

To say life was different for Zoe in Rowena was an understatement. Marshall's parents were farmers who lived along a dirt road in an isolated rural area miles from the nearest village. An Indian Reservation was down the road and there were no stores or street lights. But where others may have seen only hardship and despair, Zoe only saw the man she loved and had waited so long to marry. In March, they became man and wife.

At first they lived on the farm with Marshall's parents but, as Zoe says, 'A kitchen wasn't made for two women.' So in 1948 when Zoe went to Scotland to visit, Marshall built them a small home for $968 (Cdn), a bargain even in 1940s currency. Her mother visited often and there were other British War Brides in neighbouring communities. She had a driver's licence and access to a vehicle so she wasn't shut off from the world. She and Marshall had two boys, four grandchildren and one great-grandchild. Marshall died in 1992.

Zoe still lives in the small house that Marshall built in Rowena. Although she sometimes thinks about moving to the city, she probably never will. It's beautiful there: deer gather in the woods near her back yard and although it can be quite an experience to get snowed in during a winter storm, the summers along the Tobique River are breathtaking. When asked about the decision she made to come to Canada so long ago, Zoe says with a satisfied smile: 'I got exactly what I wanted. And there's nothing like getting exactly what you want.'

I Learned to Love This Country
Edna (Burrows) Simpson

Edna (Burrows) Simpson's boyfriend came back to England and proposed to her in 1947. In September, she followed him to Canada.

I grew up in Liverpool and I was only sixteen when war broke out. I can remember sitting in our small home in the suburbs listening to the Prime Minister telling us our country was at war.

Because Liverpool was a major port and important shipbuilding centre, heavy German bombing was expected so the high school I attended was to be evacuated to Wales. There was just me and my younger sister, and my parents wanted the family to stay together so instead of completing high school I enrolled in a commercial college and finished up with a diploma in shorthand, typing and bookkeeping.

After a few temporary positions, I was hired by the Ministry of Health, then under the leadership of Dr K.W. Monserrat, one of the most eminent surgeons of his time and father of the famous novelist Nicholas Monserrat.

I was to work in the newly formed Casualty Bureau. This branch was set up to keep track of air-raid casualties. After London, Liverpool was one of the most heavily bombed areas of the country. We had a gradually increasing number of air raids in 1940, which intensified in May, 1941, with the seven-day blitz on Liverpool when the bombers arrived at dusk and kept up a steady attack on our city each night, not leaving until dawn.

It was an exhausting time. More than 1,700 people were killed, another 1,200 seriously injured during the May Blitz. Each day we had the massive task of compiling lists of casualties, and issuing notices giving names, addresses, and the hospitals or morgues to which they had been taken.

These lists were very important as they were often the only way relatives and friends could track down their loved ones when they came home from shift work or Air Raid Precautions (ARP) duty to find homes damaged or destroyed.

Unfortunately, many victims were listed as 'unidentified'.

By the beginning of 1943, the number of raids had dwindled and our bureau was being used to keep statistics of servicemen admitted to Liverpool hospitals as well as civilian casualties. My job was no longer considered a reserved occupation.

At the same time, there were increasing calls for women to enlist to fill the jobs of servicemen serving overseas, so I decided to join the Women's Auxiliary Air Force (WAAF), thinking my commercial training might be useful in some way. After completing the tests at the recruiting centre, I was asked if I wanted to train as an RDF (Radio Direction Finder) – later called radar. It was top secret and they could not tell me what I would be doing but I presumed it would be interesting and very important for the war effort.

After initial training in marching, being outfitted in uniform and lectures on service procedure, I was sent directly to a radar station on the east coast of England north of London called Walton-on-Naze and learned on the job to be a radar operator. We were stationed in a tall tower facing the sea, with spiral steps inside which we climbed each day to our operations room on the next to top floor. There we learned to accurately read plots of the blips appearing on the radar tube and to pass them to the plotting room in our area where they were identified as hostile or friendly. It was a concentrated and demanding job, as we often plotted hostiles overhead and, in fact, were on the receiving end of the effects of a nearby bombing while at our hostel one day.

After a few months there was space for us at the training school and there we learned how the radar sets worked and the technical details of radar itself. From there I was posted to South Wales, then in 1944 to Cornwall, where I met my husband-to-be, Doug, a handsome, blonde Canadian.

Attached to every radar station were radar mechanics whose task it was to keep the sets maintained and on the air during every watch. Fortunately for me, Doug was assigned to our watch. By this time, I had taken further training on a 10 centimetre type of radar which could pick up low-flying aircraft and the periscopes of any E-Boats (rumour was that 'E' was for 'enemy') or U-boats which surfaced along the coastline. This was very important as D-Day approached.

All our stations were small and we were involved in a very hush-hush occupation so we got to know each other very well and the friends I made there have remained my friends all my life. So it was with Doug. I got to know him well from the hours when he came and talked to us as we studied and plotted the radar tube on the night shift. When his maintenance duties were done, he was on watch for any type of breakdown. In the small hours of the morning when everyone is tired, there are no masks up and I was attracted to his kindness and honesty. He talked of his family and his home in Ontario and I found it all so very interesting.

We went to a few dances together and walked home along the cliff top. Then he was posted on a course and to another station so we only met once more before he returned to Canada due to his father's illness in 1945. But we promised to write to each other and this we did for two years.

In February 1947, Doug returned to England on the *Queen Elizabeth* carrying an engagement ring on a chain around his neck. I travelled to London to meet him and we came to Liverpool where he met my family.

My mother's health had broken during the stress of wartime and she was in a nursing home but my father liked Doug and trusted him. Within a week Doug had proposed to me and the ring was on my finger. We started making plans for me to come to Canada to marry him. It was difficult to get passage across the Atlantic and finally on 1 October, I booked a berth on the SS *Nova Scotia*, a freighter ship sailing to Halifax via Newfoundland.

It took ten days to reach Halifax. We had a rough passage near Ireland but I found I was a good sailor and enjoyed the exhilaration of the fresh air and high waves. At Halifax, I can only remember being put on a train for the 1,100-mile trip to Toronto. I recall the seemingly endless trees we passed and very little sign of habitation on that long train journey. I had been introduced to this vast country.

Doug met me in Toronto and we drove to his parents' farm in Glencoe. It was a four-hour ride and I was amazed at the straight roads, huge cars and the wide open fields. We even passed a big deer with antlers.

We arrived at the farm house and I met his mother and father, who I am sure were wary of this English city girl who had come to marry their son, but they made me welcome. We were married within a month and although the weather had been clear and cold since my arrival in October, that day the winter set in and we had a very cold winter with snow on the ground until the end of February.

I was introduced to the wood stove which heated our poorly insulated farm house and I learned to cook on it without a thermometer. The farm women checked the temperature by putting their hand in the oven but I had many failures and was reduced to tears on more than one occasion. My husband was kind and loving and I gradually learned to keep the fire going at a steady pace.

I was terribly lonely but I enjoyed the beauty of that first Canadian winter and I learned to appreciate my husband's pioneer background. His ancestors had come to Canada in the early 1800s from England and Scotland and each branch had cleared land, built homes and raised families through their own hard work.

Our oldest son was born the following December and we moved into the house where he still lives today. It is a big yellow brick ten-room house with high ceilings and was quite daunting to me, having been brought up in a small, semi-detached house in Liverpool.

I had a very busy life and so much to learn. We were involved in general farm operation, raising cattle for market, feeding hens to sell eggs, and keeping a milk cow for our milk. It seemed the work never ended as chores had to be done seven days a week. At a pinch I could throw feed to the cattle and squeeze a little milk from the cow. Gathering eggs became one of my jobs each day: the eggs had to be washed and packed in trays each evening. As our family grew to three boys and a girl, gradually the chores were divided among the family.

We had a hired man most of the time when the children were growing up and I learned to cook hearty meals twice a day as the men worked hard physically. During harvest time, there were many men to feed when they were at our farm to help with the silo filling and filling the barn with hay and straw for the winter ahead. Thank goodness for good neighbours and relatives who came to help and teach me how it was done.

As the years went by I realized the advantages of bringing up a family on a farm. We depended on each other and developed a closeness that is a treasure now. I always feel my children helped me grow up as much as I helped them and through it all, my gentle Canadian Radar Mechanic proved his worth in his steadfast devotion to me and our family.

The children are all married now with families of their own and I am fortunate to have them settled around me. Sadly, when Doug was eighty-four he developed Alzheimer's Disease and I nursed him at home for three years. Finally, I had to put him in a nursing home where he died in 2005. Now I have to go on alone.

There are so many things to be thankful for in the events that brought me to this place. I was so lucky to marry my Doug and to have him with me all those years, to have a close-knit family where I was accepted and learned a new way of life. The Church has played an important part in all our lives and brought so many friendships and strengths into my life. Along the way, I learned to respect the values of those who make their living from the land and to love this country of Canada.

Postscript: Edna Simpson still lives in Glencoe.

Anything but Ordinary
Alice (McGregor) Hooker

Alice (McGregor) Hooker was born in London, England. She married her Canadian fiancé in June 1948.

At first glance Alice McGregror's life may seem ordinary, but her story is anything but.

Alice had three sisters and one brother. Her oldest sister died in 1918 of the Spanish Flu; her mother died after being struck by lightning; and her brother died in a bicycle accident. When her father died of stomach cancer in 1934, Alice was orphaned at twenty-six and became the oldest surviving sibling in charge of her two younger sisters.

In 1935 at the age of twenty-seven, she decided to go into nursing. She trained at a large hospital in London and became a registered nurse, just in time for the Second World War.

During the bombing of London she worked in her hospital and lived at home. One day, she returned home to discover her house had been bombed. She became a 'theatre nurse', meaning she worked in the operating theatre. She developed a passion for this type of nursing and felt she could have been a great surgeon herself but this ambition was never realized.

One of the surgeons she assisted was Archibald MacIndoe, the famous plastic surgery pioneer who developed innovative techniques to heal more than 600 airmen whose planes were shot down in flames during the war. These young men sustained horrible burns and needed extensive medical treatments. Alice was very proud to have worked with this brilliant surgeon, whose patients became known as The Guinea Pig Club.

In her thirties Alice was a very good-looking brunette with dark brown eyes, perfect complexion and lively personality. She was slim and energetic with a quick wit. She was also intense, practical, competent and assertive. Men found her both attractive and intimidating.

On her vacations, she liked to travel around the countryside on her bicycle. She didn't have boyfriends; she liked being independent and doing something useful with her life. She thought men were boring. She used to say, 'The best man is unworthy of the worst woman.' She loved being a nurse and doing her duty to help win the war. She often said that the years she spent nursing in the hospital as a young woman were the happiest years of her life.

Alice didn't like her name so as a nurse she went by her nickname, Mac. Mac's life changed abruptly one day in the fall of 1943. The nurses from her hospital were invited to attend a party sponsored by the Canadian High Commission, which had been relocated from Canada House to another less vulnerable site. The local English nurses added some sparkle to their social events.

There was, of course, music, dancing and singing. Mac participated in these events and enjoyed the opportunity to play the piano and sing some of the popular songs of the day. Alice had a gift for music, but her parents could not afford to pay for piano lessons for all their offspring so only the eldest were given lessons. As a youngster, Alice listened to the lessons and snuck into the parlour where she taught herself how to play by ear. She also sang in her church choir and had ambitions to become an opera singer – her choirmaster told her she had 'the voice' – but without the training and opportunity, she never realized this dream. However, throughout her life, she relied on music and song to lift her spirits and entertain her friends and family.

At one of these parties Mac met a Canadian army officer, Captain William (Bill) Hooker. He asked her to dance and later he invited her to go walking with him one Sunday afternoon.

Mac was enchanted. Capt Hooker was in his mid-forties but looked much younger. He was handsome, well spoken, well educated and very charming. It wasn't long before these two were in love. Mac often said that Bill was her one and only love, and there would never be another. It was obvious that Bill loved her too.

From 1943 to 1944 Bill worked on assignment with Canada House as a lecturer on the virtues of Canada. He was invited to speak to various schools and organizations around the UK to educate people about the country. This was part of the government's effort to encourage British emigration to Canada after the war. As a schoolteacher with two university degrees, this job assignment suited Capt Hooker quite well. He loved lecturing about Canada and travelling all over the British Isles at government expense.

As luck would have it Mac became pregnant in the spring of 1944. By this time, she was qualified as a midwife and had helped many women give birth naturally. However, her own pregnancy was not necessarily what she had in mind. To complicate matters, her lover, Capt Hooker, was a married man with a family back in Canada. Mac found herself in a very uncomfortable situation: pregnant, single and in love with a married man.

The social stigma, and her embarrassment no doubt, made her decide to leave England and take an assignment as an army nurse. She travelled on a hospital ship to Alexandria, Egypt, where her son was born in January 1945. This is how she kept her pregnancy well-hidden from her family back home. While in Egypt she worked in a MASH-like desert hospital and slept in Army tents.

Mac returned to England with her infant son, Victor (Bill's middle name was Victor) in the spring of 1945. Back in London, Mac and Bill were together again.

Meanwhile Bill's oldest daughter, Lois Hooker, had arrived in England with the Canadian Auxiliary Services Entertainment Unit. Lois had auditioned for and been accepted with an army entertainment troupe, having lied about her age (she was sixteen at the time). She did this against the wishes of both her parents but being a headstrong teenager with no fear she followed her heart and dreams to be in the entertainment industry.

Eventually, the Army discovered her real age and prepared to send her back to Canada but she went absent without leave and somehow obtained the very first Lady Louis Mountbatten Scholarship to the Royal Academy of Dramatic Arts (RADA) in London. When the Army finally caught up with her they had to deal with Lady Mountbatten, so Lois was discharged in England and stayed at RADA.

She graduated two years later and while there she met a young actor who would become her lifelong friend, Roger Moore. Her first role with him was at RADA as his uncle in *Henry V*, disguised in a flowing red beard. Later she rose to fame as Miss Moneypenny alongside him in the first fourteen James Bond films.

It's uncertain how much Lois really knew of her father's relationship with Mac but she must have figured something was up when she saw hairpins on the dresser in her father's London flat. She finally met Mac one day at a train station in London. Bill was waiting for Lois and with him was Mac holding a baby boy. Lois was not pleased to find out her father had been having an affair in England. To make matters worse, the child looked just like her youngest brother, David. Lois wanted her father to forget this 'evil woman' and return to the family in Toronto. From this point on, the two women were mortal enemies.

Bill's own situation with the Army was precarious at this point. Being overage for any actual combat positions he was originally assigned to desk jobs as an Army accountant and paymaster. He must have found this work extremely boring because he took the job as a lecturer with Canada House, which he loved, but this was a temporary position.

From December 1944 until June of 1945 Bill was uncertain about his job situation. He applied for several positions and was finally accepted as a counsellor with the Canadian Army's Wives Committee counselling wives of servicemen who were killed during the war.

However, this job opportunity was suddenly revoked in May 1945 for reasons which are not very clear, but it had something to do with his personal suitability. At a social gathering, a person told Bill's superior something about Bill's 'career history' and this information was used to revoke the job offer. When Bill found out about this he wrote a note to his superior asking for details so he could 'explain' and 'appeal' the decision. The details were not forthcoming.

Bill then applied for a scholarship to pursue his studies in education in England. This was also denied. At the brink of being sent back to Canada due to the lack of any suitable work assignment, the war ended and Capt Hooker had a stroke of luck. He was promoted to Acting Major and put in charge of processing soldiers returning to Canada at a location in northern England. This reprieve allowed Bill to stay in England with Mac and their baby son, Victor, for a while longer.

Meanwhile, Bill's wife was anxious for his return. He had left Canada for England in 1941 and it was now 1945. For four long years she alone looked after their house and their children while working in a munitions factory. Their eldest daughter Florence was now married, and their youngest son David, who was born in 1939, didn't know his father at all. The fourth child, Keith, was twelve. On top of all that, she was sick and needed an operation. In October 1945 Bill received a telegram advising him of his wife's imminent hospitalization. He was required to return home on compassionate grounds to look after the children.

One can only imagine how this news affected Bill and Mac's relationship. Bill got on the earliest flight he could find and returned to Toronto where he resumed his teaching duties with the Toronto Board of Education.

Lois remained in London after Bill left as she was still involved with her training at RADA. She was doing some acting in some local theatres when Jack Warner of Warner Brothers spotted her and offered her an acting contract which launched her career in film. In January 1947 she was already a celebrity and her arrival in Toronto was written up in local newspapers.

She was on her way to Hollywood, and would have been very happy, except for the fact that she learned her parents were getting a divorce. It seems that her mother found a letter from Mac in Bill's pocket and this was the last straw. With her divorce, Lois's mother moved to Los Angeles with the two boys, David and Keith, and changed their last name to Maxwell, the name that Lois had chosen for her acting career.

By the end of 1947 Bill had arranged for Mac to join him in Canada. He flew to England over Christmas and returned after New Year's Day. Bill and Mac married in June 1948 and their daughter, Carole Anne, was born in September 1949.

Mac arrived in Canada without her son. She had put Victor, now about three years old, into an orphanage in England. All this time, she had never disclosed his birth to her sisters or anyone else in her family and she kept his life a secret from them until she died. Victor remained in the orphanage until about the age of six when Bill and Mac finally made the arrangements to have him join the family in Canada.

Bill's divorce from his first wife caused a huge rift in his family. Bill's two daughters from his first marriage rejected their father. When Bill tried to help Lois with her career by offering to be her manager she turned him down dismissively. Lois had, at one time, adored her father, but his involvement with Mac was most hurtful to Lois and she remained loyal to her mother.

The boys, on the other hand, seemed to accept the new family arrangement more easily. Keith joined the US Army Medical Corps in Korea before returning to Canada to pursue his studies at McGill University to become a doctor.

David, when he was about fifteen, moved back to Canada to live with his father's new family in Pickering Village, a few miles outside of Toronto, where Bill and Mac had settled. It was an idyllic little place in the country, very pretty and peaceful, a far cry from the busy city streets of London.

David left LA because he needed his father's firm hand, as his mother could no longer handle him. Eventually, David joined the RCMP and obtained his law degree. The integration of David with the new family went relatively smoothly. David and Mac developed their own special relationship and in the end, David respected Mac and vice-versa.

There was never any reconciliation between Bill and his daughters. Bill's siblings – he had several brothers and sisters in Toronto – also rejected his new bride. According to Mac they were rather mean to her and she refused to have anything to do with them. Perhaps they didn't believe in divorce which was quite a stigma back then, or perhaps they felt loyal to Bill's first wife. The family was apparently embarrassed by the fact that Bill's divorce got into the local papers due to Lois's celebrity.

There was little or no contact between Bill's new family and his siblings in Toronto, except for Bill's younger brother Frank and his wife Ethel, who maintained a relationship with the family until Bill's death in 1962.

Theirs is a love story. Mac and Bill experienced hell on earth together, the fear, the deprivations, the stress, the bloodiness and human tragedy of war. Mac's dream was to share her life with Bill once the war was over. They were devoted to each other for the duration of their marriage. One of the first things Bill did when he moved the family to Pickering was to buy Mac a piano — it was a surprise for her birthday. She loved that piano, and insisted that both Victor and Carole receive formal piano lessons. This somehow made up for her own lack of formal training.

Mac and Bill had some rough spots, due mostly to Mac's difficulty in integrating herself with the local rural Ontario population and feeling trapped and bored in her role as housewife and mother. As a young woman in London, she regularly attended the theatre and opera, and she missed these cultural outlets. She thought Toronto was a crude and rude place, and that Canadians in general were lacking sophistication and manners. She didn't like gossiping with her neighbours and she valued her privacy above all.

She obviously didn't want anyone to know about her affair with Bill and the illegitimate birth of her son, and they never celebrated their wedding anniversaries. She didn't wear an engagement ring, only a simple wedding band.

She returned to England just once to attend her sister's wedding in 1958. When she returned she was happy to be back in Canada and didn't want to live in England any more. She had become Canadianized by then.

Her personal tragedy was that Bill died so young. He was sixty-four and she was just fifty-four. As a widow she mourned his passing for several years. Then she tried to return to nursing but she was too frail psychologically and physically and couldn't handle the demands of the job. She was never registered as a nurse in Canada.

Her son Victor believes that the stress of living in London during the Blitz, including the bombing of her own house, working with wounded airmen and other casualties of war had a profound affect on her that came out in later years. She suffered depression off and on and was hospitalized several times in her late sixties and seventies.

Mac died of liver cancer in 1985, in Ottawa, where her daughter Carole and granddaughter Camille lived.

This article was contributed by Mac and Bill's daughter, Carole Coplea.

The Best Thing That Ever Happened to Me
Margaret (Budge) Black

Margaret (Budge) Black was born in 1921 in Springburn, Glasgow, Scotland.

I will never forget 24 September 1943 – the day I met a stranger in uniform and my life changed forever.

It all started when my next-door neighbour invited me to a get together at her home. I had already made plans to go out with another friend so I politely declined. When we returned a few hours later the party was still going and my neighbour pressed me to join them.

I didn't really want to go, but to please her I agreed and asked my friend to accompany me for support.

There were some familiar faces in the group but I was surprised to see uniformed guests wearing Canada badges on their sleeves. My friends and I had never met Canadian soldiers before but I had relatives living in Canada: two of my uncles on Mum's side went to live in Ontario; Uncle Bill moved on to the United States but Uncle James had stayed in Ontario.

I saw a soldier standing on one side of the room. Our eyes met and I found myself being introduced to Private Don Black of the Canadian Army Service Corps (CASC). We began to talk and we just seemed to understand each other. We clicked – it was love at first sight.

Don told me that his home was on Cape Breton Island, Nova Scotia and later in the evening, when he overheard me arranging to escort my friend back home to her place, he asked if he could join us. When my friend left us she said I better direct this soldier boy to the streetcar that would take him back to the Canadian Club downtown – that was where Canadian servicemen stayed while on leave in Glasgow.

I returned home thinking about the pleasant end to an interesting evening and assumed I would never see this Canadian soldier again. But it wasn't an ending; that chance meeting was just the beginning.

Imagine my surprise when Don showed up at my doorstep the very next day. Because he knew where my neighbour lived it was just another step next door to me. He explained he was returning to England the next day and asked if he could see me again. So the next evening I went with him to the train station and we chatted until the train arrived, exchanging fond farewells.

He promised to write from England and to keep in touch which he did faithfully throughout his service in North Africa, then Italy and later to France, Germany, Belgium and finally Holland. In late 1944 he had a leave so we were together again for the first time since we met in September 1943.

I took Don home to meet my mother and gain her approval. Mum had been widowed since I was just one month old and she didn't have it easy. In the early years she worked at a jail cleaning cells and later she found a job as a domestic. I went to work at the Craig Park Electric Cable Co. on Flemington Street when I left school at fourteen and during the war it became an essential service so I stayed there and my income helped keep the house going. I was her only child and she was very protective of me but my mother liked him right away and he, in turn, treated her with utmost respect.

Mum may have been impressed with Don but one night I stayed out too late with him and she was so worried that she slapped my face when I returned. I still remember that slap!

When the war ended in May 1945 Don was in Holland waiting to return to Canada. At that time there were not enough shipping spaces available so he had to wait his turn. In the meantime we hoped that we could spend another leave together at Christmas. But when Christmas arrived I was lying in a hospital bed in the Royal Infirmary after an emergency mastoid operation.

Don and I were shattered but we made the best of it. He visited me at the infirmary and brought me a gift of oranges which had been rare during the war. Some of the younger patients had never seen an orange so we got permission to give them to the children. There were so happy and excited! But I was even happier because Don said: 'One day, you will be in Canada with me.' I realized then I would be leaving Scotland some day.

Don left for Canada and when I was released from the hospital in January 1946 I received a telegram saying he was finally back home. We continued to write to each other and Don applied to Immigration to bring me to Canada as his fiancée. I had endless paperwork at my end and medical examinations and lots and lots of questions. It all worked out happily for both of us and after one-and-a-half years of negotiation we received permission for me to come to Canada.

In July 1947 I began my very long journey by air, automobile, rail and ferry to Canada. I had no second thoughts about leaving my mother behind. I was wrapped up in myself, in love and happy.

My long and interesting trip began with a train from Glasgow to London; then I boarded an American flight from London to New York with a stopover at Gander, Newfoundland. I was supposed to fly from Gander to Halifax, Nova Scotia but due to fog in Halifax the plane was diverted to Moncton, New Brunswick. From Moncton all the passengers were transported by car to Halifax where Don and I were finally reunited. From Halifax we took a train to Canso. At Canso the trains were separated and put on a ferry to cross the narrow Strait of Canso which lies between mainland Nova Scotia and Cape Breton. On the other side the individual train cars were reconnected and we continued on by rail to Sydney, Cape Breton and my future home.

When I arrived I found that not everyone was welcoming. Don was what you would call 'a bit of a looker' and some of the local women were jealous because they thought the men would return to them.

My new home came with a mother-in-law. We got along most of the time but there were times when we didn't see eye to eye; I found her exasperating at times. People could not understand my accent so that could be frustrating. In Scotland we had running water and indoor plumbing but here we had an outhouse and I had to go to a well for water.

After my first two children were born I took them back to Scotland for a three-month-long vacation in 1952. Donalda celebrated her second birthday in Scotland; Elizabeth was five months old.

When we came back to Canada my mother was lonely by herself in Scotland so she moved to Sydney to live with us. At first she seemed to be happy but after a few years she started getting homesick. She said it was too difficult for an older person to pull up roots like that and she wanted to be buried in her home country. She decided to go back to Scotland so we bought her a one-way ticket and she began preparations to leave. A few weeks before she was to fly back home she passed away in her sleep. She was buried in Sydney.

It's true Don and I only saw each other during his leaves in 1943, 1944 and 1945 but we had a letter courtship for five years and I still have the first letter he wrote to me.

My marriage was a very happy and loving one with a great guy. Together we had eight children, four boys and four girls. Sad to say he passed on in January 1980 with lung cancer. I still miss him so much.

I'll never forget the evening my life changed when I met this stranger in uniform from Canada. He was the best thing that ever happened to me.

Postscript: Margaret Black passed away in August 2007, not long after this book was first released. Her daughter Marina read Margaret's story at the funeral.

8

Children of War Brides

When the Canadian government brought 44,000 War Brides and their 21,000 children to Canada between 1942 and 1948, it was understood that every serviceman's dependent automatically became a Canadian citizen upon landing at Pier 21 in Halifax, Nova Scotia.[1]

Certainly that's what everyone believed for the last sixty years. From the very beginning of the War Bride transportation scheme, servicemen's dependents were called citizens and except for their Immigration ID card that curiously bore the stamp 'Landed Immigrant', every single document they were ever given in the course of their transportation to Canada reinforced the comforting view that they were citizens.

A colourful little brochure called *Dock to Destination* which was handed to every War Bride upon embarking at Southampton and Liverpool contained these heart-warming instructions from Canada's Department of National Defence:

As soon as the ship docks Canadian Immigration officials will come aboard. These men will complete the formalities for your entry to Canada which automatically makes you a Canadian citizen.[2]

Even Canada's Prime Minister, William Lyon Mackenzie King, had nothing but praise for Canada's War Brides. Sailing with a group of servicemen's
dependents aboard the *Queen Mary* on 31 August 1946, he was described as
giving a most encouraging speech to the group assembled before him that
day:

> Mr King, in a short speech of welcome congratulated the brides who won the
> hearts of Canadian soldiers, the men on their choice of brides, and Canada on
> the splendid addition being made to its citizenship.[3]

War Brides and their children have worked, paid taxes, voted, served in elections and some children have even had distinguished careers in the Canadian
military. If they travelled they applied for and were given passports which
they used to travel back home to Britain over the last sixty years.

Every now and then a story will surface from the 1950s, '60s or '70s
of a War Bride who was told she wasn't a citizen and in every case, she
quickly went about clearing the matter up. In 1954, Mary Dale of Mabel
Lake, British Columbia was stopped at Customs when she went home to
Scotland with her Canadian-born son, Gordon.

> She considers herself a Canadian ... but she was surprised to learn that was
> not true on her first trip to Scotland when Gordon was five.
>   She was told she lacked a Canadian citizenship certificate and was del-
> egated to a different line than her son. She applied for the paperwork upon
> her return to Canada and learned she had to pay a fee.
>   'I'm a $2 Canadian,' Mary says with a great roll of laughter.[4]

Scottish War Bride Zoe Boone of Arthurette, New Brunswick had a similar experience travelling with her children to Britain in the 1950s, except
the fee was $5. Interestingly, English War Bride Gwen Zradicka of British
Columbia was told in 1969 that since she had divorced her first husband,
she was no longer a Canadian citizen!

> After 24 years in Canada, Zradicka divorced in 1968. She remarried the fol-
> lowing year to another Canadian. But when she went to get a passport for a
> trip to Britain, her request was denied.
>   Because of the divorce, Zradicka was told she had lost her citizenship ...
> She went through the challenging task of tracking down her ex-husband, and

getting permission to get a copy of his birth certificate. Then she had to get a copy of the British marriage certificate.[5]

If you ask a group of War Brides most will say they've had no problems with their citizenship, but from the small sample above we know that some have definitely been told they are not citizens – and they weren't very happy about it. When faced with the upsetting news, these women and their children dealt with it the best way they knew how; they filled out the paperwork and applied for their citizenship card. In the days before computers, the Internet, and 9/11, these applications were dealt with fairly efficiently and nobody ever again questioned their citizenship – that is, until a War Bride child named Joe Taylor came along.

Joe Taylor is the son of an English War Bride and a Canadian serviceman who landed on the shores of Normandy on D-Day. His parents' marriage did not survive the realities of postwar Canada and his mother returned to England with Joe after only a few months in Canada.

When Joe and his mother went back to England in 1946 they travelled on a Canadian passport because they were Canadian citizens. Joe always considered himself Canadian and as his story will show, he made every effort to come back to Canada in the 1970s when he was a young man, but bureaucratic bungling put a stop to that. In 2002 when Joe again started asking questions about his Canadian citizenship, he opened up a Pandora's Box that threatens the security of every Canadian War Bride and the children they brought with them to Canada at the end of the Second World War.

In a nutshell, Joe was told he is not a Canadian citizen because he was out of the country and failed to attest to his citizenship when he was twenty-four years old in 1969. When Joe challenged this obscure regulation, he was then told he isn't a Canadian citizen because he was born out of wedlock to a British woman and a Canadian serviceman.

According to the 1947 Citizenship Act, upon which War Brides and their children were given Canadian citizenship, when a child is born out of wedlock he inherits the nationality of his mother at the time of his birth. It doesn't seem to matter that Joe's parents did marry when Joe was five months old and that he and his mother came to Canada with the promise of citizenship in 1946.

Complicating matters is the heightened sense of security since 9/11 and the recent introduction of new passport regulations between Canada and the United States. Previous to the new regulations, a Canadian citizen did not require a passport to enter the U.S. As of January 2007 every Canadian entering the U.S. by air must produce a passport and in January 2008 the same will apply to Canadians entering the U.S. by land and sea. With these new regulations in force, Joe soon found that he wasn't the only one who was being told he's not a Canadian citizen. As War Bride children started applying for passports, they started coming forward with their own tales of woe.

It's only going to get worse; most War Bride children are nearing retirement age. As they start applying for federal benefits such as Old Age Pension and Canada Pension, they'll soon find that questions about citizenship may hold up their cheques.

In May 2006 Joe took Canada's Department of Citizenship and Immigration to British Columbia's Federal Court and he won; but the Department has appealed the ruling and in so doing has raised the spectre that every serviceman's dependent who came here in the 1940s could lose their citizenship.

It's hard to believe but it's true, and as Justice Luc Martineau said in his ruling of September 2006, if the Federal government appeals his decision to the Supreme Court the impact will have ramifications beyond Joe Taylor.[6]

'This is not a street fight; the outcome of this goes beyond the interests of Mr [Joseph] Taylor. It has huge consequences,' Justice Luc Martineau warned Crown lawyer Peter Bell, who was representing the immigration minister.[7]

In this chapter we will meet four War Bride children who have been told they are not Canadian citizens; two of them have lived their entire lives in Canada; one was abducted by her mother as a nine-year-old child and brought back to England; and the other is Joe Taylor himself.

They Can't Take My Identity Away from Me
Joe Taylor

Joe Taylor was barely two years old when his parents' wartime marriage fell apart in Canada and his mother fled back to England with little Joe in her arms. As a child, Joe knew little of the circumstances which led to his parents' divorce and cared even less: growing up on the Isle of Wight he was the apple of his grandfather's eye and had a childhood that most boys would envy.

It took many years before Joe found out what happened between his mother and father in Canada. Along the way, he came up against the power of the Canadian government, which is challenging his claim to citizenship, and he's became a beacon of hope for thousands of War Bride children who believe they are entitled to Canadian citizenship by virtue of their birth.

Joe's mother is eighty-five years old now and she still doesn't like to talk about her short time in Canada. She married an Englishman in the 1950s and went on with her life. She has never been very forthcoming about Joe's father but she's never lied to Joe either and for that he is thankful. He knows there are other children of War Brides just like him whose mothers have not been so truthful.

Much of what he's been able to find out has been pieced together from snippets of conversation over the years and from what other family members on both sides of the Atlantic have told him. Because of this delicate situation he has asked to give his mother a pseudonym so that he can be frank in the retelling of his parents' story and what happened to a love gone so very wrong.

Joe's mother, Glenys Alice Sidney (a pseudonym) was born in 1921 in East Cowes on the Isle of Wight. His grandfather was a sawmill manager and his grandmother had been a hotel employee in Ventnor before marrying.

Alice grew up in East Cowes, went to school there and like many young girls her age she found employment in the Saunders Roe (known as Saro) aircraft manufacturing plant based in Cowes. Alice worked in the office at Saro on a Hollerith machine – a leading edge tabulating machine that used cards with pre-punched holes for data entry. (The Hollerith machine was a precursor of the computer and its inventor, Herman Hollerith, eventually founded the world famous computer company International Business Machines.)

When war broke out, Saunders Roe threw its entire workforce behind the war effort and, since the aircraft industry was deemed an essential service, Alice stayed on while the plant switched over to the manufacture of Supermarine Walruses and de Havilland Sea Otters. She worked there until baby Joe was born in December 1944.

Joe's father, Cpl Joseph (Joe) H. Taylor was born in Nanaimo on Vancouver Island, British Columbia in 1923. As a teenager growing up in the depths of the Depression, with poverty and unemployment the common experience for uneducated workers, he considered himself lucky to get a job working in the Cumberland coal mines on the Island, just like his own father had before him. Ten months after war was declared, Joseph did his last shift at the mines and joined the Canadian Scottish Regiment in Courtney. After going through basic training, he was sent to the UK in 1942.

Joe doesn't know how his parents met but he figures they were introduced to each other on the Isle of Wight during the fall of 1943. He also knows that by April 1944 there was talk of Alice and Joseph marrying but getting married to a Canadian serviceman wasn't that easy: there were forms to fill out, medical examinations to take, and most important, Joe had to get permission from his commanding officer in the Canadian Scottish Regiment before anything could move forward.

At the time, Canadian military authorities tried to discourage what they considered to be hasty marriages taking place between Canadians and British women. One way of putting the brakes on these marriages was by implementing a convoluted bureaucratic process which ensured only the most determined couples applied.

Time moved swiftly in these months and weeks leading up to the invasion: before they knew it, preparations for D-Day were upon them and Joseph was gone. On 6 June 1944 he landed on the shores of Normandy and he spent most of the next year trying to survive while manning a flamethrower that incinerated everything in sight – nightmarish scenes which came back to haunt him after the war.

By mid-summer 1944 Alice knew she was pregnant and that she was in big trouble. Joseph was fighting in Normandy and there was little hope of reaching him. Being pregnant and unmarried in the 1940s was a scandal that brought shame upon the entire family and was enough to have a young woman ostracized permanently from society.

It mattered little how you were brought up, your education or family connections: women who dared to keep a so-called 'illegitimate' baby faced terrible social consequences that still reverberate today.

In today's modern society, few people care whether parents are married when children are born but back then such children were known as bastards and – in the midst of the social upheaval brought on by war and the presence of so many foreign soldiers – they were Canadian bastards at that.

Abortion was illegal and dangerous, and, if there was no support from a woman's family, there were only two options: 1) go as far away as possible to a home for unwed mothers, have the baby in secret, then give it up for adoption, or 2) marry the father of the child.

Alice was a very lucky young woman: her parents were supportive and they helped her as much as they could, going so far as to try to get a message through to Joe on the front lines in France that Alice was pregnant and that he was going to be a father.

When Joseph found out that Alice was pregnant, he tried twice to get permission to marry from his commanding officer but he was refused both times. In Joseph's military personnel record from Canada's National Archives is his request to marry Glenys Alice Sidney and a handwritten response from his commanding officer saying permission has been 'denied.'

There was little Joseph could do from the front lines and both he and Alice just accepted that if he survived the war, he would make his way back to England and they would get married. That's exactly what happened.

On 5 May 1945, shortly after Joseph returned from the Continent, they were married on the Isle of Wight. Their wedding/family picture shows a beaming Alice with a proud-looking Joseph Sr. cradling five-month-old Joe Jr, in his lap. Sadly, it is a picture of contentment that that didn't survive the test of time.

Joseph remained in Europe until February 1946 where he helped with mopping up duties in the army of occupation. Five months later, on 1 July 1946, Alice and eighteen-month-old Joe arrived at Pier 21 in Halifax, Nova Scotia on board the ocean liner *Queen Mary* with thousands of other War Brides. After a week-long journey by War Bride train to Vancouver, mother and baby landed in Cumberland on Vancouver Island.

Alice must not have known what she was coming to because the picture she described to her relatives back in England was one of utter poverty. Joseph lived in his parents' home – a tiny mineworkers' shack with no running water or electricity. There was little privacy for the young married couple and the grandparents were far from welcoming. Alice told the story of how they refused to allow other locals to arrange a baby shower for their grandson.

Joe's father was a changed man as a result of the terrible things he had experienced during the war. Today he would probably be diagnosed with post-traumatic stress disorder but sixty years ago the military did not recognize that soldiers could suffer mental disorders from the hell they had lived through in battle. Joseph took to drinking at the Legion hall and returning home in the early hours of the morning to physically assault Alice.

After three months of a rapidly disintegrating situation Alice ran away with the baby one night when Joseph was out at the Legion. It was dark and she was deathly afraid of the black bears which she had been warned were lurking in the shadows of the woods but she was desperate. Alice collapsed, but luckily she was discovered by a neighbour and his wife who took her and little Joe into the safety of their own home.

When Joseph found out they were hiding in the neighbour's home, he allegedly stomped over in a fury and hammered at the door demanding their return. But the man held his ground and said he would call the police if Joseph did not leave immediately. The couple helped Alice send a telegram to her parents in England asking for help. Alice's parents sold most of their furniture in a hurry and obtained a loan so that they could wire the money to pay for the trip back to England.

Alice and little Joe travelled across Canada by train to Montreal and then to New York which was the cheapest route at the time. At the Consulate in New York they were issued with a Canadian passport. They flew home in a small airplane that made stops in Halifax, Gander, Greenland, Iceland and Ireland before landing back in England in October 1946.

Alice was seriously ill and had to be hospitalized upon her arrival. When she was fully recovered she went back to work at Saro in order to repay the loan from her parents. Although he couldn't know it at the time, young Joe was an extremely fortunate young boy with grandparents who truly loved him. Not only did they care for him while Alice was at work and dote on him as only grandparents could, but his grandfather became a substitute father whom Joe considered his idol.

Joe was about seven years old when he first began to notice other children his age had fathers. While his mother and grandparents didn't go out of their way to tell Joe what had happened in Canada, neither did they exaggerate or lie to the young boy. So when he asked, in all his innocence, 'Why do all the other children have fathers and mothers but I do not?' he was told in a matter of fact way that his father had been a Canadian soldier who came to England to fight in the war and that the marriage had not been successful. That is why his father was in Canada while he and his mother were in England.

A couple of years later the issue came up again and Joe asked if he could write to his father in Canada. He was given his father's last known address and to everyone's surprise, Joseph replied. There followed three years of correspondence exchanging Christmas and birthday presents before communication ceased completely.

Many years later Joe found out that his father was practically illiterate and the letters were actually written by his second wife in Canada. The letters stopped around the time that Joseph's father and wife began having their own children and the little boy in England became a distant memory.

Joe was not bitter about the way things turned out. He accepted the fact that he probably would never have a relationship with his father. Nonetheless, in 1971 when Joe was twenty-five years old and married with two young children of his own, he began to think of moving his family to Canada. He was a Canadian citizen, after all, so he made inquiries at Canada House in London.

Canadian law relevant at the time that Joe landed in Canada in July 1946 stated that the children of Canadian servicemen born while they were on active service abroad were to be deemed, when landing in Canada, as non-immigrants and to have the same status as their fathers.

Joe told the officials at Canada House all about his Canadian father but they made no comment other than, 'We will send you the appropriate forms to complete.' Joe did not understand that he had been sent standard forms which any prospective immigrant with no connection to Canada would receive. Not realizing the nuances of the process he became tangled in a Kafkaesque immigration department bureaucracy over a misunderstanding of his own status and was thus perceived as an immigrant.

(Coincidentally, years later, Joe was also informed by Canada House in London that he lost his Canadian citizenship on his twenty-fourth birthday because he had not filed forms requesting the retention of his citizenship status. This has happened to many other War Bride children including well-known Canadian Senator Roméo Dallaire. Dutch-born Senator Dallaire was a General in the Canadian Army when he led the ill-fated 1995 UN mission in Rwanda that became the basis of a blockbuster Hollywood film *Hotel Rwanda*, starring Nick Nolte. The son of a War Bride and a Canadian serviceman, Dallaire came to Canada with his mother on the War Bride ship *Empire Brent* in December 1946. He was a young captain in the Canadian military when, after applying to renew his Canadian passport, he was informed that since he had not filed for retention of his citizenship by age twenty-four, he was not a Canadian citizen.)

Back in 1971 when Joe made his first application to 'immigrate' to Canada, one of the main requirements was the sponsorship of a Canadian citizen. Not realizing that as a Canadian citizen he shouldn't have to seek the sponsorship of another Canadian to come back to his home country, Joe filled out the forms and sent them to his father's last known address. But the address was years out of date and the forms never came back.

Without his father's sponsorship Joe's application could not move forward and he had to give up on the idea for the time being. But Canada was never far from his mind as Joe moved his growing family to Buckinghamshire and then later to Gloucestershire in England.

About 1996 Joe began to look for his father again to see if he was still alive. His first return to Canada was in October 1999 and he immediately felt an affinity with the land of his ancestors. Not only had his father been born on Vancouver Island but so had his paternal grandparents.

Joe wrote to Canada's Department of Veterans Affairs seeking information on his father's whereabouts and in November 2000 he received a letter regretting to inform him that his father had died on 5 February 1996. The letter said he was buried in the Royal Canadian Legion's Field of Honour in Port Alberni on Vancouver Island.

Joe made an inquiry with the City Clerk in Port Alberni who was kind enough to send the newspaper obituary. That was when Joe heard the surprising news that he had seven brothers and sisters from his father's second marriage.

In 2001 Joe and his wife came to Vancouver Island for a three-week visit and they had two things in mind: first, they wanted to buy a house somewhere on the Island to which they could retire and; second, they wanted to meet Joe's brothers and sisters. They did end up buying a house in Victoria and through an amazing stroke of luck they found his relatives instantly after visiting the miner's museum in Cumberland.

Feeling somewhat more positive about his situation and with retirement in mind, Joe did a bit more research and made a second application to come to Canada in November 2003. It took two long years but this application was eventually rejected in May 2005 by a processing officer at the Sydney, Nova Scotia Immigration Centre.

The rejection was based on the fact that Joe was born out of wedlock while his father was fighting to defeat the Nazi forces in Europe. The government's position was that the child acquires the nationality of his mother when he is 'illegitimate' and since his parents weren't married, Joe was British, not Canadian. Joe therefore has no entitlement to citizenship.

Joe challenged CIC and found himself in British Columbia's Federal Court in May 2006. In a decision that ruled staunchly in Joe's favour, Justice Luc Martineau accused Canada's Department of Citizenship and Immigration (CIC) of violating the Canadian Bill of Rights, the Charter of Rights, the due process of law and the fundamentals of justice. At the eleventh hour CIC appealed the ruling and won.

Joe's case has been reported widely in Canada over the past two years and his story has appeared in nearly every major newspaper, television and radio show nationwide. Joe and his supporters, who run the gamut from

War Brides and historians, politicians and writers, to other War Bride children who are also struggling to have their citizenship recognized, have even appeared before the travelling Parliamentary Committee on Citizenship and Immigration, then chaired by MP Andrew Telegdi, to shed light on this ridiculous situation and to plead with legislators to set the record straight.

In major cities in Canada where the Committee held hearings in 2005, people came forward with similar complaints, drawing more attention to the issue and raising the profile of Joe's case in the media. In 2007, with planned changes to passport rules between Canada and the United States coming into effect, the plight of War Bride children like Joe was back in the news again. Canadians were appalled to learn that the federal government intends to fight Joe's BC Federal Court ruling so in February 2007 he flew from England and appeared before the Committee for a second time.

All this has taken a gruelling toll on Joe's emotional health, not to mention his financial resources. To date he has spent $40,000 (Cdn) on the case and if the case goes to the Supreme Court, there is no telling how much more he'll have to spend. A certified Chartered Accountant with a successful accounting practice in England, Joe is used to dealing with numbers but he says the treatment of Canada's War Bride children by the CIC simply doesn't add up.

'Whenever I start to feel like it's a losing proposition – and that's more often than not – a new War Bride child will contact me and say "Don't give up Joe. You've come so far. We need you to fight this for us."'

Joe explains that being a Canadian is more than just a piece of paper, it's about who he is as a human being. 'It's my very soul,' he says, 'It's my identity.'

So to those bureaucrats and politicians who think a long costly battle at the Supreme Court will scare Joe away, he wants them to know he has no plans to back down: 'I am a Canadian, and I will be a Canadian until I die. No government can take my identity away from me.'

Postscript: Joe accepted a Section 5.4 Grant of Citizenship and on January 24, 2008, became a citizen in a special ceremony held in Vancouver.

'I Live, Breathe and Will Die a Canadian'
Sheila Walshe

Sheila Walshe was only nine years old when her English mother suddenly announced that she was taking the three children on holiday to England. At the time, Sheila's father was away working as a long haul truck driver in

eastern Canada and he knew nothing of his wife's plans. Once the family
arrived in England, Sheila's mother told the children their father was dead
and they were staying in the UK.

That was 1952. As Sheila found out nearly forty years later, the story of
her father's death was a complete fabrication concocted by her mother, a
woman whose actions still infuriate Sheila today.

Sheila's father certainly was not dead; in fact, when he returned to
Brookville, New Brunswick and discovered that his wife had abducted the
children he tried everything to get them back. But all he met was bureaucratic resistance and English in-laws who refused to help. Eventually, after
many years of searching he gave up.

It took thirty-nine years before Sheila was reunited with her Canadian
father in British Columbia: for the first time since she was nine years old
she finally knew where she belonged. Like her brother and sister before her,
Sheila decided to leave England forever and start a new life in Canada. But
what began as the return of an abducted daughter has turned into a fight
with the Canadian government which callously insists Sheila lost any claim
she may have had to citizenship when she turned twenty-four.

Sheila's mother was one of three sisters who married Canadian soldiers
during the Second World War. The sisters met their future husbands in
1941 when three young men were billeted in the family home at 5 Slindon
Road, Broadwater, West Sussex. It wasn't long before the women, by now
aged twenty-one, nineteen and seventeen were courting the Canadians and
in the heightened emotions brought on by the uncertainty of war, all three
of them married in 1942.

Sheila was born in Brighton in March 1943. As the dependents of a Canadian
serviceman, both she and her mother were entitled to free passage on board
the War Bride ships and upon landing, to full rights of Canadian citizenship.
In May 1946 she and her mother came to Canada on board the *Queen Mary*
where they were met at Pier 21 in Halifax, Nova Scotia by Sheila's father.

All three War Bride sisters came to Canada, but only Sheila's mother, the
middle child, had difficulty settling in. In civilian life Sheila's father was a truck
driver, a trade he learned in the Canadian Army when he served with the Three
Rivers Tank Regiment during the Second World War. At first the family lived in
Welland, Ontario where Sheila's father was born, but jobs weren't easy to come
by in postwar Canada so they moved to wherever the work could be found.

Although Sheila doesn't like to speak badly of her mother, you can read
between the lines to see that her mother wasn't happy in Canada. Even

after having two more children she pined for England and was constantly homesick. With her husband away much of the time, Sheila's mother found distractions in the small towns where they lived – and that was part of the problem.

Perhaps she married too young, had children before she should have, maybe she was just the type of person who could never settle down, but whatever the reason, when Sheila's father would come home after a couple of weeks on the road there were problems and the family would move again, eventually ending up in Brookville, NB which was a long way from Welland.

Sheila was too young to understand the reasons why her parents fought. She adored her father and that is why the news of his death hit her so hard. There wasn't even a funeral. One week they were in Canada, and the next, they were in England living with grandparents who called Sheila and her two siblings 'nothing but Canadian bits of dirt.'

It wasn't long before the family moved out on their own, with no thanks to the English relatives. For most of her growing up years in England, Sheila, her mother and two siblings lived in poverty in a small one-room flat in Worthing and then in a council house in Maybridge that was paid for by National Assistance.

Sheila always wondered if her mother's family hated the three children because they were Canadians: after all, her brother and sister were born in Canada and Sheila was a citizen too because she was born in England to a Canadian serviceman and had come to Canada with her War Bride mother in 1946.

But Sheila now realizes it was the divorce that caused so many problems as they were growing up. And even though she still doesn't know the whole story, she does know enough to say that her mother's entire family was caught up in a web of deceit that went on for generations. She says it's 'shocking' from today's perspective to believe that her grandparents, aunts and especially her mother would prefer the children believe their father was dead rather than know their mother's marriage ended in divorce.

And that is the way that Sheila and her siblings grew up: poor, fatherless and shunned by their mother's relatively well-to-do family who lived less than three miles away. It was a dismal time in Sheila's life. She married when she was seventeen. Her sister did the same. Only their little brother Lloyd was left at home and the time came when he too had to get out of that situation.

As a Canadian-born citizen, Lloyd returned to Canada in the 1970s and, still believing his father was dead, searched for his Canadian relatives with little success. In the days before the Internet it took a very long time for a breakthrough but in 1990 Lloyd finally found his step-grandfather and, through him, an uncle who told him the astounding news that their father was still alive and living in British Columbia on Canada's west coast.

Lloyd wrote to Sheila with their father's address. She was ecstatic and wrote a Christmas card to say that she had never stopped thinking of him. Sheila did not expect a reply but he wrote back. Her father had remarried and raised four more children but he wanted to see his oldest child. Sheila was reunited with her father in 1991 and it was a moment she will never forget. Both he and his new family, including his second wife, embraced Sheila with open arms. The family that she had left behind in 1952 was waiting for her in Canada.

Sheila returned to England but the urge to see her father was so great that she came back to Canada a few weeks later. Not wanting to be a burden on her father's family, she and her husband bought a mobile home in the beautiful Okanagan Valley so they would have a place to stay when they came to visit.

Meantime, Sheila put the wheels in motion to return to Canada permanently. As a nurse, she has a skill that is needed in Canada and since she was Canadian – or at least thought she was – she assumed it was just a matter of filling out some forms in order to return.

In February 1992 Sheila contacted Canada House in London for a Canadian passport. After filling in all the forms, getting all the documentation required and paying the fees, Sheila received a letter four months later which said her claim for Canadian citizenship had expired when she was twenty-four. Because she had not taken advantage of the opportunity to affirm her citizenship in the 1960s, it was too late.

> Based on the information and documents you submitted, we have determined that you had a claim to citizenship in accordance with 4 (1) (b) of the Canadian Citizenship Act because of your birth outside Canada to a Canadian born father. However, you ceased to be a Canadian citizen on March 30, 1967 because you did not reside in Canada on your twenty-fourth birthday, nor had you applied for retention of your citizenship before that date.

'I was totally unaware of the necessity to reaffirm my desire to be a Canadian,' says Sheila. 'How can they punish me for something I didn't even know?'

Added to the irony is the fact that in the ensuing years, Sheila's brother Lloyd, her sister and even her own son, daughter and granddaughter have moved to Canada and are Canadian citizens or permanent residents.

Sheila and her husband still live in the mobile home in the Okanagan, existing on their British pensions and hoping for a day when her citizenship will be validated by the Canadian government. She is not allowed to work and it is difficult financially but her husband is by her side and they're not willing to give up. Her father has since passed away and his dying wish was that Sheila would have her citizenship.

In 2005, soon after her father died, Sheila testified before the Canadian Parliamentary Committee on Citizenship and Immigration in Vancouver, BC. In her brief appearance, she told the story of being abducted as a child and her frustrating experiences with the Canadian government as it continues to deny her citizenship. These are her closing remarks:

> My father missed his first Remembrance Day parade this November. I marched for his memory. Help me make his wishes become fact please. He was a great man, and always very proud of being a Canadian … I live, breathe and will die, a CANADIAN. I ask you, help me.

Postscript: On October 14, 2007, Sheila Walshe accepted a Section 5.4 Grant of Citizenship, thus ending her struggle with the Department of Citizenship and Immigration.

I Feel Bad for My Parents
Marion Vermeersch

Marion Vermeersch and her brother, Peter Brammah, are the children of English War Bride, Doris Barr.

In May 1946 I sailed to Canada on board the *Queen Mary* with my older brother Peter and my mother, English War Bride Doris Barr. I was only seventeen months old so I don't have any memory of the trip but at nine years Peter was old enough to remember that my mother was terribly seasick so he spent a lot of time playing with another boy and almost fell out the porthole!

My mother had been married before the war and Peter was the son of that marriage. My father, Sgt Sandy Barr of Lynn Valley area, Norfolk County, Ontario was fighting in Europe when she found out she was pregnant with me so I was born in Steyning, Sussex, England, before they were married in March 1945.

We settled into life in Ontario and grew up enjoying all the things of a typically Canadian childhood – skating, hockey, baseball, swimming, and camping. Living in a rural area, we enjoyed our small farm with its animals and gardens. Peter was raised as my parents' first son and was well-loved and accepted by everyone in the family. But my parents were the sort of people who never paid much attention to formality and for one reason or another my father never officially adopted Peter.

My dad came from a family of tenant farmers in Scotland. In 1924 his mother and siblings dreamed of a better life abroad and the Dominion wanted immigrants. It was a struggle to keep things going so he and his brother Andy were sent to Canada with a group of Home Children. The Home Children were mainly orphans but also included the poor and street children from Britain who were gathered up and shipped to Canada in the thousands during the nineteenth and twentieth centuries to work as farm labourers. My father was thirteen and my uncle eleven years old and they were very lucky to be taken in together by a farmer near Guelph, Ontario, who was very good to them.

My brother Peter joined the Canadian Navy at sixteen, retiring twenty-five years later with the rank of Chief Petty Officer. He went on to spend ten years with Dome Petroleum in the Canadian Arctic and then worked with the city police in Calgary, Alberta where he lives today. I worked at various jobs throughout my life and still work today in child welfare in Simcoe, Ontario. Over the years we have voted in elections, paid taxes, and in Peter's case, even served our country.

All those years that Peter was in the Navy and with Dome he travelled the world on his Canadian seaman's papers without any problem what-soever. He even went to England many times to see our relatives and his citizenship status was never once raised as an issue when he'd come back to this country. That all changed after 9/11.

In 2003 Peter was planning a trip to Britain and since he was no longer in the Navy he had to apply for his first real passport. Thinking it was just a matter of filling out a few forms, he went to the Passport Office in Calgary, Alberta and was sent to the federal Department of Citizenship and Immigration Canada (CIC). To his complete and utter shock, he was told that he was not a Canadian.

There was no reason given and certainly nothing has ever been put in writing. Peter was just told that he's not a Canadian and had to apply for a permanent residence card if he wants to stay in the country. Peter went back to the office several times, met with his Member of Parliament and other officials, he even appeared on a radio talk show in Calgary but he continued to be told the same thing. He was not a citizen and he had to apply for a permanent resident card. We found out he could get a British passport so at least he could go on his trip. However, no amount of references or discussion would convince CIC that Peter was Canadian.

In a panic, I went to the CIC office in Hamilton, Ontario, and got almost exactly the same answer to my request for a passport. After looking through some of my mother's old documents I returned with a booklet that was given to my mother when she boarded the *Queen Mary* in July 1946. The booklet clearly states that when Peter and I and our War Bride mother arrived in Canada in 1946 we were considered Canadian. It says: 'As soon as the ship docks, Canadian Immigration officials will come aboard. These men will complete the formalities for your entry into Canada which automatically make you a Canadian citizen.'

The documents didn't matter. They insisted that I am not a Canadian and furthermore I had no status in Canada at this point. Like Peter, I was told that I was British and had to apply for a permanent residence card.

At the time, I contacted the office of my MP, Diane Finley in Simcoe, Ontario. As I write this story, Ms Finley is the Minister of Citizenship and Immigration in the Conservative Federal government of Stephen Harper, but in 2004 she was just a backbencher in the opposition.

I found that her office did not even know what a War Bride was, had never heard of such a situation and advised me that there was no way for me to avoid going through the entire immigration process. I was advised that I should not expect any special treatment because, 'After all, we have to have security in the immigration process.'

All Diane Finley's office would do was offer to give me forms to get started applying for permanent residence status.

My next step was to contact the neighbouring MP, Lloyd St Amand, in Brant, Ontario. He was very understanding, felt a mistake was made and assured me that the federal Parliamentary Committee on Citizenship and Immigration was working on the problem and that surely a resolution to this situation would be forthcoming.

Peter and I applied for permanent residence cards which we finally received at the end of December 2005. After you obtain the cards, you have to wait three years to apply for citizenship. In the meantime we cannot legally vote. I was told by CIC to contact Elections Canada and have my name taken off the voters' list! We also found out that we may have difficulty with certain benefits for which we have worked all our lives such as Old Age Pension and Canada Pension Plan.

So that is the situation we are in today – two of a quickly growing number of War Bride children who are being told we are not Canadians. Ironically, our children are entitled to the British Citizenship we hold by birth; my daughter Leslie has both Canadian and British passports. I am worried that should Peter and I obtain Canadian citizenship, we will have to continually apply for renewal: it may not be permanent, in spite of all our years in this country.

I feel bad for my parents, who are not with us today. They would be appalled to learn of this shabby treatment by the country for which they fought and worked for so many years.

Postscript: Although it would make their lives a lot easier, Marion Veermeersch and her brother Peter Brammah have refused on principle to apply for a Section 5.4 discretionary Grant of Citizenship from the Minister of Citizenship and Immigration. Marion and Peter represent a large number of War Bride children who believe the discretionary grants do not fully recognize their Canadian citizenship from the date of their arrival in Canada more than sixty years ago. They say they will accept nothing less than the recognition of that status from the Canadian government and are prepared to wait for Bill C-37, the so-called 'Lost Canadian' legislation to become law on 17 April 2009.

Update: On 10 December 2007, International Human Rights Day, Canada's Minister of Citizenship and Immigration introduced Bill C-37, an Act to Amend the Citizenship Act. Called the 'Lost Canadian' Bill, it was so named after the group 'Lost Canadians' led by Don Chapman of Gibsons, British Columbia. After a long struggle through Parliamentary and Senate Committees, the House of Commons and the Senate, Bill C-37 finally received Royal Assent on 17 April 2008 with an amendment stating that it be enacted within one year, on 17 April 2009. Chapman, who led the call for changes to the Citizenship Act after discovering he had been stripped of his citizenship as a child, believes Bill C-37 will solve the problems facing Canadian War Brides and War Bride children by recognizing their status as Canadian citizens. Those who are not covered by Bill C-37 can still apply for a Section 5.4 grant of Citizenship from the Minister.

9

Canadian War Brides of the First World War

The Canadian War Brides of the First World War
by Annette Fulford

Almost ninety years have passed since the end of the First World War yet comparatively little is known about the women who married Canadian servicemen they met in Britain during the war and then came to Canada to live.

Like the War Brides of the Second World War, thousands of British women and their children were brought to Canada after the First World War in a government sponsored immigration scheme that set a precedent for future military plans of its kind. The Canadian government offered free repatriation to the wives and children of its soldiers living overseas, as well as to British and European War Brides who had never set foot on Canadian soil and had married Canadian soldiers during the war.

Each woman was given a one-way ticket to join her husband in the country he lived in prior to joining the war effort. Many of these women had no idea what their life would be like when they arrived in Canada.

What became of War Brides who arrived in Canada during this era? Did they live healthy, productive lives in Canada or did circumstances beyond their control force them to return to their native country? We are lucky that a few of these women wrote about their experiences for a new generation of War Brides arriving in Canada after the Second World War. For the most part, however, their collective history remains to be told.

Meeting Canadian Soldiers in England

Over 600,000 men enlisted with the Canadian Expeditionary Force (CEF) during the First World War and as many as 424,000 of them served overseas.[1] Although the majority of the men were Canadian born, there were also a large percentage of newly immigrated British men who enlisted in the CEF. Most went overseas to fight in Europe or were housed at military training camps in England.

With a large majority of British men fighting in the war, women were needed to work in jobs that were considered traditional male occupations. British women joined the war effort in various organizations such as the Women's Land Army, Volunteer Aid Detachments, Women's Legion, Women's Army Auxiliary Corps, Women's Royal Air Force and First Aid Nursing Yeomanry to name a few. Many women found employment in the war industries and worked in factories producing munitions and related equipment.

The War Brides of the First World War met their Canadian husbands in all manner of ways: at social events like dances, in hospitals where the soldier was recovering from his wounds, or when he was on leave. One War Bride met and married her school friend's older brother who returned to England from Canada with the CEF. Another War Bride worked as a Volunteer Aid Detachment nurse when she met her soldier. My grandmother, Grace Gibson, met Hugh Clark when her sister brought him home for a meal.

Dependents Living Overseas

At the end of the First World War there were thousands of soldiers' dependents living overseas in Britain and Europe. Many of these dependents were the Canadian wives and children of servicemen who travelled overseas and were living in the United Kingdom to be near their soldier husbands. In addition, there were thousands of Canadian soldiers who married women they met abroad during their extended stay and planned to return to Canada with their new brides.

Repatriation Becomes Official

After 11 November 1918 the main task of the Canadian government was to bring the soldiers home quickly and safely. However, it became apparent that many soldiers with families still in Europe could not afford to pay for their return trip to Canada.

In January 1919 the Government of Canada passed an Order in Council (P.C. 179), offering military dependents of Canadian servicemen, including War Brides and their children under the age of eighteen, free third class ocean and rail passage from their home in Britain to their final destination in Canada. The family only had to pay for meals and other incidentals on board ship and train. There was no distinction made between women who had already lived in Canada and those who were travelling there for the first time.[2] The Order in Council, which was passed on 29 January, would set a precedent for future schemes.

Each woman who married a Canadian soldier and planned to live in Canada was required to submit an Application for Repatriation form which was sent out by the Minister of Overseas Immigration in London. Most military dependents were given the option to travel to Canada with their husbands or fathers. This was not always possible due to illness or for women in the later stages of pregnancy.

About a week before a War Bride was to make her journey to Canada she was sent a circular letter or telegram from the Department of Immigration and Colonisation in London. It would give details stating the name of the ship she was to sail on, the date of departure, and where it would embark.

The repatriation scheme was revised several times over the course of the year. In March another line was added to exclude any dependents who intended to travel overseas after this plan came into effect. In November it was revised to include reimbursement for those who sailed to Canada before the Armistice.

Transporting Military Dependents to Canada

The Department of Immigration and Colonisation assumed the task of coordinating the return of military dependents from its London emigration office. Even before the Armistice, the department encouraged dependents to travel back to Canada through letters enclosed with their separation allowance cheques.

On the advice of the Canadian government many dependents returned to Canada prior to the Armistice. Over 17,000 women and children took advantage of this offer and returned to Canada between mid-1917 and November 1918. The government at this time did not pay for their passage but offered them a special rate on a secure ship.

At the Armistice there were still a large number of dependents living abroad. In an article on the front page of the *Calgary Herald* on 27 December 1918 a military official 'estimated the number at close to 60,000 or 70,000, not all whom wish to return to Canada.'

He goes on to say, 'It is interesting to know that approximately 20,000 of the soldiers' dependents now in England have never been in Canada.'

However, Canadian soldiers were marrying British women well in to 1919 so this number could be much higher. The *Globe and Mail* on 7 April 1944 compared the total number of marriages between the two world wars at the time and stated that, 'In the four years of the last war the number of Canadian-British marriages made in Great Britain was 25,000.'

These statistics are for the number of soldiers' dependents that arrived in Canada after the First World War. There are no official figures given for the total number of Canadian soldiers who married abroad and returned to Canada with a War Bride and/or children. Also not included are the many young women who travelled to Canada after the war to be married at their own expense.

In all, 54,500 First World War servicemen's dependents arrived on Canadian shores: the majority (37,748) of dependents crossing the Atlantic to Canada between 15 November 1918 and 31 December 1919.[3]

Shipboard Accommodations

All soldiers' dependents were provided with free third class passage aboard the troopships. It was possible to get superior class passage but it would likely involve a long delay so rather than wait most chose third class passage in order to get to Canada as soon as possible.

Despite careful planning, the transportation of soldiers' dependents to Canada still experienced problems. At the beginning of the repatriation scheme there are many complaints in the immigration files about conditions in the third class accommodations as most families were not used to travelling in steerage.

Once on the ship though, most passengers preferred to be on the deck in the fresh air, not stuck in their cramped berths. A common complaint was the lack of seating on deck for those who wanted to escape their berths.

There were additional complaints about seasickness, overcrowded, dirty accommodation, and lack of amenities. Most of these complaints were dealt with quickly while on board.

The *Saskatoon StarPhoenix* in May 1919 reported one bride's criticism about her journey on the *Corsican*. 'The conditions below were so repulsive that we could not stand it, and had to spend the time on deck, where there were no chairs, and nothing but the mouldy, dirty deck to sit on.'

Insufficient deckchairs were still a problem that had not been alleviated when my grandmother, Grace Clark, sailed on the troopship *Melita* in early autumn 1919. In a letter to her parents back home in England she describes the events that happened each day while on board the ship.

Although many soldiers travelled to Canada with their families, they were berthed in different locations on the ship. The soldier was still in the Army and the ship was under military command until landing in Canada. The officer commanding the troops had control over whether these families could associate on board.

When my grandparents sailed to Canada they were able to spend the majority of their time together. My grandmother wrote about many of the activities on board, which were organized by a YMCA representative. The YMCA captain delivered a lecture on Bolshevism to an interested crowd. There were also children's sports, a baby show, a whist drive, church services, a sing song, a special concert, and a boxing match.

My grandfather entered the boxing match and won! He was awarded £1, which my grandmother used to purchase a large postcard print of the ship and a souvenir spoon, items that are treasured family heirlooms today.

Arriving on Canadian Shores

The government booklet *Information For Wives of Soldiers Coming from Overseas*, written *c.* 1919, outlines the steps the War Brides should take once they arrive in Canada. During the winter months they would arrive at Halifax, Nova Scotia or Saint John, New Brunswick where a Women's Welcome Committee met them. For the remainder of the year troopships arrived at Quebec City where similar groups attended to their needs once they passed through immigration.

The committee at each port was made up of various women's organizations such as the Red Cross, Salvation Army, Young Women's Christian Association (YWCA), Imperial Order of the Daughters of the Empire

(IODE) and the Canadian Patriotic Fund. These groups offered relief to the travel-weary bride, as many were travelling with small children or infants.

Later the families boarded trains to their final destination. Rotary Clubs across Canada organized automobiles to drive the soldier and their families home from the local train station or dispersal depot.

One group of 300 War Brides and children were given a special welcome in Sudbury, Ontario when their train had a brief stop there. The local IODE treated them to home cooking, fruit, magazines and toys were given to their children.

The majority of soldiers and their dependents arrived in Canada by the end of 1919, much earlier than planned despite being hampered by unrest at demobilization camps in England, shipyard strikes, a shortage of coal, and a worldwide flu epidemic.

Life in Canada

The majority of these women worked hard to settle into their new life in Canada. Many War Brides like my grandmother had to adjust to a completely new way of life. They worked hard at home and in their communities to make it a better place to raise their children. Their perseverance and determination paid off. Nearly a century after these pioneering women blazed a trail across Canada, hundreds of thousands of their descendents are proud to say that they have a First World War War Bride in their family tree.

I Am a Canadian Already
Grace (Gibson) Clark

Grace (Gibson) Clark came from Sheffield, England to an isolated farming community in southern Saskatchewan in 1919.

My grandmother Grace (Gibson) Clark was just one of many English city girls who married a Canadian soldier from a farm community and embarked on a completely different way of life in the Dominion.

Grace Gibson was from Sheffield, England. She met twenty-three-year-old Hugh Clark in 1919 when he was stationed at the Ripon military camp in North Yorkshire. Hugh had actually met Grace's younger sister first, but once he and Grace were introduced, her sister stepped aside.

Hugh lived in a tiny rural community called Storthoaks in southern Saskatchewan where he worked on his parents' farm. He was drafted in May 1918 and travelled to England that August but he never saw action because once the military found out he knew how to box, he was called upon to entertain the troops in the boxing ring.

Hugh and Grace were married in Sheffield on 15 April 1919. In September, they boarded the RMS *Melita,* a Canadian Pacific Railway ship that was carrying returning Canadian soldiers and their dependents. The *Melita* set sail from Liverpool, England and arrived at the Port of Quebec on 25 September.

During the voyage Grace wrote a long letter (or as she described it, her 'epistle') to her family back in Sheffield. The letter was more like a journal of her trip. It was written in pencil on both sides of five by eight inch paper, more than sixty-eight pages in all. Although it is tattered and torn, and the last entries are missing, the majority of the letter is still intact and is fascinating to read.

In this excerpt from 18 September Grace describes how she and Hugh are settling in on the boat:

At present I am sitting on the upper deck and the waves are continually spraying us with 'showers of blessing.' The sea is awfully rough and has been for some hours. — Quite a large number of people have been sick already, but I am pleased to say I feel o.k. I eat a hearty breakfast consisting of bacon & liver. Of course that does not say I shall not be sick but I am hoping not. The sun is shining gloriously, although the wind is very sharp & piercing, thanks to my nice warm coat mother, dear, I don't feel cold. Hugh is sitting beside me reading one of the books you bought him. There is no doubt about it, the 'Melita' is a very fine boat, and 'runs' along fairly smoothly.

Of the other War Bride passengers and their children, Grace wrote:

There are heaps of young children and babies, and the poor mothers are having a trying time of it, trying to nurse, when they should be lying down. However from what I see the Canadian soldiers are very attentive to their sick wives, & do their share of nursing.

We have some fine musical concerts below deck, among the 'baby passengers' and I can assure you there is some fine talent among them. Their lungs are very powerful, and the sound carries a long way, especially at night time, when we 'single uns' don't appreciate it.

Off of Newfoundland, they see their first icebergs and are witness to a burial at sea.

> Quite a lot has happened today, and in fact it has been a very eventful one …
> Word spread along the deck that there were icebergs to be seen, this was as
> we were passing between Labrador, & Newfoundland, before we struck the
> Bell Isle Straits. In the distance, we saw a huge iceberg, it looked like some
> great building, with a tower to it. We passed not very far from it. A gentleman
> standing near, gave us his 'eye glasses' (or rather 'spy glasses') to look through.
> You have no idea what a grand thing it looked, I was surprised, for I had no
> idea they were so fine. We passed two others, shortly after.
>   … we had a sad, burial at sea. A blind officer on board lost his three-month-
> old baby, it died the day before. The minister on board conducted the burial,
> and many hearts were touched. — The Mother & Father were there, and
> were greatly upset. It was all the more sad, seeing the man was blind.

Two days before the *Melita* lands at Quebec, the passengers sight *terra firma*
and there is a celebratory mood on board. As they pass through the St.
Lawrence, they can see Quebec's fall landscape alongside the river's edge.

> Have just had my first sight of the Maple leaf, a way on the Hills, just tinged
> with red. The scenery is beautiful now … This is the best part of the journey.
> —There is no wind at all, & everything is so calm, while 'his majesty the sun'
> is shining 'to beat the band.' —You see I am Canadian already, now we are at
> 'God's Land'.

The diary ends in mid-sentence at the bottom of page sixty-eight, so we'll
never know Grace's first impressions of Canada. I know that once they
landed at Quebec my grandparents boarded a train for Toronto to visit
with family nearby. A few days later they caught the train to Storthoaks,
Saskatchewan where they stayed for seven years.

Grace and Hugh lived with his parents in a small house on the farm
where the mode of transportation was horse and buggy and cooking was
done on a wood stove. Grace was a city girl from an affluent middle-class
family in England and she had a lot to learn about rural life. Many years later
she told her daughter, 'I had hardly seen a cow before, let alone milk one!'

For the first half of her long marriage to Hugh Clark, Grace lived without electricity, running water or an indoor bathroom. It wasn't until the

family moved to Langley, British Columbia in 1942 that life became easier when they purchased a house that had all the amenities.

Grace learned how to run a farm household and was able to produce enough food for her husband and four children each year. She kept three gardens and became skilled at preserving what she grew. She supported the community through her volunteer activities and made many lifelong friends. Grace died in 1968, after living in Canada a total of forty-nine years.

Postscript: Grace and Hugh Clark had four children, eighteen grandchildren, twenty-two great-grandchildren and six great-great-grandchildren. Her granddaughter, Annette Fulford, contributed this article.

A Remarkable Woman
Peggy (Lewis) Holmes

Peggy (Lewis) Holmes made a name for herself in Canada as a writer, painter and radio broadcaster after she retired.

Peggy Holmes was born Maud Lewis in Hull, Yorkshire in 1897, the only daughter of Fred and Rosa Lewis. She met British-born Alfred (Harry) Holmes at her school friend Phyllis's home early on in the war.

Harry was Phyllis's older brother and he had immigrated to Canada in 1911 to a homestead in Alberta. Harry joined the Canadian Expeditionary Forces (CEF) shortly after war was declared in November 1914 and was promptly sent back to England.

Peggy wrote about meeting Harry many years later in her first book titled, *It Could Have Been Worse*:

> My first meeting with Harry was in a romantic setting in the drawing room of the Holmes' house. Here, in front of a blazing fire with his ancestors staring down at us from the walls, stood a tall, handsome soldier in Canadian uniform, which was much smarter than the British outfits.
>
> We didn't fall in love at first sight as Phyllis had romantically predicted, but we were attracted to each other. I was ten years younger and admired his sophistication, while he was amused by my frivolous chatter and zest for life.

Peggy and Harry were engaged the next year and they married at All Saint's Church in Hull on 23 September 1917. They came to Canada in 1919 on the troopship SS *Scandinavian* which set sail from Liverpool in October. The plan was to reclaim Harry's homestead in northern Alberta, then return to England after two years.

In her book Peggy wrote how unprepared she was for life in Canada:

Being a city girl I was totally ignorant of pioneer life. Apart from what Harry had told me, which sounded quite unreal, my slim information had been gained from maps and movies. I remember shivering through one show watching mountains of snow, husky dogs and howling winds. My one thought was, 'I must pack some extra sweaters' – or 'jumpers' as we called them. So I arrived in Canada with more woollies than any Hollywood sweater girl ever dreamed of possessing!

The couple spent the first winter in Calgary. Later, they worked on a ranch nearby so Peggy could 'get acclimatized to Canadian life before being plunged into the wilds ... ' The couple didn't reclaim Harry's homestead in northern Alberta until the spring of 1921. By then Harry's small shack had been destroyed by fire which meant they had to start all over again.

I had a glowing picture of our new home ahead of us, and couldn't wait to get there. But to our horror and dismay, when we finally arrived there was no shack – just a heap of charred ruins. Everything of any use had been pilfered. Nothing was left, and our only welcome was the croaking of frogs and the buzzing of flies and mosquitoes.

About a mile back on the trail Harry had seen a deserted shack, so tired and depressed we had to backtrack to find shelter.

It was very dilapidated and dirty, and nailed to the door was a weather-beaten note: HAVE GIVEN UP THE UNEQUAL STRUGGLE. HELP YOURSELF. What a sense of humour!

Later that evening Peggy reflected on the events of the day:

I tried to be brave and calm and to accept all this with aplomb, but we bedded down very deflated and unhappy.

Harry had brought yards of cheesecloth with him which I couldn't understand until the mosquitoes started their nightly raid. We slept under a mosquito bar as they loved our English blood! But we were so tired that we slept in spite of the nocturnal lullaby.

Suddenly I woke up screaming. 'What is it?' The whole shack was rocking.

Harry, cool and calm as always, pulled me back under the blankets and holding me tight said quietly, 'It's only a stray horse scratching himself on the corner of the shack.' He knew instinctively the sights and sounds of this primitive country.

Awaking the following morning, after the gruelling shakeup on the wagon seat the day before, I was bewildered, scared and stiff in every joint. 'Where was I? Who was I? Why was I in a wooden box?' It was quite a time before I could answer myself, 'You are on a homestead. You are Peggy Holmes, a war bride. The wooden box is your log shack.'

It was constant struggle to work the land while building a home to live in. When Peggy's father came from England to join them, he became ill and this prompted the couple to reconsider living in the Canadian north. Peggy, Harry and her father moved to Edmonton where Peggy volunteered in many organizations such as the YWCA, the Victorian Order of Nurses and the Red Cross.

Peggy lived on a farm for only a short period of time in the 1920s, but it made a lasting impression on her. Many years later at the age of seventy-seven, she began her own radio programme based on her memories of life on the homestead. The Canadian Broadcasting Corporation radio show, *The Way It Was*, lasted three years.

She went on to co-author three books on her life in Canada during her eighties and is listed as one of 200 remarkable Alberta women in the book by the same name.

Postscript: Peggy and Harry Holmes had four children; but only one son survived. All three daughters died at birth.

Just You Wait and See
Dorothy (Allard) Abraham

Dorothy (Allard) Abraham wrote a book about her experiences coming to Vancouver Island as a as War Bride in 1919 in order to educate a new generation of British wives about Canada.

Dorothy Abraham was a First World War Bride from Chirk, Denbighshire, Wales who kept a journal about her experiences settling into life on Vancouver

Island, British Columbia. During the Second World War, with thousands of War Brides arriving in Canada from Britain, Dorothy self-published her journal, which she called *Lone Cone: Life on the West Coast of Vancouver Island*.

Dorothy was born at Shipbourne, Kent, England in 1894 and the following year her family moved to Chirk in Wales. During the First World War Dorothy worked as a nurse for the Voluntary Aid Detachment (VAD) at Brynkinalt Auxiliary Hospital, in the parish of Chirk. There she met and married Edward (Ted) Abraham, a British-born member of the Canadian Expeditionary Force (CEF).

Ted Abraham lived on Vargas Island near Tofino, on the northwest coast of Vancouver Island, British Columbia. Ted had immigrated to Canada from England shortly before the war to farm on Vancouver Island. Like many other British ex-pats, he returned to his homeland with the CEF after war was declared in 1914.

Dorothy and Ted came to Canada in May 1919 on the SS *Olympic*, which at the time was being used as a troopship. The trip took six days and they sailed from Southampton to Halifax, Nova Scotia. The couple travelled by train across Canada to Vancouver, BC and then boarded a coastal steamer to Victoria, on Vancouver Island where Dorothy met her husband's family for the first time.

It is hard to imagine just how isolated Vargas Island was in 1919. In this excerpt from *Lone Cone,* Dorothy describes her first impressions of the place her husband called home:

My husband's place was on the open beach, beautiful, rugged, terrifyingly lonely, with a little shack on the beach, about two miles through dense bush from my in-laws ... It was all so very different from what I had imagined, if I had really imagined it at all ... I shall never forget the first walk to our bay, or the wild loveliness when we got there, with the sea dashing madly against the rocks, but the awful loneliness of it all frightened me. I am not a very timid sort of person, and love being alone at times, but this was a loneliness unknown and unheard of. My heart sank, and I remember having an argument with myself – whether to tell my husband straight out that I could not live there or to pretend that I liked it – but you cannot pretend with your husband, can you? So then and there I told him I could not endure such loneliness. I am afraid my husband was very disappointed. However, we decided right away to build a house on the other side of the island, next door to my in-laws. Not far away from them lived one other white man, which made that part of the island seem like a town compared to the lonely open beach.

The couple farmed near Tofino, a village with about 300 people, for a decade before her husband was transferred to Victoria with his government job as customs officer. In this hilarious excerpt, Peggy recalls her first encounter with the local Haida Indians:

I had been terribly frightened of the Indians at first, though I had been assured time and again that they were harmless, but somehow they always scared me and I would fly into the house if I saw them coming. One day my husband and I went down to the Indian Reserve to look for some cattle that had strayed and leaving me on the beach with the boat, my husband went off, saying he would not be long.

No sooner had he gone out of sight than almost immediately some Indians came along. I was so frightened. I dare not run into the bush, as I did not know the trails. ... so there I stayed, whilst more and more Indians came along till it seemed that all the Indians on the coast were surrounding me. Then one of the women came up and said, 'You come with me.'

What could I do? By this time they were gathered around me and were jabbering away in their guttural tones. I was desperate, but meekly followed them, thinking of all the gruesome stories I had read of people being scalped. ... Upon reaching the village, we proceeded to a house where the fence was covered with fish hanging up to dry, smelling to high heaven. As I gazed frantically towards the bush, I wondered if my husband would hear me if I screamed, but I think I was too frightened to even scream ... Then an Indian brought out a chair, upon which I sank ... I remember thinking that as I was very tall they could not reach to scalp me if I was standing up ... I remember too thinking that my husband would come back to find my red head sitting on a pole (the Indians used to do that with heads in the olden days) and how awful he would feel – and what a terribly tragic end to my life – and what would my people and my friends say? When suddenly there appeared before me an Indian maid, who in the most charming manner presented me with a lovely vase covered with the finest Indian basket work and I found out that I was not going to be scalped at all. I was so overcome I nearly wept, and to this day I do not know if I said 'Thank you' properly.

Dorothy wanted her book to be read by War Brides of the Second World War so that they might learn from her insight and experience settling into rural Canada. She had great hopes for the new generation of British Brides and foresaw a future where poverty would be eliminated and prosperity and happiness would sweep across the land. In the closing paragraphs of *Lone Cone*, she gave this sage advice:

> So to every war bride of today, I send a wish that you may be as happy in this great land as I have been. You will find it very different, of course; Canada is a young country, comparatively, with little or none of the traditions of the Old Land, and there will be many things you may not like at first, and perhaps be inclined to criticize. You may be homesick, as I was many times, and many problems and difficulties will arise: but as brides we promised 'for better, for worse,' and as women we have a great part to play in the building of a new world. … you will find 'Love and laughter, peace ever after, tomorrow – just you wait and see.'

Postscript: Dorothy Abraham died in 1990 and is buried at Ross Bay Cemetery in Victoria.

Appendices

Table I
Résumé of Marriages and Births of Known Marriages and Births for Servicemen Married While Serving Outside Canada to 31 December 1946

Country	Wives	Children	Total
Britain	44,886	21,358	66,244
Holland	1,886	428	2,314
Belgium	649	131	780
France	100	15	115
Italy	26	10	36
Denmark	7	1	8
Germany	6	0	6
Norway	1	0	1
North Africa	1	0	1
South Africa	1	0	1
Greece	1	0	0
Algiers	1	0	1
Hungary	0	3	3
Russia	1	0	1
India	1	0	1
Malay	2	0	2
Australia	24	2	26
Newfoundland and Caribbean Area	190	0	190
Total	47,783	21,950	69,733

Table II
Marriages and Births by Branch of Service

Service	Wives	Children
Army	80%	85.5%
RCAF	18%	13.1%
Navy	2%	1.4%
Total	100%	100%

These totals are of the known cases only of marriage and children including the ones brought to Canada by the Department of Immigration previous to August 1944. There are however, a considerable number of cases in which marriages were not reported or Dependents Allowances asked for and also others for which no applications for transportation were made but private arrangements completed to come to Canada and the dependents are now putting for claims for refund. It is understood there were other marriages in various countries such as Norway etc. of which we have no record but which will turn up at a later date.

Since the above figures were compiled (Note: The statistics above refer to marriages and births up to December 31, 1946. This historical report of the Directorate of Repatriation is not dated but it was written sometime after the last sailing of War Brides in January, 1947) there have been reported 87 marriages and 32 births a total of 119 not included in above. It is therefore anticipated that the correct figures when other facts are available will bring the grand total well over 70,000.

Source: History of Directorate of Repatriation, Department of National Defence, p. 34. February, 1947, Library and Archives of Canada.

Table III
Immigration to Canada by War Brides and Their Children 1942–1948

Year	Total no. of Immigrants*	No. of Brides and Dependents**	% of Total
1942–43	7,756	188***	2.4%
1943–44	8,504	1,255	14.75%
1944–45	12,801	6,442	50.3%
1945–46	22,722	16,133	71%
1946–47	71,719	39,092	54.5%
1947–48	64,127	1,336	2%
Total	187,449	64,446****	34.3%

Sources: This table originally appeared in Melynda Jarratt, *The War Brides of New Brunswick*, (University of New Brunswick, Masters Report, 1995), p. 12.

*Valerie Knowles, *Strangers at Our Gates: Canadian Immigration and Immigration Policy 1540–1990* (Toronto: Dundurn Press, 1992), p. 190.

** Fiscal year 1 April to 31 March.

*** Department of Mines and Resources Annual Report 1944–45 reported 7,885 dependents admitted from 1 April, 1942 to 31 March, 1945, of whom 5,009 were adults and 2,876 were children. Given the figures for 1943–44 and 1944–45, it appears that only 188 Canadian servicemen's dependents came to Canada in the fiscal year 1942–43, which was the first year in which the Canadian government officially provided transportation for the brides and their children.

**** 'Immigration Branch' Department of Mines and Resources Annual Report 1947–48, p. 243. The Director reported that a total of 64,451 dependents had come to Canada since 1942, a difference of five dependants.

Table IV
Canadian Wives Bureau Flow Chart

Information & Welfare Section	
Welfare Department	Duties: interviewing, giving welfare assistance, counsel, guidance, to Dependents, etc.
Clubs Dept	Duties: Organization of clubs, lectures, films, library (6,000 volumes). Supervision of social activities, etc.
Civilian Repat Section	
Administration Section	
Repat 1	Duties: Repat and clearing new applications, Service verifications, liaisons with Records, D.B.T. liaison, investigations.
Repat 2	Duties: DA&AP questions, Transfer funds, insurance policies & Savings certificates, Customs and export permits, Transportation accounts, Priorities & gradings, Records & Statistics.
Repat 3	Duties: Personal interviews, general correspondence, pre-traffic documentation, special compassionate cases, medical certificates, preparation of passports & visas, Board of Trade matters, Service discharges of Wives (in British forces generally).
Repat 4a	Duties: Dependents drafts, Berthing, Nominal rolls, Train rolls, Train schedules, Traffic index cards, Declaration forms, Embarkation cards, Roll warrants, S.S. Tickets, Medical cards, Warning orders and Movement instructions.
Repat 4b	Duties: Drafts other than Dependents (generally as for Repat 4a, plus collection of cash payments).
Repat 5	Duties: Liaison with immigration branch and health department.
Repat 6	Duties: Legal matters and liaison with AJAG Branch.
Central Registry	
Repat 7	Continental Establishment
Repat 7a	The Hague
Repat 7b	Brussels
Repat 7c	Paris

Source: Canadian Wives Bureau, Flow Chart, Department of National Defence, Library and Archives of Canada.

Bibliography

War Brides of the Second World War
Primary Sources

Anonymous. 'British Bride Speaks Out' *Maclean's*. 15 January 1945.

Allen, Ralph. 'War Cupid Defended, British Brides of Canadian Servicemen Merit Hand of Friendliness' *Globe and Mail*. Toronto, Ontario. 7 April 1944, p. 13.

Auld, Allisson. 'War brides Commemorate 60-year Anniversary' *Canadian Press*. 9 February 2006.

Bellett, Gerry. 'Judge Asked to Rule on Status of War Brides, Kids' *Vancouver Sun*. 31 May 2006, p A3.

Bezeau, Joyce. *A Bench in the Park*. Unpublished memoirs, 2001. Copy in the author's possession.

Boone, Zoe. Interview with author. Rowena, New Brunswick. 19 January 2007.

'British Brides' *The Legionnaire*. January 1945.

Brooks, Vera. 'In the Same Boat.' *Legion Magazine*. December/January, 1987–88, p. 12.

Campbell, Betty. *Her Story*. Unpublished memoirs. 2007. Copy in author's possession.

Canadian Red Cross Society Annual Reports. Toronto: The Canadian Red Cross Society, 1944, 1945, 1946, 1947 and 1948.

Cribbens, Norman. '31,000 War Brides 8000 Children Have Been Safely Moved' London, 11 June 1946, C.P. Cable in Ruddick, Kay. *Diary of Her Work as an Escort Officer in London, England in 1946*.

Department of Mines and Resources Annual Reports. (Ottawa: Edmund Cloutier, Kings Printer), 1941–42, 42–43, 43–44, 44–45, 45–46, 46–47, 47–48.

Department of National Defence Annual Reports. (Ottawa: Edmund Cloutier, Kings Printer), 1940, 1941, 1942, 1943, 1944, 1945, 1946, 1947, 1948.

Department of Veterans' Affairs Annual Reports. (Ottawa: Edmund Cloutier, Kings Printer), 1944, 1945, 1946, 1947, 1948.

Dock to Destination. Department of National Defence. 1946.

Eaton, Margaret (Perkins) Bristow. *Margaret's War 1939–45*. Unpublished memoirs. 2007. Copy in author's possession.

Eighth Census of Canada 1941 – Volume 1: General Review and Summary Tables. (Published by
    C.D. Howe, Minister of Trade and Commerce, Ottawa: Dominion Bureau of Statistics)
Foy, Vernie. Letter to author, 15 February 2007.
Hall, Gwendolen (Cliburn). Letter to author, 18 January 2007.
Hunter, Mrs Valreia. 'Train-Meeting Journal of Mrs. Valreia Hunter of the McAdam Red
    Cross Train Meeting Committee' *McAdam Branch of the New Brunswick Division of the
    Canadian Red Cross Society.* 19 March 1945 to 26 December 1946. Original in author's
    possession.
Hyslop, Dorothy. Letter to author. St Stephen, New Brunswick, 9 January 1988.
Jarratt, Melynda. 'Canadian War Brides: Good Canadian Citizens' Speech to the
    Colchester Historical Society Annual General Meeting. Truro, Nova Scotia: 28 May
    2006. Unpublished. Copy in the author's possession.
Jarratt, Melynda. 'Johan DeWitt: Scottish War Bride' as found on http://www.canadian-
    warbrides.com/dewittj1.asp, 1999.
Jarratt, Melynda. *The War Brides of New Brunswick: Questionnaire Results.* Privately published,
    Fredericton, New Brunswick, September 1990. Copy in the author's possession.
Jarratt, Melynda. *Operation Daddy.* Ottawa: The Canadian Red Cross Society, May 1995.
Johnston, Ann (Biles) Lawrence. *The Story of the Biles Clan.* Unpublished memoirs,
    Fredericton, New Brunswick: 2005. Copy in the author's possession.
'Large Contingent of Brides Arrive' Press Release issued by the Press Relations Office of
    the HMT *Queen Mary*, 31 August 1946. Copy in the author's possession.
Library and Archives Canada, RG 76, *Repatriation to Canada of soldiers' dependents.*
Library and Archives Canada, RG 76, *Regulations re admission of fiancées or prospective brides,
    1922–1946.*
Library and Archives Canada, RG 24, *Nominal rolls of dependents returning from overseas,
    1944–1947.*
Library and Archives Canada, RG 24, *Repatriation. Dependents of Cdn. Army Personnel in
    Canada. Social Service policy.*
Library and Archives Canada, RG 24, *Public Relations, Publicity, repatriation, 1945–1948.*
Library and Archives Canada, RG 24, *Public Relations, Publicity, war brides and dependents,
    generally, 1946.*
Library and Archives Canada, RG 24, *Transportation of soldiers' wives from overseas to Canada
    1916–1938.*
Library and Archives Canada, RG 24, *Assistance to dependents re desertion, bigamy illegitimacy,
    1940–1947.*
Library and Archives Canada, RG 24, *Policy, wives and families overseas to return to Canada,
    1943–1945.*
Library and Archives Canada, RG 24, *History Directorate of Repatriation.*
Library and Archives Canada, RG 24, *Canadian Wives Bureau.*
Lloyd, Doris. Letter to author. Plaster Rock, New Brunswick, 9 February 1995.
Lloyd, Doris. Interview with author. Plaster Rock, New Brunswick, 20 January 2007.
Lyster, Eswyn. Letter to author. 27 September 2004.
MacIntosh, Beatrice. *Memoirs of a Cape Breton War Bride.* (Privately published, Dingwall,
    South Harbour, Cape Breton: 2004.) Copy in the author's possession.
MacLennan, Hugh. *The Two Solitudes.* (Canada: First Macmillan Paperbacks Edition, 1986.)
Mott, Gloria. 'Dora and Dude Addison' *Carberry News-Express.* (Carberry, Manitoba. 1999.)
—. 'A War Bride Story: Doris (Shelton) Butt' *Carberry News-Express.* (Carberry, Manitoba. 2006.)
Panter, Kathy, 'Barbara Kate Warriner (née Cornwell)' in Clark, Marilyn and Courtney.
    War Brides: Our Sentimental Journey. (Regina: Saskatchewan, 2005.)

Pearase, Jackie. 'Mary Dale: From Glasgow Girl to Mabel Lake Girl' *North Valley Echo Remembrance Day Special*, (Enderby: British Columbia, 7 November 2006.)

Pyne, Patricia. *Letitia Diary*. 21 February 1946 to 3 March 1946. Unpublished, copy in the author's possession.

Ruddick, Kay. *Diary of her work as an Escort Officer in London, England in 1946*. Unpublished, copy in the author's possession.

Simpson, Edna (Burrows). Letter to the author, 18 January 2007.

Spear, Jean. *ESWIC Club*, (Ottawa, Ontario, 3 October 2004.)

Stewart, Laverne. 'Adventurous Spirit Delice Wilby, 86, has lived an interesting, dramatic life' *The Daily Gleaner*. (Fredericton: New Brunswick, 13 June 2006.)

Surgeson, Bea, *Autobiography*. Unpublished memoirs, 2001. Copy in the author's possession.

'Survey Shows Canadian War Brides Contented: NB Taken As Example' *Telegraph Journal*, 22 May 1947, p. 1.

Taped interviews with war brides and Red Cross Corp (Overseas) Escort Officers in the author's possession.

Taylor v. Canada (Minister of Citizenship and Immigration) 2006 FC 1053, as found on http://decisions.fct-cf.gc.ca/en/2006/2006fc1053/2006fc1053.html.

Vankoughnett, Mary (Mitchell). *Autobiography*. Unpublished memoirs, copy in the author's possession.

'Warbrides Live in Mayfair Mansion Before Starting Trip' *Ottawa Morning Journal*. 4 February 1946.

Welcome to War Brides. Department of National Defence, December 1944.

'Women and War' Imperial War Museum. http://www.iwm.org.uk/upload/package/41/women/WomenWarThemes.pdf

Worthington, Peter. 'The shameful citizenship debacle' *Toronto Sun*, 24 January 2007.

Young, Victor and Edward Heyman. *Love Letters*, 1945.

Secondary Sources

Abraham, Dorothy. *Romantic Vancouver Island: Victoria: Yesterday and Today*. 3rd edition. (Victoria: Hebden Printing, n.d.)

Burnet, Jean R. with Howard Palmer. *Coming Canadians: An Introduction to a History of Canada's Peoples*. (Toronto: McClelland & Stewart, 1988.)

Dear, ICB, General Editor, MRD Foot, Consultant Editor. *The Oxford Companion to World War Two*. (Oxford: Oxford University Press, 1995.)

Denton, V.L. Ed. *Dent's Canadian School Atlas*. (Toronto, Ontario: J.M. Dent & Sons [Canada] Limited. 1940.)

Costello, John. *Love, Sex and War: Changing Values 1939–45*. (Suffolk, England: William Collins, Sons and Company Ltd. 1985.)

Duivenvoorden-Mitic, Trudy and J.P. LeBlanc. *Pier 21: The Gateway that Changed Canada*. (Hantsport, Nova Scotia: Lancelot Press, 1988.)

Hickey, Rev. Father James Myles. *The Scarlet Dawn*. (Campbellton, NB: Tribune Publishers, 1949.)

Jarratt, Melynda, Masters Thesis, *The War Brides of New Brunswick*. (Fredericton: University of New Brunswick, 1995.)

Knowles, Valerie. *Strangers at our Gates: Canadian Immigration and Immigration Policy, 1540–1990*. (Toronto: Dundurn Press, 1992.)

Landry, Raymond. *En passant par les îles*. (Saint Hubert, Quebec: Éditions REPER, 2003.)

MacAuley, Peggy and Horace, eds. Revised Edition, *Surrey Girl: Not Just Another War Bride.* (Nepean, Ontario: HRM Publishing, 2006.)

Rains, Olga, Lloyd Rains and Melynda Jarratt. *Voices of the Left Behind: Project Roots and the Canadian War Children of World War Two.* (Toronto: Dundurn Press, 2006.)

Stacey, C.P. and Barbara M. Wilson. *The Half Million: The Canadians in Britain, 1939–1946.* (Toronto: University of Toronto Press, 1987.)

Summerfield, Penny. *Woman Workers in the Second World War: Production and Patriarchy in Conflict.* (London, England: Croom Helm Ltd., 1984.)

Walker, Joan. *Pardon My Parka.* (Winnipeg, Manitoba: Harlequin, 1958.)

Recommended Reading

Aikens, Gwladys M. Rees. *Nurses in Battledress – The World War II Story of a Member of the Q.A. Reserves.* (Halifax, Nova Scotia: Cymru Press, 1998.)

Barrett, Barbara B. and Eileen Dicks, Isobel Brown, Hilda Chaulk Murray and Helen Fogwill Porter, eds. *We Came from over the Sea: British War Brides in Newfoundland.* British War Brides Association of NL. (Portugal Cove: ESPress, 1996.)

Bebbington, Graham. *The Fledglings.* (Staffordshire, England: Churney Valley Books, 2003.)

Broadfoot, Barry. *Six War Years 1939–1945 Memories of Canadians at Home and Abroad.* (Toronto: PaperJacks Ltd., 1985.)

Campbell, Gray. *We Found Peace.* (Toronto: Thomas Allen Limited, 1953.)

Clark, Marilyn and Courtney, *War Brides: Our Sentimental Journey.* (Regina: Saskatchewan, 2005.)

Faryon, Cynthia J. *A War Bride's Story: Risking It All for Love After World War II.* (Canmore, Alberta: Altitude Publishing Canada Ltd, 2004.)

Granfield, Linda. *Brass Buttons and Silver Horseshoes: Stories from Canada's British War Brides.* (Toronto: McClelland & Stewart Ltd., 2002.)

Hibbert, Joyce, ed. *The War Brides.* (Toronto: Peter Martin Associates Limited, 1978)

Ladouceur, Barbara, ed. and Phyllis Spence, ed. *Blackouts to Bright Lights: Canadian War Bride Stories.* (Vancouver: Ronsdale Press, 1995.)

Latta, Ruth. *The Memory of All That: Canadian Women Remember World War Two.* (Burnstown, Ontario : General Store Publishing, 1992.)

Lee, Helene. *Bittersweet Decisions: The War Brides 40 Years Later.* (Lockport, New York: Roselee Publications, 1985.)

Kochan, Pearl Colis (with Kevin Quirk). *To Johnnie, with Love.* (St. John's, Flanker Press. 2003.)

Maclay, Michael. *Aldershots' Canadians in Love and War 1939–1945.* (Farnborough, Hampshire: Appin Publications, 1997.)

McNeil, Bill. *Voices of a War Remembered: An Oral History of Canadians in World War Two.* (Toronto, Ontario: Doubleday Canada Limited, 1992.)

O'Hara, Peggy. *From Romance to Reality: Stories of Canadian War Brides.* Second Printing. (Cobalt, Ontario: Highway Book Shop. 1985.)

O'Neill Dahm, Jacqueline. *The Last of the War Brides.* (Canada: Trafford Publishing, nd.)

Rains, Olga. *We Became Canadians.* (Hyde Park, Ontario: Overnight Copy Service, 1984.)

Shewchuk, Helen. *If Kisses Were Roses: A 50th Anniversary Tribute to War Brides.* (Sudbury, Ontario: Helen Hall Shewchuk, 1996.)

Wicks, Ben. *Promise You'll Take Care of My Daughter: The Remarkable War Brides of World War II.* (Toronto: Stoddart, 1992.)

First World War
Primary Sources

'300 War Brides at C.P.R Station.' *Sudbury Star*. 22 February 1919, p. 2.

'A Serious Situation.' *Minnedosa Tribune*, 9 November 1916, p. 4.

'Canadian Soldiers'Wives Not Wanted in England.' *Minnedosa Tribune*. 7 December 1916, p. 2.

'Canadian Wives Should Stay in Canada.' *Minnedosa Tribune*. 23 November 1916, p. 1.

Clark, Grace (Gibson), letter. 17 September to 24 September 1919, from on board the Canadian Pacific Railway ship RMS *Melita*, to Mr and Mrs FO Gibson. Held since 1992 by Annette Fulford.

Canada. Department of Militia and Defence. *The Return of the Troops: A Plain Account of the Demobilization of the Canadian Expeditionary Force*. Ottawa: Government Printing Bureau, 1920.

Library and Archives Canada, RG 76, *Applications for Refunds of Passage Money (For Soldiers' Dependents), 1919*.

Library and Archives Canada, RG 76, *Policy of government for refunding passage money to soldiers' dependents, 1919–1925, 1931, 1934*.

Library and Archives Canada, RG 76, *Soldiers' dependents returning to Canada, 1919, 1921–1934*.

Library and Archives Canada, RG 76, *Soldiers' dependents returning to Canada, 1919*.

Library and Archives Canada, RG 76, *Women and children leaving Canada to go to England (Soldiers' dependents)*.

'Movement Should Be Quicker.' *Calgary Daily Herald*. 27 December 1918, p. 1.

'Rats Drive Women Up on Decks, Women Afraid to go to Their Berths.' *Calgary Daily Herald*. 9 January 1919, p. 1.

Repatriation Committee. *Information for Wives of Soldiers Coming From Overseas*. np: nd.

'"Rotten Trip" Says Passengers from the Corsican.' *Saskatoon StarPhoenix*. 3 May 1919, p.1.

'Troops Overseas Marrying Rate Three Hundred a Week.' *Toronto World*. 9 December 1918, p. 1.

'Wives of Canadian Soldiers Should Not Go to England.' *Minnedosa Tribune*. 19 October 1916, p. 4.

'Women Must Return.' *Minnedosa Tribune*. 15 February 1917, p. 1.

'Y.W.C.A. to Look After War Brides.' *Toronto World*. 6 December 1918, p. 5.

Secondary Sources

Department of Soldiers' Civil Re-Establishment. *Returned Soldiers' Handbook – contains valuable information and tells you where to get more*. (London: St. Clements Press, Ltd., nd.)

Morton, Desmond. *Fight or Pay: Soldiers' Families in the Great War*. (Vancouver: UBC Press, 2004.)

Repatriation Committee. *The Programme of Repatriation*. (Ottawa: Allied Press, nd. Issued by the Department of Public Information.)

Recommended Reading

Abraham, Dorothy. *Lone Cone: A Journal of Life on the West Coast of Vancouver Island*. Third Edition. np: nd.

Gould, Florence E. 'A War Bride Journey in 1917.' *Okanagan History: The Thirty-seventh Report of the Okanagan Historical Society*, 1974, 48–51.

Holmes, Peggy and Joy Roberts. *It Could Have Been Worse.* (Don Mills, Ontario: Collins Publishers, 1980.)

Holmes, Peggy and Andrea Spalding. *Never a Dull Moment.* (Toronto: Collins, 1984.)

Holmes, Peggy. *Still Soaring.*(Edmonton: Loon Books, 1987.)

McKenna, M. Olga. *Micmac by Choice: Elsie Sark–An Island Legend.* (Halifax, Nova Scotia: Formac, 1990.)

Strange, Kathleen. *With the West in Her Eyes: The Story of a Modern Pioneer.* (Toronto: Macmillian Company of Canada Limited, 1945)

Notes

Preface

1 Letter to author from Dorothy Hyslop, St Stephen, New Brunswick, 9 January 1988.
2 C.P. Stacey and Barbara M. Wilson, *The Half Million: The Canadians in Britain, 1939–1946* (Toronto: University of Toronto Press, 1987), p. 136.
3 Although there were nearly 48,000 marriages to the end of December 1946, not all War Brides came to Canada on the government sponsored War Bride transportation scheme. Nearly 4,500 refused the offer of free passage to Canada for various reasons, including the fact that their husbands had found work in Britain and Europe. Many War Brides, however, refused to come to Canada because their marriages had broken down or they were refused admission by Immigration officials who determined that their settlement arrangements in Canada were 'unsatisfactory'.
4 Stacey and Wilson, *The Half Million*, p. 141. Stacey and Wilson quote an official British analysis as saying: 'At the time, public interest was concentrated on the arrangements made for those who were popularly known as "G.I. Brides," yet in fact it was the dependents of Canadian servicemen who provided the largest number of travellers … over 40,000 wives and nearly 20,000 children, as compared with 34,000 wives and 14,000 children of United States servicemen.' p. 141.
5 *Ibid*, p. 138.
6 A report on the History of the Directorate of Repatriation contains a widely circulated 'RESUME OF MARRIAGES AND BIRTHS' for servicemen married while serving outside Canada to 31 December 1946 which shows that of the total 47,783 marriages, 44,886 were to British women. Library and Archives of Canada, Immigration Branch, History of the Directory of Repatriation.
7 'One of Them, "British War Bride Speaks Out"', *Maclean's*, 15 January 144, p. 10.
8 Ralph Allen, 'War Cupid Defended, British Brides of Canadian Servicemen Merit Hand of Friendliness', *Globe and Mail*, 7 April 1944, p. 13. Other editorials appeared in the *Vancouver Sun*, the *Brockville Recorder Times*, the *New Brunswick Telegraph Journal*, etc.
9 *Welcome to War Brides*, Department of National Defence, December 1944.
10 Vera Brooks, 'In the Same Boat', *Legion*, December/January, 1987–88, p. 12.

11 ICB Dear, General Editor, MRD Foot, Consultant Editor, *The Oxford Companion to World War Two,* (Oxford: Oxford University Press) 1995, p. 1133.

12 John Costello, *Love, Sex and War Changing Values 1939–45,* (London: William Collins, Sons and Co. Ltd.), p. 40.

13 Melynda Jarratt, 'Johan Dewitt, Scottish War Bride', www.canadianwarbrides.com/dewitt1.html

14 'Bigamous Marriages' Code Letter C, Library and Archives of Canada.

15 Olga Rains, Lloyd Rains and Melynda Jarratt, *Voices of the Left Behind: Project Roots and the Canadian War Children of World War Two,* (Canada: The Dundurn Group), p. 31.

16 Stacey and Wilson, *The Half Million,* p. 174.

17 *Ibid,* p. 175.

18 'British War Bride Speaks Out', *Maclean's,* p. 10.

19 Stacey and Wilson, *The Half Million,* pp. 174–178.

20 Acadians are the descendents of the original French settlers of the region called Acadia which was the former French colony located in eastern Canada, mainly in Nova Scotia but also including New Brunswick, Prince Edward Island, Cape Breton Island, and the coastal area from the St Lawrence River south into Maine. In 1755, the British deported the Acadians to southern territories, including Louisiana, where their descendants came to be known as Cajuns. H.W. Longfellow's narrative poem *Evangeline* made famous the story of the deportation of the Acadian peoples.

21 Rev. Father James Myles Hickey, *The Scarlet Dawn,* (Campbellton, New Brunswick: Tribune Publishers, 1949), pp 131–132.

22 'Warbrides Live in Mayfair Mansion Before Starting Trip', *Ottawa Morning Journal,* 4 February 1946.

23 Eswyn Lyster, Letter to author, 27 September 2004.

24 'Operation Daddy Begins as Liner Mauretania Arrives', *Telegraph Journal,* Saint John, New Brunswick, 11 February 1946.

25 Doris Lloyd, Letter to author, Plaster Rock, NB, 9 February, 1995, as cited in Melynda Jarratt, *The War Brides of New Brunswick.*

26 Norman Cribbens, '31,000 War Brides 8000 Children Have Been Safely Moved'. London, 11 June 1946, C.P. Cable in 1946 Diary of Kay Ruddick Red Cross Escort Officer.

27 24 February 1946, Pat Pyne, Letitia Diary. Copy in author's possession.

28 27 August 1946, Diary of Kay Ruddick. Copy in author's possession.

29 An exception is the ESWIC (England, Scotland, Wales, Ireland and Canada) Club in Ottawa, Ontario, which was founded in July 1944 by the Canadian Red Cross Soldiers' Dependents Committee. The ESWIC club eventually became independent of the Red Cross and marked its 60th anniversary in June 2005 in Ottawa: Source: Jean Spears, ESWIC Club, Ottawa, Ontario, 3 October 2004.

30 'Survey Shows Canadian War Brides Contented: NB Taken as Example', *Telegraph Journal,* 22 May 1947, p. 1.

31 *Ibid.* The article stated that of 1,820 marriages, 1,760 brides were still in the province as of January 1947. Of the sixty who had left New Brunswick, thirty-eight had moved to other parts of Canada or the United States, one had died, and twenty-one had returned overseas. Of the twenty-one who returned, six went with husbands who planned to settle down over there; one was a widow; another widow had only come to meet her husband's people; another wife was called home because of her father's death; only twelve left Canada because they did not like it and only two obtained divorces.

32 Letter from Mrs J.H. Thompson, Springbrook, Ontario, 14 January 1947, Library and Archives of Canada.
33 Henrietta Pronovost, correspondence with the author, February 2007.
34 Betty Campbell, Her Story, 2007. Copy in author's possession.
35 Stacey and Wilson, *The Half Million*, p. 141.

Chapter One

1 Alisson Auld, 'War Brides Commemorate 60-Year Anniversary', 9 February 2006, Canadian Press.
2 Table II, Population, Numerical and Percentage Increase for Each Ten-Year Period, for Canada and the Provinces, 1851–1941, in *Eighth Census of Canada 1941 – Volume 1: General Review and Summary Tables*, Published by C.D. Howe, Minister of Trade and Commerce, Ottawa: Dominion Bureau of Statistics, p. 5.
3 Table VII, Rural Population Classifed by Farm and Non-Farm for Canada and the Provinces, 1931–1941, in *Eighth Census of Canada*, p. 36.
4 *Ibid*, p. 36.
5 The term 'Atlantic Canada' is used to refer to the region consisting of Newfoundland, Nova Scotia, New Brunswick and PEI. Geographically, and historically, Newfoundland and the Maritimes have much in common and they are viewed as one when we think of Atlantic Canada as a whole.
6 Beatrice MacIntosh, *Memoirs of a Cape Breton War Bride*, Dingwall, South Harbour, Cape Breton, 2004. Copy in the author's possession.

Chapter Two

1 Eswyn (Ellinor) Lyster, as quoted in a speech given at Pier 21, Halifax, Nova Scotia on 9 February 2006.
2 C.P. Stacey and Barbara M. Wilson, *The Half Million: The Canadians in Britain, 1939–1946* (Toronto: University of Toronto Press, 1987), p. 138.
3 Hugh MacLennan, *The Two Solitudes* (First Macmillan Paperbacks Edition 1986), Dedication.
4 Letter from A.L. Jolliffe, Director of Repatriation to Major J.H. Neeland, 26 January 1945, p. 1, Library and Archives Canada, Immigration Branch (RG 76, Volume 461, File 705870, pt. 6).
5 *Ibid*, p. 2.
6 Table II, Percentage Distribution of the Population Classified According to Sex, by Official Language for Canada and the Provinces 1941, in *Eighth Census of Canada 1941 – Volume 1: General Review and Summary Tables*. Published by C.D. Howe, Minister of Trade and Commerce, (Ottawa: Dominion Bureau of Statistics), p. 257.
7 Joan Walker, *Pardon My Parka* (Winnipeg, Canada: Harlequin, 1958), pp. 41–42.

Chapter Three

1 Table II, Population Numerical and Percentage Increase for each Ten Year period, for Canada and the Provinces, 1951-1941, in *Eighth Census of Canada 1941 – Volume 1: General Review and Summary Tables*. Published by C.D. Howe, Minister of Trade and Commerce, Ottawa: Dominion Bureau of Statistics, p. 5.

2 *Ibid*, p. 295.
3 Excerpt from the Diary of Mary (Mitchell) Vankonnaught. Copy in the author's possession.
4 Vernie Foy, letter to author, February 2007. Copy in author's possession.

Chapter Four

1 Peggy and Horace MacAuley, *Surrey Girl: Not Just Another War Bride,* Revised Edition, (Nepean, Ontario: HRM Publishing, 2006), pp. 45–46.
2 Table II. Population, Numerical and Percentage Increase for Each Ten Year Period, for Canada and the Provinces, 1951-1941, in *Eighth Census of Canada 1941 – Volume 1: General Review and Summary Tables*. Published by C.D. Howe, Minister of Trade and Commerce, Ottawa: Dominion Bureau of Statistics, p. 5.
3 Table VII, Rural Population Classified by Farm and Non-Farm, for Canada and the Provinces, 1931–1941, p. 36.
4 *Ibid*, p. 36.
5 Table II, Population, Numerical and Percentage Increase for Each Ten Year Period, for Canada and the Provinces, 1951–1941, p. 5.
6 Dorothy Abraham, Romantic Vancouver Island, (Victoria: Allied Printing, n.d.).

Chapter Five

1 In December 1941 the National Service Act made British women liable for compulsory military service for the first time. Under the Act women were liable for conscription between the ages of 19 and 31. Married women and women with children under fourteen living with them were exempt and there was a provision in the Act that no woman called up for service would be required to use any lethal weapon, unless she had signified in writing her willingness to do so. *Women and War*, Imperial War Museum, http://www.iwm. org.uk/upload/package/41/women/WomenWarThemes.pdf
2 Penny Summerfield, *Women Workers in the Second World War Production and Patriarchy in Conflict* (London: Routledge, 1989), p. 29. Since there was not a census in 1941, the number of 7.5 million women workers in 1943 is based on the Wartime Social Survey of 1944 by Geoffrey Thomas. The number of women recorded as 'occupied' in the 1931 census (the last pre-war census) was 6,265,000, a difference of 1.35 million between 1931 and 1943.
3 *Women and War*, Imperial War Museum.
4 PRO CAB 67/9, WP (G)(41)115, 'MOS Labour Needs', memo by Minister of Supply, 20 October, 1941, as cited in Penny Summerfield, *Women Workers in the Second World War*, (London: Routledge, 1984), pp 34–35.
5 Penny Summerfield, *Women Workers in the Second World War*, pp 35–36.

Chapter Six

1 '946 Dependents Start for Canada: Women and Children Reach Liverpool to Sail on Mauretania', *New Brunswick Telegraph Journal*, (Saint John, New Brunswick), 5 February 1946.
2 Unwilling to Proceed, Applied, Code Letter B, Lists 1–10, Library and Archives Canada, Immigration Branch files.

Chapter Seven

1 A song that was popular in 1945–46, 'Love Letters', written by Victor Young/Edward Heyman (1945).
2 Memorandum to Deputy Minister (Army) Transportation of Fiancees of Canadian Servicemen and ex-Servicemen to Canada.
3 Memorandum to the Minister of National Defence, re: Overseas Fiancees of Army Personnel.
4 Letter from G. Congdon, Commissioner, Department of Mines and Resources to the Director, Immigration Branch, 15 December 1945.
5 Autobiography of Bernadette Surgeson, unpublished. Copy in possession of the author.

Chapter Eight

1 S.3. of Privy Council Order in Council 858 of 9 February 1945 specifically states: Every dependent who is permitted to enter Canada pursuant to Section of this order shall for the purpose of Canadian immigration law be deemed to be a Canadian citizen if the member of the forces upon who he is dependent is a Canadian citizen and shall be deemed to have Canadian domicile if the said member has Canadian domicile. LAC, PC 858. History of the Directorate of Immigration, Immigration Branch, RG 76.
2 *Dock to Destination*, nd. Department of National Defence, copy in author's possession.
3 'Large Contingent of Brides Arrive', Press Release from PRO aboard HMS *Queen Mary*, 31 August 1946, as found in Kay Ruddick, Diary 1946.
4 Jackie Pearase, 'From Glasgow Girl to Mabel Lake Girl', *North Valley Echo* (Enderby, British Columbia) 11 November 2006.
5 Peter Worthington, 'The Shameful Citizenship Debacle', *Toronto Sun*, (Toronto, Ontario) 24 January 2007.
6 Taylor v. Canada (Minister of Citizenship and Immigration) 2006 FC 1053, as found on http://decisions.fct-cf.gc.ca/en/2006/2006fc1053/2006fc1053.html
7 Gerry Bellett, 'Judge Asked to Rule on Status of War Brides, Kids', *Vancouver Sun* 31 May 2006.

Chapter Nine

1 Desmond Morton, *Fight or Pay: Soldiers' Families in the Great War* (Vancouver: UBC Press, 2004), p. 244.
2 Soldiers' dependents returning to Canada, Library and Archives of Canada, Immigration Branch, RG 76, Immigration, Series I-A-1, Volume 614, Reel C-10434, File: 908571, Parts 15–17.
3 Canada. *Department of Militia and Defence, the Return of the Troops: A Plain Account of the Demobilization of the Canadian Expeditionary Force* (Ottawa: The Government Printing Bureau, 1920), p. 28.

Index